HEART OF FIRE

'A haunting and eye-opening read by an amazingly brave woman'
Sunday Express

'*Heart of Fire* is a moving account of a female suffering' *Marie Claire*

'Her description has the starkness of a bitter personal experience ... a
simple and quite extraordinary story' *Sydney Morning Herald*

'An insightful read into the psychological effects of being a child soldier'
Witness

'A remarkable biography' *Harper's Bazaar*

'Passionate and revealing […] leaves a permanent impression' *Time Out*

'The reader is enticed by the phenomenal story of Senait Mehari ...
Heart of Fire sheds light on a situation that seems out of our intellectual
grasp, and thus becomes an education. It warrants more than a quick
read' *Seed*

'Mehari tells a story that is, at times, terribly painful to read, but the
ultimate triumph of the human spirit wills you on' *Sunday Telegraph*

'Normally with memoirs such as these it's the tale that carries the reader
along, but Mehari is a very good writer, too – evocative, confessional yet
detached and quite heart-wrenching' *The Age*

'A powerful and inspirational testimony to her refusal to be a victim of
her past' *Sunday Tasmanian*

'A griping account of triumph over adversity' *Reach*

SENAIT MEHARI was born in Asmara, the capital of Eritrea, in 1974, and grew up amid the thirty-year-war between her homeland and Ethiopia. A child soldier for three years, Senait escaped to Khartoum, in Sudan, and was then summoned to Germany by her father. She now lives in Berlin where she is a well-known singer songwriter. Her first album *Mein Weg* (*My Way*) was released by Universal Records in 2005 to considerable acclaim. *Heart of Fire* is her first book and is a European bestseller. Senait is a spokesperson for UNICEF and works with White Band of Peace, campaigning against the use of child soldiers.

HEART OF FIRE

From Child Soldier to Soul Singer

SENAIT MEHARI

Translated by
Christine Lo

This paperback edition published in 2007

First published in Great Britain in 2006 by
Profile Books Ltd
3A Exmouth House
Pine Street
London ECIR OJH
www.profilebooks.com

First published in Germany in 2004 under the title Feuerherz by
Droemer Verlag, Munich
www.droemer.de

Published by agreement with Literary Agency Lianne Kolf, Munich and
Literary Agency Andrew Nurnberg, London.

1 3 5 7 9 10 8 6 4 2

Typeset in Bembo by MacGuru Ltd
info@macguru.org.uk

Printed in the UK by CPI Bookmarque, Croydon, CR0 4TD

nberg

Now that I have written everything down, I am free.
This book will give me peace.
The story I have to tell is a terrible one.
But I do not want those who read it
to see only the darkness.
I want a door to open as they read it.
So light comes through – and hope.

Senait Mehari

Contents

Suitcase Baby

The first time I walked out of my grandparents' house into the dusty alley between the low, windswept houses that made up the neighbourhood, the local children gathered round and screamed, 'Senait, the suitcase baby! Here's the suitcase baby!'

I was very frightened. Although the children were shouting with all their might, they had as little idea as I did of what they were saying – 'suitcase baby'. What did it mean? They were simply repeating what they had heard from the grown-ups. It was only later that I found out why they were calling me that.

Not long after I was born, my mother, Adhanet, had a breakdown. She had already had three children before me: two from an earlier, unhappy marriage, and one from the marriage to my father, which had ended before my birth. My father wanted nothing more to do with her, or with me. My mother was new to Asmara, and there wasn't much money to go round. On top of this, there was the fact that my father was Eritrean – his family came from a small town in the highlands, Adi Keyh – while my mother was Ethiopian, from Addis Ababa. This was an unhappy combination: Eritrea was still an Ethiopian province at the time, and the two peoples had been at war for fifteen hundred years. A child of mixed heritage was considered a scandal.

So there were several reasons why my mother felt I was too much to cope with. A few weeks after my birth she resolved to get rid of me. But she couldn't bring herself to do it with her bare hands, so she chose a half-hearted mixture of murder and abandonment.

One morning, she dressed me just as she did every day, shut me in a suitcase, put it on top of a wardrobe and went into town. Our neighbour heard me crying and wondered why my mother didn't come, so she came over to have a look but couldn't find me. She thought something terrible had happened, and ran down the street to the police station, screaming. The police didn't want to come at first – they didn't believe the screeching, near-hysterical woman. But she refused to go away until two policemen agreed to follow her. They finally found me in the scuffed suitcase on top of the wardrobe.

I was already having great difficulty breathing when they found me. The policemen took me to the public orphanage, the 'Orfan', and arrested my mother as soon as she came home.

Adhanet was jailed for six years for attempted infanticide. A newspaper reporter, alerted by the neighbour, took a photo of me, and the picture duly appeared on the front page of the Asmara daily. The story of the 'suitcase baby' was born.

2

Orfan

My very first memory is of sitting with a nun from the orphanage on the steps of the porch of the shack in which we lived. Paint peeled off its wooden railings – we children loved scratching it off and rubbing it between our fingers until it splintered into different colours. From the shade, the nun and I looked out at the heat shimmering in the parched garden and over the stony plains beyond. The blurred outline of a mountain range could be made out on the horizon.

The other children were inside having their afternoon nap. 'Why are there lions and monkeys?' I asked.

She looked at me in surprise and replied, after a pause, 'Our leader made them for us.'

I stared at her in obvious astonishment.

'Our leader made the lions, and everything else too,' she continued. 'All the animals and plants. And all the houses. Our leader takes good care of us.' She was not speaking of God – either the Christian god or Allah – but of Megistu Haile Mariam, the Communist leader of Ethiopia.

Orfan, the orphanage in Asmara, was run by the state, and that state was Ethiopia. It was 1977 and I was probably three years old. An independent Eritrea was still a distant prospect – Eritrea gained independence in 1991 – and, as the nuns told us, 'Mengistu is your god.'

'He made the lions to punish bad people,' my companion continued in a threatening tone, 'to frighten them.'

Her words filled me with fear. Immediately I thought that I was surely a wicked person, and I felt a deep sense of shame. The nun was not to know that, even now, she was laying the ground for the two emotions that would come to dominate my childhood: fear and shame.

I loved sitting on those steps, looking out at the view. I stared, fascinated, at the endless, shimmering expanse of rocks, sand and scrub. On the steps I could feel the wind that often swept down from the mountains over the plains. The air was dusty, filled with the odours of camel dung and of the fires from the desert caravans that had struck camp outside the town. No buildings interrupted the view from the terrace – the town of Asmara stood behind us, while the desert stretched out in front. In the evenings we watched the long lines of camels plod out of town. They walked in single file, with loads piled high, decorated with multicoloured strips of fabric. The camel herders ran alongside them waving big sticks over their heads, urging the animals on with their throaty cries.

At night we heard the hyenas laughing. There was a chorus of animals that we seldom saw, but we heard them: howling, yapping, cackling, snarling and whistling. The lean, mangy ones nosed around the kitchen refuse. Even the lions sniffed our food and the rubbish piled up behind our shack. They came mostly at twilight, sometimes at night. Only their shadows could be seen. When they were about the other animals lurking around the orphanage would vanish into the bushes or under a porch, tails tucked between their legs. We were warned about the lions. 'Stay in the garden,' said the nuns, 'or the lions might get you.' We hardly needed to be told – we were even frightened of the monkeys swarming in the trees in the garden.

So we stayed in the middle of the garden, between the wooden shacks in which we lived and the enormous building next door. This was the hospital, an Italian colonial building with high windows and a long flight of steps. The garden had hedges of oleander alongside vegetable beds and some dense undergrowth.

Orfan, the state orphanage in which I spent the first two years of my life.

It also contained a football field and our playground, consisting of a see-saw and a brightly coloured iron slide. We played with the pebbles we found on the ground, the twigs we broke off from the bushes and with the old tins and other discards from the grown-up world. We fought with each other one minute and made up the next, hugging each other. We hid for hours pressed up against each other, skipped through the garden with arms linked, or danced to a tune that only we could hear in our heads.

Most of all we loved to play on the porch. We wore cords which we attached to the posts of the railing, and hung rag balls from them, then spent hours kicking the balls. Up in the air. Down again. The balls swung back and forth. And another half day would go by ...

The egg thief
Apart from when we were in bed or eating, we spent almost all

day outdoors. We had our meals in a room next to the kitchen, where we sat under a picture of a beautiful white lady with golden hair. I had never seen a woman like this in real life. She looked down over us, and the head nun said she was watching everything we did. Sometimes the lady in the picture even turned her head and followed me with her eyes as I tried to creep away, full of guilt over something I had done. There they were again – fear and shame.

Take the incident with the eggs, for example. Sometimes, we were given a hard-boiled egg in the evenings, which was always a special treat. The head nun used to say, 'If you're late, the lady will have your egg.' So I always hurried to dinner so as not to miss out on the eggs, but I was late a few times and, sure enough, there was no egg left for me. I burst into tears, looking up at the lady all the time but she never moved, she just stared into the distance, pretending not to notice me. I didn't like her at all then. I hated her, even though the nuns constantly tried to drum a love of the lady into us. Why should I love her when she had taken my eggs?

One day I decided to keep watch on her to catch her in the act. I wanted to see how she did it: steal eggs from where she stood in a picture hanging high up in a corner of the room. I took out the egg I had set aside secretly from the previous evening and put it down on the table as I walked past. Then I crept into the next room, hid behind a table and waited. But nothing happened. The strange white lady didn't react. Suddenly, one of the children's nurses from the hospital came in – an African woman whom most of us disliked. She spotted the egg and pocketed it immediately. The egg that I had sacrificed as bait for the white lady! I was crushed.

I dashed outside and told the other children about my sensational discovery. But they didn't believe a word of it. I was very hurt by their reaction – after all, I'd witnessed the heinous act with my own eyes. I kept the knowledge in my heart and resolved never to be late for dinner again.

Death in a bottle

My first experience of death was also in Orfan. My friend Helen was just old enough to start school and, although she was much older than me, we spent a lot of time together. But she became ill and was moved to the large hospital building next to our huts. We were allowed into the hospital at all times because our dining room was in there – the huts were only for sleeping in. Helen lay in a large bed with a tall stand next to it. A bottle hung from the stand, and a tube dripped water from the bottle into her. Or at least it looked like water. I was fascinated by this apparatus, and watched transfixed, as drop after drop of liquid swelled in the tube.

One day, I was sitting on the edge of Helen's bed when the drip ran out. She told me to fetch a nurse because the drip should never be empty. 'If that happens, my blood will start flowing the wrong way and I'll die.' I had no idea what she meant but I knew that it was something serious. So I ran off to get a nurse, but no one came. One of them was too busy, another one didn't want to come with me, and the third said she would come later. Soon after, I had to leave to join the other children of my age.

Early the next morning I went to visit Helen again. Before I reached her room someone pushed a child past me on a trolley-bed. I was surprised to see an older child sleeping peacefully so late in the morning. There was a large bloodstain on the bed. I began to cry because I didn't understand what was going on. I didn't realise that that child was Helen – all I knew was that something bad was happening. Then someone said that Helen was dead.

From that moment on I hated the nurses – shuffling along the corridors in slow motion, going about their work with no sense of urgency. I didn't know whom to trust or whom to tell that the nurses hadn't reacted when I had tried to raise the alarm about Helen. Later, I mentioned it to one of the nuns, but I don't think anything came of it. The nurses continued as before, as if nothing had happened.

For days, the children in the orphanage sang a song for Helen, one that we'd made up ourselves. We re-enacted her funeral, burying a doll and singing our song all the time. Everyone cried except me. One of the girls slapped me for not crying. I hadn't meant to offend anyone – I just couldn't cry, and that was that. I felt as if the tears, breath, everything, had been cut off. The girl who hit me before got into a rage, striking me over and over again until I started to cry, but only from the pain and the humiliation.

Some time later, when I was playing in the garden with this same girl, she swallowed a small coin. In a panic, I went off to fetch a nurse again. This time one came, but it was too late. The girl died of suffocation. My second experience of death.

Helen's death affected me more deeply, however, and for a longer time than the death of this girl. Helen was my friend; I wanted to avenge her death. So, carrying a container of water, I crept into the babies' ward where the nurses who I had tried to fetch to Helen's bedside also worked. I walked along the row of cots and poured water over the babies: soaking their nappies, their little gowns and mattresses. The nurses had to spend hours changing nappies and bedclothes.

When I did the same thing again, I was caught and given a sound beating. I never ventured in the babies' ward after that.

Parents and orphans

Over and over again, I looked on as children around me were taken away by grown-ups who had come especially for them. These adults only ever hugged one child. Unlike the nurses, who passed through the bed-lined rooms giving everyone equal attention, these people walked straight up to one particular child and took him or her with them into the mysterious world out there on the other side of the fence. 'Out there' was an unim-aginably wide expanse, the desert into which you were never allowed to go by yourself. Only in the company of an adult. And even then, only the adult who came for you – and for you in particular.

Gradually, I realised that no one came for many of the children because there was no one to come for them. I was one of those children. All of us who slept in the huts stayed behind, while those in the hospital stayed for only a few weeks or months. There must be a difference between us and the other children, I thought, between those who stay and those who go. When I decided to ask about it, a nun explained to me: 'It's simple. The children in the hospital have parents, but you don't. You're orphans.'

Orphans or children. So these two words determined whether you stayed or you went, happiness and unhappiness. How could it be that some children were orphans and not others? Had orphans ever had parents? Had they done something bad? There were no answers to these questions, only the uneasy feeling that something was missing. Every time that another child left to join its parents and I had to stay behind came as a fresh blow to me.

I couldn't make any sense of it – I was only three years old. At least I assume that I was three at the end of my time in Orfan – I could have been four. To this day, no one knows when I was born. This is not unusual in Africa. Almost nobody knows their birth date, especially if, like me, they were born to poor families or in the countryside. There is no formal documentation of births. Ordinary people have neither a birth certificate, a certificate of baptism, a passport or an identity card. And why should they? These things cost money, and official confirmation of having been born brings nothing tangible: there is no baby bonus, maternity pay, child benefit, welfare payment or medical benefit to claim.

Later in life, I managed to establish, from my mother and from other relatives' memories, that I had been born 3 December but no one knew which year. It was easier for them to remember the day than the year, for the Ethiopian calendar brings additional complications. For instance, according to the Ethiopian calendar, 2004 is 1997. A year or two can easily be lost in converting dates. As I understand it, I could have been born on 3 December 1976,

1975, 1974, or even 1973. Nineteen seventy-four seems most likely to me. But it could just as easily be 1973.

I am not even sure what I was called when I was born – my early childhood is obscured in mystery, just as the Eritrean highlands are shrouded in mist in winter. I was probably named Saba after the famous queen. The first name I use today, Senait, was given to me later by my grandparents. My second name, Mehari, is my grandfather's first name. Children in Eritrea are given a first name, then they take their father's first name as a second name. The father will have a first name and take the first name of his father as a second name. So instead of distinguishing between first names and surnames, we have a very long succession of different first names. Since my father was not around, I took my grandfather's.

3

Comboni

At last the day came when I, too, was fetched from the home. Not by a set of parents, though, but by two men in uniform. They were in a great hurry and did not give me any time to say goodbye to anyone.

I suddenly felt a great longing for my parents. I knew instinctively that neither of the two soldiers was my father, for they barely glanced at me. Despite this, I sat in the small van hoping that they were taking me to my parents. I hoped it would be a long journey, for I wanted to see the desert and the mountains and the great expanse that I had only glimpsed from the veranda.

But the van did not head for the plains, it travelled into the city instead. My eyes opened wide. I had never left the grounds of the orphanage before, and now I saw people everywhere, buildings, palm trees, carts on the streets and traffic junctions. I was not looking through a fence this time; these things were all around me. I pressed myself to the window absorbed in a world that I had not seen before.

But my pleasure did not last for long. A few minutes later the van drove through a gate and I was in familiar surroundings again: a wall, a garden, a large building, lots of children, nuns and a gate that shut off the outside world. The building was larger, older and more beautiful than the one I had lived in until then. It was built of brick and had a gabled roof, which I had never seen before. It even had a tower with a bell, which sometimes rang. But I didn't notice any of that. I only saw the wall around us, rising unbelievably high above me; impossible to climb, even for a grown-up. It was much higher than the fence at Orfan and was built of stone. A solid wall that restricted my field of vision to the sky above rather than the wide reaches of the desert to which I had been accustomed.

A deep sadness overcame me when I realised that I had not been set free. Those soldiers had not brought me into the big wide world, or to my parents, but to another home. The nuns here wore strange uniforms: high-collared grey dresses with gigantic white caps that looked as solid and as heavy as stone. And I was practically the only black girl in this orphanage, too. Almost everyone else was white, nuns and children included.

The nun who came to meet me introduced herself as Florina, a name I had never heard before. Her face was white, as was her clothing – a dazzling white dress that swept the floor. Florina had thin, hard hands, which she laid on my shoulders. I shrank from her, partly because her hands were so pale and white that the veins beneath the skin could be seen. I stared at her in disbelief. She was very tall and thin, and wore glasses. I knew about glasses, but this was the first time I had ever seen them.

Filled with a kind of horrified fascination, I realised that the few hairs escaping from Florina's stony head-cloth were also pale. They were golden, like the hair of the lady in the painting in the orphanage refectory. All in all, Florina looked very much like the lady in the painting, except that her headdress was larger and whiter and stiffer. She folded her hands just like the lady in the painting, but she did not look gentle when she did so. I was immediately frightened of her, and knew that she had to be treated with respect. Florina spoke words that I understood, but in a harsh manner. Her words sounded quite different from anything anyone else had said to me before.

I looked around in wonder. Until then, the only white person I had ever seen was the lady in the painting, and now I was to live among white people. It was only then that I realised that there really were people with light-coloured hair and skin. I was filled with a sense of coldness and alienation, more clearly and deeply than ever before. Overcome with sadness, I was not even able to cry.

A strange place

Everything seemed even stranger to me when I realised that the white people spoke among themselves in a language that I did not understand. Not one word did I recognise. They produced completely strange sounds; only rarely did I hear the familiar rasp, coo, click and rhythm of my own language, Tigrinya. Their language was an exotic sounding singsong that was lovely and melodic to listen to, but also very fast and vigorously spoken. The language the nuns were speaking was Italian, both among themselves and with those in their care – white children and the odd African child like me.

Things were very different in this orphanage. Instead of raving about Mengistu Haile Mariam, they worshipped Daniel Comboni, a white man with a long beard and a stony face. A picture of him hung above the inner door. The nuns said he was from Italy, their home country, and that he had come here to help children. That was why he had built this place.

I noticed that the man with the strange name wanted to help the white children more than the black children, though. For the first rule of the orphanage was that pale-skinned people were allowed to do more than those with dark skins. No one told me that explicitly, it became clear to me from living there. In the courtyard was a large playground containing a colourful merry-go-round with horses, a couple of swings and a slide. It was paradise. I had never seen such a wonderful playground. But we black children were not allowed to use it.

At mealtimes, the black children sat at a small table set apart in a tiny anteroom connected to our dormitory, while the white children ate in the large dining hall, with a ceiling so high that you could barely see it. This room, which we were allowed into on special occasions, was covered in murals. The pictures on the walls showed strange things: green forests, mountains, lakes, and large brown animals wandering amidst them. There were short white men with beards and pointed hats, girls wearing long dresses and a hyena wearing a red headscarf. The nuns sometimes told us stories relating to the pictures, but I barely understood them. I did not know if all these things were real or if they came from a place which the nuns called 'heaven'.

In the beginning, the white children stared at us constantly, but they soon found out that they were better than us and treated us accordingly. They once forced me to eat my own lice, which crunched between my teeth, crawled, tickled and tasted bitter and revolting.

There were very few pleasant things about life at Comboni, things that I encountered there for the first time. However, 'Formaggio' was one of them. The Italian word for cheese still sounds wonderful to me. Also, the beds had sheets which were changed regularly, not mattresses or sacks with blankets, beneath which I had to huddle at night. (Winter nights could be terribly cold in Asmara, and the temperature could sink to five or ten degrees.) We were given a bright red drink, too – diluted raspberry cordial. All these pleasures had been unknown to me before. But best of all was being able to eat my fill every day. In Orfan we were always hungry, or went to bed with half-empty bellies, because there wasn't enough food to eat in the evenings. This was such a matter of course that I used to think that it was normal for my stomach to growl in the evenings. Even though I didn't like much about the rest of life in the convent, it was wonderful to have a fully belly at night.

I also liked the trips they took us on. We were packed into a bus every few days and driven into the city centre, to a much larger building, with an even higher tower than the one in which we lived. This was the cathedral of Asmara, where we had Tigrinya lessons with some white children. I had to study my own language as a foreign language, for in the year that had now passed, during which I had been speaking Italian to the

When I was in Eritrea in 2004 re-visiting my childhood, I went to the Daniel Comboni Catholic Convent as well.

other children and to the nuns, my mother tongue had become alien to me. I even spoke Italian to some black children because they came from regions in which Tigrinya was not spoken. They spoke other African languages, but I did not understand a word of them.

This babel of languages meant that I had no friend in the convent. So I spoke to an invisible friend that only I could see. He existed solely in my imagination, but all the more vividly for that. I spoke to him for hours, fought with him, let him explain things to me, comforted him, and let myself be reassured by him. I was not to have such a practical, patient and kind friend for a long time to come.

The white women told me I had other friends. One of them appeared often in my new home. He was pinned to a wooden cross with gigantic nails, so that blood streamed from his hands and feet. He even had blood on his head from wearing a crown of thorns. This white man with the tortured, morose looking expression on his face meant nothing to me, and I did not take anything the nuns said about him seriously. Jesus, as he was called, was nothing more than a distant, white stranger who was much to be pitied.

Salvation

I felt quite differently about the white lady in the beautiful long dress, however. There were statues of her all over the place. There she was in the corridor to the nuns' residence, above the entrance to the children's dormitories, and again and again in the church next door. This lady with the pale glowing skin, the blonde hair and the light blue eyes was very strange to me, but I liked her. I had never seen a woman remotely as beautiful as her. Almost all the nuns were Italian, as were most of the children – or they had at least one Italian parent. So, apart from Florina, they had dark hair and olive skin, although they were still very pale in comparison to Africans like me. But theirs was not the glowing white of the lady in the blue cloak with the golden circle round her head.

It was not only the lady's appearance that drew me to her, but the nuns telling me that she was my mother. I did not understand. This lady did not do anything for me that a mother would do: she did not take me out of the home; she did not punish my tormentors; she did not make sure that black and white children were treated equally, and she did not help me get over my loneliness. She did nothing but stand by looking friendly and beautifully pensive. Despite this, I pricked my ears up when the nuns said this. Was she really? If so, why was my mother pale-skinned? I had already realised that black women had black children and white women white. Was I an exception? It didn't seem very convincing, for it just couldn't be right – different children had different mothers; I had seen it with my own eyes. Was everything the nuns said a lie?

Although I wasn't sure about this lady, I still tried to talk to her. When no one could see me, I went up to her, stroked her, whispered to her and touched her to see if she was alive. But I never got a reply. Nothing happened, and the mother stayed silent.

Then another mother suddenly turned up. A flesh and blood mother. A black mother – my mum. Or at least a woman who claimed to be my mum. That was more than enough for me. Was I to be saved, too?

Mbrat just came into the Mother Superior's office one day and told her that she was my mother. The nun was convinced, and agreed to let Mbrat take me with her. Neither the nuns nor I showed any sadness at parting. While Mbrat exchanged a last few words with the nuns, I could hardly wait for the gate – which was always closed and watched over by a uniformed guard – to open and let me and Mbrat out, not into a new home this time, but finally into the wide world beyond all walls.

Mbrat took me by the arm and I went happily. I had never seen her before, but I called her 'Mama' from that day onwards. I brushed away any doubts about whether she was really my mother. She was good to me: she had taken me away from the horrible orphanage, she wanted to look after me and she smiled at me – I had never been so happy.

4

Grandparents

When Mbrat led me through the gate of the Comboni convent, she took me not only outside the wall at last, but also into a completely new world, which I found even stranger than the one I had seen on the streets of Asmara: the world of the family. I now lived in one of the small houses that I had only ever previously seen from the outside. I was part of a group of people held together by one thing: common descent. I was suddenly a member of a family, and a proper African family at that, with at least twenty people.

At only four or five, I was the youngest of eleven children, the baby of the family and I lived with my grandparents while my aunt and uncle lived in the house next door with their children, aged between ten and twenty years old. To me, this was a perfect family. I did not know that my father, a deserter and adulterer, had run off with another woman. I never asked after him. Only one thing counted for me: Mbrat, my long-absent mother, had taken me back into the bosom of her family.

It was like paradise. My grandparents' house was in Maitermenai, one of the better areas of Asmara. Maitermenai was not one of the exclusive residential districts that had been built by the Italians in colonial times, but slightly out of the city, on a gentle hill, where the houses had originally been built round a large hospital. Also there were only houses there, all with small gardens or courtyards, without slums, barracks or any industrial buildings in between.

My grandparents' house in Asmara is on this street.

My grandparents' house was the last in the street. Cars could barely pass through it, firstly because it was so narrow but also because the rocks jutted so high out of the sand that drivers feared for the undercarriage of their cars. Most people didn't have cars, though, only a bicycle at most, or perhaps a donkey or a horse, which they harnessed to a wooden cart. One room in our house was used for cooking, eating, living and sleeping in. Another room served as a storeroom and a bedroom. In a third room, which was very small and with no windows, were stored a few blankets, a cooker, wood and the washing tubs. In front of the house there was a yard no bigger than a room, surrounded by a wall. Unlike Comboni, this wall was not threatening, for you could walk through its gate at any time. Rather, it was protection from the world outside, for you could close the gate whenever you wanted. I loved this wall as I had never done a wall before.

There were animal sheds at the other end of the yard – small stalls in which two cows, two goats and a few hens were kept. The lean-tos were so low that the grown-ups could not stand upright in them, though I could. But the rooms we lived in had high ceilings so the heat didn't build up too much. There was space for beds, a table, a couple of chairs and a small cupboard. Our windows did not have glass in them, but they had tin shutters to keep out the heat. The floor was bare concrete – pleasantly cool – and a light bulb dangled from the ceiling. The beds were our seating in the daytime; apart from them we only had the two chairs and a low table, which we ate from seated on the floor.

Before every meal, we fetched a few bowls, pots, pans and the spirit cooker from the storeroom. We brought all this into the middle room to cook with. Everything happened in this room: preparing the food, eating it, living and chatting. We girls and women squatted on the floor or on low stools to chop the vegetables and cook the soups and sauces. After eating, we washed up in the courtyard and put everything back in the storeroom so all traces of eating or cooking were gone. The central room was once again pleasingly empty and tidy, for there was nothing in it. We only had a few things, and there was room for them all in one cupboard and a couple of boxes containing clothes and miscellaneous things.

I loved it. I had my very own kingdom for the first time ever. The tall iron gate protected me from the neighbourhood children roaming the street, donkeys, camels and dogs. My kingdom also had many colonies beyond its protective wall. The house was at the edge of the city, which ended just behind it. Herdsmen grazed their animals there and women tended vegetable allotments and small crop fields. This was where we children played. Everyone living in the area came here to a small wood for their ablutions, for there was no running water in the houses. Going to the toilet meant walking out into the bushes, squatting in floor-length robes while chatting with others, cleaning oneself with a few stones and then strolling back. It took me some time to get used to this, for the convent had had flushable toilets with spotless porcelain lavatories.

For us children, the rocky hillside that rose directly behind the fields to a small forest was an endless source of entertainment. You could look out over almost the whole city from the top of the hill. We hid in holes in the ground, played tag among the thickly clustered trees or simply hid in the bushes when we wanted to be left alone. I had my own special hiding place, a little hollow at the top of the hillside which no one else knew about. I loved creeping off there to dream a little, doze off, or simply gaze into the hazy heat of the day from the shade.

Sometimes, I herded my grandparents' cows, goats and chickens through the fields. They were kept in the tiny stalls next to the house at night, but spent the daytime outdoors. My family slaughtered the animals themselves and sold the meat, skins and everything else of value from the cows. There were also a dog and a cat, which I claimed for myself with no objection from anyone else – for dogs and cats were not of especial interest to anyone. So I could call them *my* dog and *my* cat with a clear conscience, which was a wonderful feeling. For the first time in my life, I felt that I could make decisions for something.

Fights with my siblings – not really my brothers and sisters, of course, but my uncles, aunts and cousins – did not bother me, for the street was full of other children I could play with at any time. It was not just like paradise, it was paradise.

The period I spent with my grandparents was indeed the most wonderful time of my childhood, if not my life. I felt nurtured and secure and loved as I never would feel again. This was despite the fact that moving in with my family was quite hard for me initially – although I eagerly overcame my difficulties. For instance, I found the school I went to strict and difficult because I hardly understood Tigrinya any longer, and I had to take great pains to relearn the vocabulary I had lost while I had been with the Italian nuns. This made me an outsider in my class, and I had to fight for my place in it.

I found the food strange, too. I was used to European food. Everyone ate with their fingers here, as well, instead of with a knife and fork, as the nuns had taught us to do. There was no cheese, bread or eggs, but *injera* instead. *Injera* in the mornings, afternoons and evenings, if there were three meals (there were often only two). *Injera* is the staple food of Eritrea, a thin, soft, sourdough pancake eaten with sauce. You can tell how well-off a family is by its sauce – poor families eat their *injera* with a simple tomato gravy or vegetable soup. If the family has a bit more money, the gravy contains chunks of meat, onions, diced vegetables or even eggs and chicken drumsticks. We had sauces of all sorts, not always with meat, but everything was extremely spicy – as spicy as anywhere else in Africa.

We sat round a circular tray to eat *injera* – tearing pieces of injera off and dipping them in sauce, or wrapping them round chunks of meat, carrying them to our mouths by hand. To everyone else's amusement, children and adults alike, my hand always jerked away from my mouth because the sauce was too spicy for me. I was very ashamed of this, and tried to switch my handful of *injera* from one hand to another without attracting attention because I thought the burning sensation came from my hand and not from the food. I used to panic when the food tasted just as spicy from the other hand, and examine my hands thoroughly to see if there was anything on them that made them taste that way. It was not possible to just stand up, leave the room and wash my hands, for this was only done after the meal. Later, I learned to scoop up less gravy, and got used to the hot spices. Looking back, I must have seemed like a European who was eating African food for the first time.

The christening

Although they were farmers, my grandparents were not in the least provincial. They lived in a town; they were not like people who lived in a village in the mountains who only knew their immediate environment, their animals, the landlord and the priest. They were educated people, Coptic Christians who spoke not only Tigrinya but Hebrew. My grandmother's mother had been raised in the Jewish faith – Judaism, like Christianity, had been brought over the Red Sea to Ethiopia over a thousand years ago by traders. We celebrated Chanukah as well as the Christian festivals, and my grandmother taught me a few Hebrew phrases. But soon after my arrival, my grandparents decided I should be christened – no one had thought about christening me before, not even the Catholic nuns. Perhaps they thought I had already been christened.

For my grandparents, only a christening in the centre of Christianity – Jerusalem – would do. This was tradition among the Coptic Christians in Ethiopia and Eritrea, though many people could not afford the journey to the Holy Land. All who are christened in Jerusalem are thus very proud of the fact throughout their lives, as I am.

There have been Christians in Ethiopia for a very long time, much longer than in central Europe, for instance. Soon after Jesus's death, Syrian traders brought Christianity with them to Ethiopia, where by the third or fourth century, a time when pagan Europeans still danced round their fires in Europe, it had become the state religion. It was because of this that Ethiopia was the only country in Africa that was never colonised by Europe – it was only occupied by the fascist Italians for a few years. The Italians must have marvelled at what they found on their arrival: no black savages here, but churches hundreds of years old, robed priests and devout Christians. It was not possible to claim that Ethiopians were inferior beings who had to be enslaved and converted in order for eternal life in God's kingdom to be open to them. My grandfather told me all this with great pride, and passed on a closeness to God that I feel to this day.

My grandparents had already travelled to Jerusalem many times for their own children, but made the journey once again for me. It was late at night when we boarded the ship in the large port of Massawa to start our voyage of thousands of kilometres, over the Red Sea, past Sudan and Egypt. We had spent the night before on a bus from Asmara to Massawa, negotiating hundreds of hairpin bends on the road down to the sea, a descent of almost 2,500 metres. After the ship docked at our destination, we boarded another bus that took us across the Sinai peninsula to Jerusalem, where my grandparents christened me 'Senait' – Tigrinya for 'Sinai', the tongue of land between Egypt and Israel.

From then on, I was called Senait, like Mount Sinai, from which the Ten Commandments had been proclaimed. Many girls in Eritrea carry this name, which means 'place of peace' or simply 'peace'. The Eritrean war of independence against Ethiopia had been underway for more than twenty years at the time, claiming thousands of lives on both sides. Many towns, especially in Eritrea, had suffered great destruction, and vast stretches of land were minefields, totally off limits. But there was still no end in sight. So there were good reasons to name a child 'peace'.

My grandparents did not give me my name lightly. Like most of my family, they were deeply religious Christians, from whom I learned to believe in God. We read from the Bible together, and I listened to the stories of Jesus and Mary in church.

When I returned from my christening, I went back to school exhausted but bursting with pride. My classmates clearly treated me with more respect after that. This was important to me, for I had never had an easy time at school. My Tigrinya was improving only very slowly, and I still did not understand a great deal of what the teacher or my classmates said. Apart from this, I was left-handed, but the teacher insisted that I learned everything from scratch and write, draw and sew with my right hand instead. Sewing was the most difficult of all – needle in the right hand, fabric in the left. I just couldn't get the hang of it.

We were taught in Tigrinya and English, and at five years old we had already started on fractions, music and geography. We learned everything by heart. In Africa, knowledge is a rare luxury, to be taken maximum advantage of. 'Be grateful for your education,' our teacher told us over and over again. Laziness was out of the question, for the teacher and for us.

Our teacher was especially committed – she saw me as a challenge. She took me home after school every day herself as a gesture of thanks for the bananas or other small gifts my grandparents sent through me. My grandparents were well aware of how to help their granddaughter along in school. Despite this, the teacher complained about me almost every day. 'This child is a monster!' – I still hear that sentence ringing in my ears. I was an impossible child who just could not sit still or leave my classmates alone, constantly asked questions that the teacher could not answer.

I was a rebel, a whirlwind, the terror of the classroom and of the entire neighbourhood. I even managed to beat up the boys in my street. Girls were not meant to hit each other, but for a girl to hit a boy was so unthinkable that it wasn't even on the list of taboos.

Martin, a boy in my street, was very fat, and I had it in for him. I used to chase him through the neighbourhood yelling, 'Fatty! Lose some weight!' I must have driven him crazy. Sometimes I decided I liked him and would ask him to marry me, but the next day I would hunt him down only to beat him up again. His fatness was a source of boundless irritation. How could anyone just go on eating like that? I wondered.

My behaviour made my grandmother anxious. 'She's got that gleam in her eye again,' she would say, 'look out! But don't worry, she isn't angry with you.' She was right, for I was honest and straightforward: if I liked someone, I would tell them so baldly, and if I didn't, I would say so too, equally openly.

Some grown-ups took offence at my frankness. My grandmother only punished me once for it, with a couple of smacks on my behind that didn't really hurt. Nothing like a real beating that left black and blue marks, after which sitting down became impossible because of the weals and bruises. I was very lucky, for whenever I was rude to a grown-up, my grandmother said, 'Of course I'll see to it that she learns her lesson', but the punishment never came. I was only so naughty because I knew my actions would have no consequence.

We had one particularly detestable neighbour who we children called 'Haregu', that is to say, 'dung beetle'. She was old and decrepit looking, stingy, and altogether stupid. Haregu hated children, and we hated her. Her eyesight wasn't very good, so we often jumped out from hiding places to frighten her. Haregu complained to my grandmother all the time, 'She's a little beast, not a child!' My grandmother promised to punish me, but as soon we got home, she would pat me on the back and say, 'Well done, well done!'

Meat

I got up to all manner of mischief at that time, such as washing meat with soap. My grandmother used to put our washing in a pot of water on top of the fire, add detergent and boil it all up, stirring a few times. We only had a few pots, which were put to every possible use, so one day, she put some meat to pickle in the same pot used for washing.

While running around in the courtyard that evening, I noticed this pot with some meat in the pickling fluid. It occurred to me that it would be good to give the meat a wash, so I shook some washing powder into the pot and gave the mixture a good stir so it foamed beautifully.

All hell broke loose the next morning. Bellowing with rage, my grandmother stormed into the room that served as the kitchen, sitting room and children's bedroom, and screamed at me like a fury. She realised that only I could have done such a thing.

'But what's wrong with that?' I asked, perfectly unaware. 'You wash everything else. I only wanted to help wash the meat.' I meant this quite seriously. Although I, too, knew there was something not quite right about putting detergent and meat together, it had never occurred to me that the meat would be made inedible. The meat – beef from a freshly slaughtered cow – was the most expensive food conceivable in an African household. In any other family, I would have been beaten to within an inch of my life for this misdemeanour, but I can no longer remember what my punishment was, so it cannot have been too bad.

My decision to stop eating meat was unrelated to this incident. It came about after I saw a chicken being slaughtered. This was an everyday event; everyone slaughtered their own chickens, goats, sheep or cows at home if they had them. Those who had no fowl of their own bought them live at the market and slaughtered them at home. With no refrigerators, it was easier to transport and store living animals than meat.

My grandparents had their own chickens. Once, my grandfather decided that I should watch him slaughter a chicken so I would know how it was done, even though I would never be allowed to do it myself. Only men were allowed to slaughter animals in Eritrea. Women were considered impure – and no one would have eaten meat from an animal slaughtered by a woman. But women were allowed to do everything else after the slaughter: plucking, washing, gutting, skinning, butchering and cooking. I sometimes thought that men had apportioned things this way to suit themselves: they spent thirty seconds slaughtering the chicken while the women spent three hours doing everything else. Perhaps I was right.

When my grandfather pulled me into the yard to watch him slaughter the chicken, the other children were already gathered round, for they loved watching a slaughter. It was precisely because I didn't like watching it that my grandfather brushed away my excuses and insisted that I stay and watch.

My grandfather was an old hand at this, and had the lives of a few hundred chickens on his conscience. With practised ease, he grabbed the chicken by its legs, turned it upside down and placed it on top of a rock. He pressed the bird down with one hand and slit its throat with a sharp knife that seemed to pass into the flesh more smoothly than through a tomato. Blood spurted and the bird jerked wildly. The other children cheered while I hid my face with my hands and sobbed uncontrollably.

My reaction annoyed my grandfather. He popped a red plastic bowl over the flailing chicken to protect it from the dirt and from our dog – who was already looking on greedily – in its dying throes. But even before the corpse was covered from my eyes, I had resolved that I would not touch a bite of that chicken, and I would never eat meat again. I have held to this.

My decision was taken as evidence of madness by everyone else. Meat was such a rare luxury, so delicious and sought-after, that I had surely lost my mind to be refusing it. It was months before my family got used to me not eating meat. I was probably the only vegetarian in Eritrea – everyone who learned of it from my grandparents shook their head wonderingly. My grandmother had a glimmer of understanding for me, but even she still offered me meat whenever it was being served – in vain.

Little did I know it, but the time was soon to come when I would no longer be offered meat – and would be happy for anything to eat at all.

Questions

If I had had any choice in the matter, life at my grandparents' could have gone on for ever. I did not miss my father, and neither did my grandparents. Having left a trail of women and children behind him, he was no favourite.

My father knew nothing about my life. He knew that Mbrat had come to fetch me from the home, but had showed no interest in visiting me. His family blamed him for leaving his parents to look after me.

I was still known as the 'suitcase baby'. My grandparents' neighbours knew the story, as did everyone else except me. My grandparents never explained, only saying that I should ignore the cries of the children. I am sure they thought I wouldn't have understood, and I am glad that they kept the truth from me.

While I lived with my grandparents, I called Mbrat, who lived in the same house, 'Mama'. Mbrat had two daughters of her own: Senait and Frehiwet, who were both older than me. Senait had already moved out by the time I arrived, so Frehiwet was the sister I got to know. She said to me once, 'Senait, you have another sister, who is also called Senait.'

This got me thinking, so I asked Mbrat: 'Mama, why have you called two daughters Senait? How will we know who you mean when you call us?'

She didn't reply at first, then said, 'I've always found the name beautiful.' But of course she would never have named me Senait if I had been her child.

Her reply didn't make sense to me, but I took it at face value because I wanted it to be true. I didn't want to have to ask any more questions.

Soldiers

During the years I spent in that perfect, sheltered world at my grandparents', the world of the grown-ups outside the walls of my little paradise had changed, and not for the better. The war between Eritrea and Ethiopia had become increasingly violent, and Eritrea seemed to be staring defeat in the face as the two forces fighting for the country's freedom – the Eritrean Liberation Front (ELF) and the Eritrean People's Liberation Front (EPLF) – conflicted with each other more and more instead of against the common enemy. The Ethiopian dictator Haile Mengistu Selassie can only have rubbed his hands in glee at seeing his enemies in such disarray, and must have felt that victory was his. Almost all the larger towns and cities in Eritrea were under the control of Ethiopian government troops, so the rebels had to retreat to the impassable mountain regions or the malaria-infested west on the border with Sudan.

The Eritreans were subject to constant harassment. Ethiopian soldiers came to my grandparents' house several times, not merely to visit or search the place, but to plunder it. They barged in at all times of the day and night and took whatever they liked. Once, they even set fire to the house, leaving my grandparents to expend great effort in putting it out. Their protestations that they were neither hiding weapons nor harbouring rebels were brushed aside by the soldiers. They may just have been following orders, but the results were the same for us: repeated harassment.

I was old enough by now to understand that all this was no game, but deadly serious. These men in uniform were not ordinary people, and my grandparents, aunt and uncle – not to mention I myself – were powerless against them.

Asmara was under a strict curfew. The tanks rumbled out of the barracks every evening to take their places at all the major intersections in the city. Soldiers patrolled the streets and the sound of gunfire echoed around the houses. Anyone caught on the streets after eight in the evening was arrested, if not immediately shot in the name of 'self-defence'. Women were raped and children were abused – this was all part of a war of attrition being played out in towns and villages. Over and over again, I asked the grown-ups what was happening, but got no reply.

One day, I decided to find out for myself what was going on outside the protective wall of our house. I had no idea what violence and danger the world outside held, even for a small girl. In the evening light, as everyone made for home and all children ought to have been in their houses long ago, I climbed over the wall. I crept down our little side street and out on to the main road, making my way uphill a little to a spot where some soldiers were standing. I'd brought them something to eat as a present. I imagined that these men in their barracks, tents and other shelters couldn't afford anything to eat, but this was quite wrong. Soldiers were much better off than ordinary people because they were able to plunder and snatch food and cattle entirely at whim.

Unlike the grown-ups and other children, I was fascinated by these soldiers rather than frightened by them. This cannot be attributed to courage, for I was a timid child and ran off whenever there was a hint of trouble. I simply had no idea who the soldiers were or what they did.

The grown-ups knew very well, and kept their distance

from them. They knew that there is no justice and no law in wartime. They also knew that other people's lives meant little to these men – who had little education, were aggressive, hungry, drunk or addicted to drugs, and capable of killing anyone who got in their way, got on their nerves or made them frightened. They knew that the soldiers thought exactly as their enemies did: shoot first, ask later. So the adults around me gave these shabby figures a wide berth, and pulled me away whenever I tried to get near them, which only fired my curiosity all the more.

I found the soldiers interesting because they looked no different from us, but had much more to say. Most of the soldiers were quite young – still in their teens – but to children like us they seemed almost grown up. It was perfectly normal for a twenty-year-old woman to have two or three children, so she would appear middle-aged in our eyes. Most of the soldiers started training at the age of eleven, and, from the age of fourteen, wore proper uniforms and were sent to the front in regular troops. The occupying forces in Asmara were a little older. This followed the pattern of all wars in Africa, which still holds true today: the young hotheads are packed off to the front while the older soldiers are called to duty in the less dangerous areas – places that are already occupied, or the hinterland. The battle on the front was no child's play, but it was children who fought it.

I wanted to see what the soldiers in the square were doing, and find out more about them. I carried with me some *injera*, a corn cob and a little fruit from our garden for them. I couldn't have brought more food without attracting attention at home – we were not so comfortably off that food would not be missed.

The soldiers shouted a hearty welcome as they beckoned me out to their guard posts. They had built provisional barricades, which commanded a good view of the main road from the city centre to Maitemenai. We sat together in their shelters and they

A view of Maitemenai in Asmara, where I used to live.

chatted with me, showing me their weapons and letting me look out of their spy-holes. They were very surprised to receive a visit from a small girl bearing gifts of food who wanted to talk to them.

After my first visit had gone so well, I visited the soldiers more often. They were always very friendly to me. Once, when night had fallen during one of our chats, two or three of them accompanied me home, for I was not supposed to be walking about on my own because of the curfew. Even the soldiers themselves did not dare to walk the streets alone for fear of snipers. When I look back now, I think it was naïve of the soldiers to trust me and accompany me home, for I could easily have led them into an ambush.

My grandmother was completely beside herself when I arrived home with the soldiers. She had been extremely worried when I hadn't returned home by the time darkness fell. She now feared that the soldiers had caught me doing something stupid, and would do something terrible to me or the family as punishment. She started to cry and fell prostrate before the soldiers, pleading, 'Please don't do anything to her, she's still a child! Please!'

The Ethiopian soldiers were used to spreading fear and terror. Although they were still in Ethiopia, they were in enemy territory, for the inhabitants of Eritrea wanted independence, and regarded Ethiopian soldiers as the hated occupiers, even when they were from the same tribe.

But these soldiers were very kind. 'We don't mean to do anything,' they reassured my grandmother. 'Now calm down and stop screaming. If someone sees us here, we'll be thrown in jail. We should be manning our posts. But this girl always brings us food, so we wanted to say thank you. Tell her not to come to us any longer – she's putting herself and you in danger.' Still sobbing, my grandmother swore that she would never let me out in the evening again.

This incident made a great impression on me. Afterwards, my grandmother said to me, 'If they catch you, and a nasty commander is there, they'll shoot you.' Instilled with fear, I never went out to see the soldiers again after that.

That night, I had a very strange, vivid dream. It was New Year's Day and soldiers had come to raise hell in our house. They were not looking for my father this time, but had come to kill my grandmother. They were shouting about wanting blood. Panic-stricken, I screamed, 'Don't kill my grandmother!' and 'Hide her!' I woke in a sweat and ran crying to my grandmother in the next room to tell her about my dream. She let me get into bed with her, but nothing could comfort me.

We re-enacted the dream together the next day. I insisted that my grandmother hide herself somewhere in the house so I could look for her. Whenever she did not hide herself well enough, I would say, 'They'll find you there', and look for a better hiding place. Then I would pull her out and scream at her, 'No, not here, in the living room!', and so on in the yard, the pantry and every other room until I had driven her through the whole house.

There were few hiding places because the house was small and had no nooks and crannies to hide in. But shooing my grandmother from place to place helped me drive away my fear. It was typical of my grandmother's remarkable nature that she agreed to play along with me. No one else I have met before or since understood children so well.

5

With my Father

The first sign that the wonderful time in my grandparents' house would end came one evening when my grandmother said, 'Senait, you must get to know your father.' This came as a shock rather than as a happy surprise to me. My father did not interest me in the least. I had my grandfather, my grandmother and Mbrat. I associated my father with bad things: the soldiers searching for him who regularly turned our house upside down; other children constantly asking me who and where my father was; the uneasy knowledge that Mbrat had fetched me from the home and that my father had done nothing to help.

The last thing in the world I wanted was to live with my father. I wanted to live with my mother and my grandparents for ever. So I told my grandmother the very same evening that I did not want to meet my father. She was genuinely surprised and asked why not.

'I don't like him,' I said.

'But you don't know him,' she replied.

'I don't like him anyway,' I retorted.

'Why? At least say why you don't like him,' my grandmother countered.

'I feel it here,' I said, pointing to my belly. My dislike sprang from deep within me. I disliked him without even knowing him.

My grandmother did not bring up the subject again for another few days, but then I was suddenly told that Mbrat had

Mbrat, my aunt, who pretended to be my mother when she fetched me from the orphanage.

left on a journey. I shot out of the house like an arrow, through the yard, and up the street. But Mbrat was gone. I asked everyone I met if they had seen her, but she seemed to have been swallowed up by the ground. No one told me where she had gone. No one from our household went anywhere normally. No one went on holiday, or away to work or to visit relatives who lived far away. The only journey I could remember was the trip to Jerusalem for my christening, and Mbrat had been christened a long time ago. She had simply disappeared.

Then I was told that I, too, had to set off on a journey the next day, and that my great aunt would come to fetch me. I knew immediately where I was going – to my father. I put up great resistance: thrashing around, arms and legs flailing, crying and sobbing, but all in vain. The grown-ups had made their decision.

The great aunt took me on an overcrowded bus, and we travelled towards Keren, a town in the west of Eritrea, and then onwards to Barka province. The journey was not without danger, for some of the fiercest battles between Ethiopian government troops and Eritrean resistance fighters were taking place in Barka.

The government troops only controlled the main roads and some of the larger towns in the region, while the rest was in the hands of the Eritreans. The partisans often blockaded roads – either to disrupt traffic or to lie in wait for Ethiopian troops. The Ethiopians often attacked non-military properties if they were suspected of harbouring the enemy. Neither side could be accused of timidity in this war.

Despite this, I enjoyed the journey, but only because of one particular event. When we changed buses late in the evening, my great aunt carried me in her arms all the way across a large square. She thought I was asleep, but I was only pretending. Being carried by her was the most wonderful thing, and I decided that this woman was not evil after all. Perhaps there was hope for me in my father's house. Perhaps I would not have to stay there for ever, and would be able to return to my grandparents soon.

Father

We reached my father's house late in the evening on the second day of our journey. One hardly ever has to travel very far in Eritrea, but it is always a long-winded business. A mere two hundred kilometres can take a whole day, what with waiting and transfer time and tyre punctures on the creaking, overloaded buses.

When we stumbled, half-dead from exhaustion, into my father's house, I saw Mbrat. She was suddenly there again, the mother who had abandoned me. I flew into her arms ecstatically, but she must have been feeling guilty, for she did not give me a very warm welcome. Instead, she introduced to a woman called Werhid, who was to be my new mother.

Confusion came over me, and only increased as Mbrat introduced me to a host of new brothers and sisters. It was an effort to remember the names of my new family. Werhid was my stepmother, whom my father had married after he had left my birth mother and then his second wife Ahrehet. Werhid had four children of her own and also looked after her sister's child. She also cared for Yaldiyan and Tzegehana, daughters of my father's second wife, who were to become my companions for many years.

Then my father came in. He looked a wreck: tall, haggard and jittery, wearing a gloomy expression. His features were similar to mine. It was a shock to suddenly come face to face with the man whom I had feared so much but was also fascinated by. I had never imagined him to look this way, and could do nothing but stare. I shied away from his greeting by hiding in Mbrat's skirt, but she pushed me towards him. I turned away, hunched and silent. The dislike was mutual from the first instant, for I had showed my father what he hated most – resistance.

My antipathy towards my father grew from that moment onwards, a product of the stubborn nature for which we were both well known. This nature sprang from our desire to control our own lives and subsequent mistrust of anyone who threatened our freedom. I knew from the moment I met my father that my life was going to change, though I did not know how to put it in words. I said to Mbrat, 'Mama, I feel that I will never see you again. You're going to go away, and I'll never see you again.'

Startled, she replied, 'Why do you say that? Of course we'll see each other again. I'm here with you now!'

Just in case, I stayed close by for the next few hours, hanging from her skirts when she went from one room to the other, even following her to the edge of the village when she went to relieve herself.

When the others lay down on mattresses or on the floor to sleep, I stayed wide awake, despite my utter exhaustion, for I felt that my beloved mother could disappear at any minute. She had disappeared from my grandparents' house two days ago with no warning, and that could happen again. I curled up next to her and clung on to her with my arms and legs as best as I could, only relaxing my grip as sleep gradually overcame me.

At first light, I sat up bolt upright and saw that Mbrat was no longer there. I knew she had gone. I didn't bother to look round the sleeping bodies in the room, but shot out into the yard on to the street and ran down it, hoping against hope to catch a glimpse of her. It was a misty morning, for it had rained heavily in the night. My mother was nowhere to be seen. I saw a few villagers on their way to fetch water and a couple of children herding goats, nothing else. No buses, no cars, and no sign of my mother.

Had I made a mistake? Was she still in the house after all? I ran back to check. But she was not there.

My throat was tight, I found it impossible to cry. Something broke in me then, a gaping wound opened deep inside me. I have no memory of the rest of that day.

New sisters

The next morning, my father's thin voice roused us, 'Get up, all of you!'

That was the first thing I remember him saying. It gave me a shock, and I huddled deeper into my mattress, my heart pounding. Then Yaldiyan, my new sister, who was five years older than me, came and whispered something in my ear. In my fright, I didn't understand her at first. She repeated, in a louder voice, 'Come, let's go and fetch the water.'

I looked around at the others, and gestured at the children of Werhid, my new stepmother. 'Aren't they coming too?'

Yaldiyan shook her head and beckoned me towards her. 'Fetching water is our job. Father said you were to come with me.'

But I put up further resistance. 'Why aren't the others working as well? Why do we have to do it?'

My father had come back in and overheard this exchange, but the first I knew of it was when I was slapped in the face and fell to the floor. I was not surprised, though, for I had guessed that my father would hit me.

All Eritrean men hit their children, and their wives, too, from time to time. Being hit is part of children's day-to-day upbringing, which mainly consists of keeping quiet and being put to useful work.

From that moment on, everything became clear to me. My father had declared himself as an enemy, and made explicitly clear that I was to obey him. That was all I had to know. Undemurring, I stood up promptly and went to fetch water with my sister. My new life as my father's daughter had begun, and it would be almost two decades before it came to an end.

Fetching water is hard work, so it is left almost solely to women, girls and, if necessary, small boys. There were no water pipes in the country – we fetched water directly from the wells, at least in theory. The wells were often empty, though, which meant we had to look for water in other places, most likely in dried-up river beds, water holes or deep valleys. A little digging brought us to a brown liquid which was only drinkable after boiling.

My sister and I were in luck this time, though. It had been raining, so the river bed was wet. All we had to do was look for a place where the water had gathered and scoop it up with a couple of old cooking oil tins. Yaldiyan had chosen a place far from home to collect water. Down in the river bed, she whispered to me, 'Just play dumb! Pretend you're a clumsy dolt ! That's the only way!' She must have been terrified of our father, to keep her voice to a whisper even then.

I took her advice and dropped one of the two containers of water within sight of the house, so that everyone could see the precious water running into the dirt. From then on, I often dropped things, so I quickly got labelled as too clumsy and nervous for most serious work.

My father was horrible not only to us but to people outside the family. He was fond of crude jokes and used to tell us how he had unmasked a fortune teller when he was a boy. This fortune teller had had a very good reputation in the area and used to be paid for diagnosing people's illnesses. My father had always suspected her of being an impostor, so he decided to put her to the test. One day, he cut a lemon in half, tied one half to his leg, pushed his trouser leg down over it and hobbled out of the house. On the street, he fell to the ground, struggled up, fell again, and pretended to be writhing in agony. In no time, half the village gathered round, as he shrieked, 'I want the fortune teller! Take me to her!'

He was carried to the fortune teller and everyone gathered round her hut. He showed her the lump on his leg and wailed, 'Oh God, it's getting bigger every day!'

The fortune teller touched the lemon through his trousers, but did not dare to lift the trouser leg of a young man of about twelve. Her face took on a grave expression. 'This is incurable,' she said portentously. 'Your leg will have to be amputated.'

My father grinned widely and pulled his trouser leg up so that everyone could see the lemon. There was an uproar, and a few people wanted to lynch the fortune teller on the spot, but she was merely given a beating and hounded out of the village.

My father related all such exploits with great relish. The high spirits of his youth had not left him. But he knew how to command respect, and I soon understood that in the village he was regarded as an important person, whose opinion on everything counted. This was good in a way, for his children were, if not exactly treated with respect, then not dismissed summarily. This went some way to helping me get used to my new surroundings.

Despite my unhappiness, I laughed a great deal – which seemed to get on my father's nerves much more than my sadness. Like my sisters, I was frightened of my father, but whereas they constantly strove to do everything exactly as he wished, I was more disruptive.

We flee

The security and regular rhythm of everyday life at my grandparents' house was gone. Life at my father's was insecure and transitory. We packed up and moved half a year after my arrival there, just as I had begun to get used to things. A few plastic bags and jute sacks sufficed for our possessions: a couple of bowls and pans, a cooker, a coffee pot, a transistor radio, a folder of documents and photos, a couple of blankets and the few clothes we had that weren't already on our backs.

We had to move because more and more soldiers had been coming to our village and threatening us. Shots rang out in the night – something I had been used to in Asmara – but there was also a low rumble, which frightened me a great deal at first. I thought it was an earthquake or a great storm until my sisters explained that it was the sound of heavy artillery.

We were a pathetic sight as we set off: my father, his wife and the motley collection of children, all laden with sacks, blankets and other odds and ends. We had neither a camel nor a car; even if we had been able to afford a car, they were simply not available to ordinary people then. So, along with everyone else, we had to squash into the backs of the overcrowded lorries which had replaced bus services disrupted by the war.

Life on the road was hard. There was nothing to eat, hardly anything to drink, no sleep to be had, and no certainty as to where our journey would end. My father let out his frustration at the situation by hitting, kicking or spitting at us at the slightest provocation.

We rested by the roadside at night, listening to the rumble of artillery and the drone of aircraft overhead heading for the towns to drop their cargo of bombs. The planes flew without navigation lights, so the sound of their engines was the only indication of their presence. The grown-ups ducked fearfully, while I became more and more frightened.

This was no mere journey from one place to another. We were fleeing for our lives. As we passed by foot or on the lorry, I saw the consequences of war for the first time: villages destroyed, burnt houses, blackened, misshapen vehicles and artillery cannons riddled with gunshot holes. But there was more, much more, that we didn't see.

Eventually we stopped travelling and came to rest in another hut built from odd bits of wood, on the outskirts of a remote village in a mountainous region. The village could practically have been a town – though the buildings were only single-storeyed, they were built of brick and lined a main street and a couple of side streets.

We started going to school again in this village. The school premises were nothing more than a corrugated iron roof held up by building scraps, casting shade over a patch of rocky ground on which we sat, facing our teacher. There were no textbooks or jotters or any other school material, only a tiny slate board on which the teacher scratched numbers and letters in chalk. Despite these meagre resources, we clung to her every word. There was no disruption or fooling around in that classroom – everyone listened, for going to school had the character of a church service about it. We were happy to be occupied with something other than war and horror.

These schools in the country were organised by the freedom fighters, this particular one by the Eritrean Liberation Front (ELF), for which my father had fought. It was under that corrugated iron roof that we first learned about the ELF vision of a free Eritrea, a socialist state for a better future, and absorbed their slogans, songs and dreams. Beyond that roof lay the murderous heat of the day, rocks and thorny undergrowth. And the war, which made itself felt not only in gunfire, misery and hunger, but in the behaviour of the grown-ups around us, which ranged from the merely tense to the outright aggressive. Paying attention in class was an escape into a better world.

I was six years old.

The war approaches

The war advanced inexorably, announcing its arrival in the days and nights before it reached us. A siren sounded in the village every night, and sometimes even during the day. Then planes droned overhead, flying so low that we could read the lettering on their tails or cockpits. Sometimes the planes arrived before the wail of the siren. In either case, there was no defence against the bombs. As soon as the enemy planes appeared, everyone ran helplessly through the village; some even ran out to the mountains, though for no particular reason. It was complete chaos.

We children had no idea what bombs were. All we were told was that they were very dangerous and that they killed everything around them. This was enough to make us extremely frightened.

Of course, the pilots were not going to waste their bombs on an unimportant village in the mountains. They were en route to Keren, Akurdet or Asmara, where the partisans had been concentrating their efforts to overthrow the Ethiopian occupiers.

On the afternoon the war arrived in the village, we children had finished lessons for the day. Some of us still had chores to do at school, though. We were doing the washing or collecting firewood, while others lingered in the shade of the school roof whiling away the time.

The siren was silent when the planes came. The drone of the engines sounded clearly like a swarm of buzzing bees, growing louder and louder. There were only two or three planes. The grown-ups started running around in panic again, and only us children stayed where we were. Our fear had been dulled by nothing ever having come of the sirens before.

This time it was different. The planes unloaded their cargo directly over us, and it looked like small animals or children were falling to the ground like stones a few hundred metres from the school. We ran off in different directions, but nothing happened. The planes disappeared into the distance, the drone faded and the silence of the desert fell again.

We raised our heads warily and crept out of our hiding places behind rocks or under thorn bushes. The grown-ups also returned to the village slowly. The planes' cargo had dropped into a small hollow not far from the school, so no one else apart from the children had seen it.

Curious, we edged towards the strange objects lying in the hollow, some of which had broken apart from their hard landing on the stones. Before we could look any closer, the teacher called all the children who had been attending to chores to come back and finish our work. We trailed back unwillingly.

Suddenly, there was a mighty explosion in the hollow, followed by screams of pain. Smoke billowed and flames shot out of the bushes. Bleeding children staggered out from the smoke and screaming mothers ran towards them. Crying and screaming filled the air. We ran over, and were greeted by a picture of desolation: blackened children, broken bodies and unidentifiable burning objects. And dolls. There were dolls lying everywhere: some a little damaged, some broken, and others whole. One of the children who had just arrived picked up one of the dolls and was engulfed in a fiery explosion. The child fell to the floor in a fireball, writhing and screaming, and then fell silent. As we stood there transfixed with horror, the grown-ups pulled us away. The dolls were filled with explosives; they had been specially constructed and scattered to maim and kill children.

That day resounded with screams of pain. Children died of burns in their mothers' arms. There was no medication, no bandages, no disinfectant in the village. A few of the injured were taken away to other places. Twenty children died that day. The village was in uproar, but nobody could do anything. Crying and shivering with fear, I and my sisters huddled together, uncomprehending. In our shock, we even forgot our hunger.

No one dared to sleep when darkness fell. Moans of grief could be heard throughout the night. I cried for hours, howling like I had never done before. There was no one to comfort me. My sisters were also inconsolable while my father tore through the village in a tornado of rage and aggression. My stepmother was comforting friends whose children had been killed. For the first time in my life, I felt how completely alone I was in the world. I realised that the only person I could rely on was myself.

In the desert

The village never returned to normal after this tragedy. School resumed, but many places were empty. The teacher often squatted silently on the ground, scratching the sand with a stick as if she was drawing something, though no one could make out what it was. My father became more restless than ever. He could barely sit still for five minutes, but was constantly going to the neighbours or out into the mountains, back on to the main road, into the local bar and out on to the street again. A few families had gathered their belongings and left the village. It was not long before we did the same. No one asked why or where we were going. Everyone knew this was no place to stay.

We set off on foot, with no animals or other companions, just us: father, stepmother and eight children altogether. The sun beat down on us mercilessly during the day, but our teeth chattered with cold at night as we slept in the open some way off the road to avoid passing soldiers.

One night, the lions came to us. We felt something different in the air; there was something missing. The quiet hum of the night had stilled. Father did not let the fire go out this time, but added a couple of sticks to it instead.

We had to be careful with our firewood, which consisted of odds and ends of brushwood, laboriously sawn off with a blunt cleaver. Apart from this, both animal and human enemy had to be considered when building a fire. A bright fire kept animals away but might draw the human attention, not always friendly. If the flames were low, people would not be drawn to the camp, but lions, hyenas and coyotes would pace in narrowing circles round the sleeping group.

The lions had come too close for comfort this time; the vigorous flames leaping from the fire had made no impression on them. They were a pair of full-grown lionesses, pacing silently fifteen or twenty metres away from us in the shadows.

A few of the children were already asleep. Werhid and my father were still awake, as was I, the greatest coward of them all. I was convinced that my hour had come and that the lions would gobble us – or certainly me – up.

I knew that you were not supposed to run away from a lion, or it would chase you and eat you. I also knew that you were supposed to keep quiet and not scream or make any gestures, which would make a lion aggressive. We had nothing to frighten a lion off with – no guns or weapons of any sort, except for our blunt cleaver. Knowing all this was no help. I started trembling and whimpering quietly.

There we lay: the little ones asleep, the older ones frozen with fear while I shivered. The lions were now two or three metres away from us. They sniffed the blankets and the empty pans and pushed a few plastic bags aside. They stood undecidedly for a moment, looking around them, stared at us and looked around again. This is it, I thought; now they are going to eat me. Those few seconds seemed like an eternity.

Then they suddenly dropped their heads and trotted off. I had peed in my pants from fear, as I often did. Where I had been freezing a few moments ago, I was now bathed in sweat. Relief washed over me as the lions padded off into the night.

The danger had probably not even been that great. Lions do not attack human beings when they do not feel threatened by them. 'A lion does not eat anything that it does not know,' said our father. 'Human beings, for example. We smell too strange. Lions eat antelope or goats or other wild animals. Human beings are a last resort.'

Beatings

After a few days, we found temporary shelter in a much smaller village, where we were able to stay for a little longer. Moving had taken its toll on us, though. A couple of the children had come down with a fever from the exhaustion of it all.

We stayed with relatives this time, but it did not make life any easier. There was not enough to eat, too little space, too many children and an abundance of beatings. My father lashed out with blows whenever anything displeased him, which happened often. Anyone making too much noise was hit, and when I did not spring up at once to fetch water because I wanted to finish playing a game first, I was slapped vigorously and pushed out of the house. If my father was hungry and dinner was not ready yet, he hit us on our heads, our faces, backs or punched us in our stomachs. While smacking children is commonplace in Africa, few fathers could have made their blows so brutal or so frequent as ours did.

I was my father's favourite victim. The longer I lived with him, the clearer it became that he had it in for me. He beat his other children, too, naturally. He beat Werhid's children too, and even the neighbours' or his friends' children, when they crossed his path. This happened as a matter of course, and was nothing out of the ordinary. Every adult had the right to smack a child who did anything to disturb or displease him or her.

My father did not beat me merely as a matter of course, though, but with a directed vindictiveness, regardless of whether I had done anything wrong. If he thought that I ought to have gathered firewood by a certain time, he would drag me into the hut when I came back from school and beat me. 'But I was in school!' I would cry. 'What do you want from me? Why didn't the others go? You can't expect me to just walk out of school! I can't go and collect firewood before school, it's too early!' My protests fell on deaf ears – he beat me until all resistance died.

He only stopped when I lay whimpering on the floor, curled up in agony, gritting my teeth against the pain.

He was not quite so violent with his other children or Yaldiyan and Tzegehana, my elder sisters. He beat them, too, but never lost control to the same extent. While Yaldiyan did not escape punishment, she was his favourite daughter because she was the quietest and most obedient one, who rarely talked back. He beat Tzegehana least because she showed him respect in her way, and managed to bring him round better than I could, for I clung to my opinions even when he beat me; I put up a fight and never simply submitted to him. Tzegehana would always give in after a couple of blows, but I hung on until pain or fear got the better of me. I used to think my father would beat me to death one day if I continued resisting. When the blood ran from my arms, my nose and my ears from a beating, I thought the very life was seeping out of me. I had watched children bleeding to death that day the dolls had fallen from the sky, and I feared that the same would happen to me after being beaten by my father.

It was an accepted fact that girls had to be beaten more than boys. Boys were generally just slapped once – around the head, for example. Girls were given a proper beating because they were worth less and because they had become better at dodging blows. And also because they were not expected to have minds of their own, let alone show that they did. Boys were given a beating if they caused mischief, such as setting the animal shed on fire by accident while playing. Girls were thrashed for everyday matters such as arriving late or losing something. There was no margin of error for girls.

The difference between the way girls and boys were treated was accepted fact. I was made to feel that I was in the wrong when I felt myself to be in the right, and I was made to feel ashamed when I had done no wrong. I learned that it was possible to escape beating by giving in, but giving in was not one of my strengths.

My father's regime of terror served one purpose: to save him from doing any work. I and my two sisters did all the heavy work around the house, for Werhid managed to save her children from the worst drudgery. Werhid spoke warmly to me, but was not so kind to my sisters. Yaldiyan, the oldest of us, had to fetch water and gather firewood, while Tzegehana had to do the washing because she was good at it. As the youngest, it was my job to light the fire and chop firewood.

The rest of the work – shopping, cooking and cleaning – was done by Werhid and her children. My father lived like a pasha. I never saw him lift a finger – he was always lying or sitting down, smoking or chatting and drinking with other men. He had fought too long in the war as an officer to contemplate earning a living as a civilian. A few generations of men – and, latterly, women – in Eritrea had known no occupation other than war. They cobbled together a living for themselves and their families from meagre army wages, plunder and international aid. Apart from the plunder, my family was no exception. My father's looting days were over.

Staring death in the face

One day, I had a strong sense that my time had come. I can't explain why I felt this, but when I saw my father pacing the yard restlessly I said to my sisters, 'He's going to kill me today.'

Yaldiyan and Tzegehana stared uncomprehendingly. 'Kill you? What are you thinking? He'd never do that!' I just shook my head and went off to chop wood. Something must have sparked off my father's particular vengeance towards me that day, but I have no idea what it was. I only knew that he kept glancing at me with rage in his eyes, which got all my alarm bells ringing.

He suddenly came up to me and said, 'Senait, come with me to gather wood!'

We never went to gather wood together. It was always the children who went, by themselves never with him. Apart from that, we had enough wood in the house for the moment – we never kept stores of anything. Families in Africa do not do this. Food is bought and cooked on the same day, and wood is collected as it is needed, just for the day, not for the day after. So I wondered why my father wanted to go and collect wood.

But I went along. Not going would have meant being beaten to death. As we approached a hollow in which a couple of bare trees stood, my father took out a gigantic machete which was used for chopping wood, but only by grown-ups, for it was so large and heavy. My father hefted the machete and looked around him, but said nothing. I was nauseous with fear. He looked at me, and I saw that flicker in his eyes again. When he spoke, the fact that his voice was quiet rather than full of anger made it sound more dangerous than ever. 'Stand in front of a tree,' he said. I stared at him, dumbfounded, and did not move, so he raised his voice a little. 'Stand in front of a tree!'

I was paralysed. I couldn't have obeyed him if I'd wanted to – I couldn't even lift my arm. Questions thudded in my head. Does he want to kill me? Or does he just want to give me a fright? Does he want to see how far he can go?

Just then, Werhid came running up to us, screaming at my father. 'Stop! Stop it!' she shrieked hysterically. 'Please, stop! We'll send Senait, Yaldiyan and Tzegehana to the Jebha!'

My father froze. After a few moments, he let the machete fall, sighed loudly, muttered something and turned away from me. I burst into tears. My father almost seemed relieved that Werhid had stopped him.

I heard Werhid say, 'Please, don't commit such a sin ...' before I fainted. Werhid must have carried me back to the house. When I regained consciousness, my head was spinning. Did a new life await me? What was that Werhid had said about the Jebha?

It was impossible to imagine that life could get any worse, but I would come to look back on life with my father with longing.

6

Morning Stars

The day after the incident with the machete, my father took Yaldiyan, Tzegehana and myself to another village by bus. He did not tell us where we were going, and we followed him without demur. We knew it was no good asking him, he wouldn't have told us anyway. I was glad my two sisters were with me, though, because I was afraid that he would take me into the woods again.

On the bus, I stared out of the window into the desert landscape, oblivious to the heat and to the stink of the chickens, their legs tied together, lying beneath the seat in front of me. I felt nothing except an overpowering longing for quiet, and a dull fear of what awaited me.

After a couple of hours, the bus stopped in a village dotted with large army tents. Our father had brought us straight to an Eritrean Liberation Front (ELF) recruitment office. The ELF was the older of the two guerrilla armies that were fighting for Eritrea's independence. My father had fought in the ELF before he had retired a couple of years earlier as a result of his severe injuries.

'Here's the ELF office,' he said. 'You'll stay here. My friends will look after you and your education.'

The 'office' was a table standing beneath a rough shelter in the middle of the village street, round which a couple of bored-looking men in crumpled uniforms sat. There was a book and a sheet of paper on the table. I loved drawing, but, because of the great shortage of paper, had not been able to do any since my short time with the Italian nuns.

A couple of steps behind this 'office' led up to a bar, a little room in which palm wine and beer were served. The men in uniform had already had a good deal to drink – they stank of booze, and their movements were unsteady. One of them was cradling a machine gun in his lap like a child.

The men welcomed us as if we were a delivery of sheep or goats. My father and they shook hands briefly before clapping each other on the shoulders in the customary male greeting. Next they exchanged a few words, then pressed each other on the shoulders again. The deal was closed – we had reached our destination.

We barely spoke as we took leave of our father. We knew this separation was not for mere hours or days, but for much longer. I had no idea what was going to happen to us and, to be honest, I didn't care. I knew my father would not come with us, and that was all that mattered to me. My sisters were also happy to be rid of him, though they had not suffered under him as much as I had. 'We're leaving Ghebrehiwet,' they said, not, 'We're leaving our father.' They didn't sound very sad.

We had clearly been handed over to the care of these men. But they were soldiers and we were children – surely even my father must have realised that we were too young for what awaited us? Yet what mattered most to him was that he had three fewer hungry mouths to feed, which could make the difference between the family surviving or starving to death.

As one of the men led us to a car a few metres away, our father walked in the other direction without turning back to look at us. He strode off as if he would be seeing us again in a few minutes. We watched him walk away, none of us making any effort to stop him or call after him. Instead, we turned and followed the man who was already waiting in the car.

That was the day on which I became a child soldier. All it meant to me, though, was that my father would leave me alone at last. Tzegehana was about eight years old and Yaldiyan about eleven. I was six, maybe seven.

The littlest soldier

After a short ride in the clapped-out vehicle, we arrived at a military camp. I looked around wonderingly. The soldiers here were not like the ones I had seen in Asmara, where they had all been dressed in the same uniform. The camp was like a temporary village in which men, women and children milled about, all armed, but not looking anything like an army. Only some of them wore uniforms. Others wore camouflage gear, T-shirts, jackets and vests. Others still were bare-chested, as they would be in a normal village.

Despite this, it was clear that this was no civilian village, for it lacked many of the elements you would expect to find in one. There were no animals grazing, no permanent huts, no wells. And it was not just the presence of the many camels that gave the impression that everyone was ready to pack up and leave at a moment's notice – as in the countless Bedouin camps I had seen on our journey there. The lorries parked in the middle of the camp – which could transport far more than the camels – and the faces and clothing of the people in the camp all helped to create that impression. No one was in traditional dress here – no headscarves, no robes sweeping to the ground.

The atmosphere was also quite different from that of any of the other Eritrean villages I had lived in over the past few months. There was no friendly chatter, no men sitting around idly, no children playing. Everyone looked tired, hungry and drained. I had learned to recognise hunger in the restless darting of people's eyes, in their sunken cheeks and fidgety movements.

I marvelled at the number of weapons in the camp, which even children carried. The older children could manage their machine guns quite well, but the younger ones had quite a struggle just carrying them. The older ones also had ammunition belts slung over their shoulders. Most of the soldiers were between seven and seventeen years of age, although perhaps only two or three out of the couple of hundred there were my age. The oldest, who included the leaders, were between eighteen and twenty-five.

The few uniforms I saw – even those of the leaders – did not look the same. But you could tell immediately who the leaders were by the way the others treated them – falling back, making way for them and saluting them. Two or three soldiers trailed behind every leader, eager to ask about something or ready to help in case they needed anything. But the leaders appeared to ignore those in their wake – seemingly in a hurry all the time, they gazed into the distance as if they had spotted something important there. When they spoke, their voices seemed louder than everyone else's.

To my surprise, quite a few of the leaders were women. It had always been men giving commands in loud voices in the villages in which I had lived. It was only later that I realised that the women were only middle-ranking leaders and that men were in ultimate command, just as they were in the villages. Among the top commanders there was only one woman.

The leaders were also the only ones who wore complete uniforms. Everyone else wore just part of a uniform – a pair of army trousers or a camouflage or khaki T-shirt, along with assorted shorts, trousers and shirts or T-shirts in colourful prints. These were all clothes sent by the Red Cross in Europe. There had been Red Cross clothes in Asmara as well, which had been distributed to everyone. Only shoes were in short supply, though these were needed most urgently of all – for the ground was hard, rocky, and littered with painful thorns. Many soldiers even went into battle wearing the rubber flip-flops which were the cheapest, most common form of footwear in Eritrea. But there were times when I did not even have these to protect my feet. Over time, the soles of my feet grew tough as leather, but it was still far from pleasant to walk barefoot over stony ground in the blistering heat.

Retreat

The ELF troops were constantly on the move, fleeing the enemy. At the time, Ethiopian troops were no longer very active where we were, in Barka province in western Eritrea. This rural area near the Sudanese border was firmly in the hands of rebels – not the ELF, though, but a splinter group called the Eritrean People's Liberation Front (EPLF). The ELF were fleeing their own countrymen – although a 'strategic retreat' was spoken of, rather than flight.

The camp was preparing to move on once again when we arrived. Pots and pans, poles, maps, guns, sacks, tins and boxes were being tossed frenziedly on to lorries and on to piles beside the camels. A couple of soldiers were responsible for sorting through these piles and packing them properly on the lorries or camels. But it wasn't a very good system, for the piles kept growing as the packing went on, and the packers sometimes had to jump to one side to avoid being hit by the objects being tossed on to the piles. It was chaos: people were running around and screaming things we did not understand.

Suddenly, someone shoved Yaldiyan so hard that she almost fell to the ground. 'What are you staring at, children? Get up there!' A man was pointing at another lorry, on to which dozens of other children were climbing.

In the back of the lorry were some struts across which a tarpaulin could be spread but, as there was no tarpaulin, even more people were being squeezed on than usual. People were hanging over the sides and clinging to every surface of the lorry, even on to the driver's door, with one man sitting on top of the driver's cabin. We managed to push our way on to the back, struggling for breath, as the lorry started moving.

The camel drivers chose the direct route, taking the steep mule tracks over the mountains, while the old lorries raced over bumpy dirt roads, rattling and shaking as they went. We stood or kneeled in the back, pressed up so close against each other that no one fell over – if anyone had fallen over, he or she would have been trampled to death. Above the racket the lorry was making, could be heard shots and the roar of artillery. In the midst of this chaos, I knelt with my hands pressed against my head, taking in everything around me, praying that nothing would happen to us.

I was used to thinking about God often, praying to Him for things that I needed urgently, or blaming Him for whatever had upset me. The nuns in the convent at Comboni had often tried to get me to talk to God, but I hadn't started praying there. It was my grandmother who helped me find the right tone of voice in which to speak to God. She spoke to Him exactly as she did to everyone else, and that seemed to me to be the right way to communicate with a distant God.

Despite the crush, the juddering and the stink of sweat and diesel, I eventually fell asleep, and only woke up when we stopped in the middle of the night. Everyone started climbing off the lorry immediately. My legs were so stiff that I could hardly move at first, and all but tumbled off the lorry like a deadweight. My sisters were no better. It was pitch black – I could only make out the contours of bushes, rocks and a few trees. Someone said that this was our new home. We were about to set up camp in the middle of nowhere, in the wilderness.

Wilderness

I stole a glance at Yaldiyan and Tzegehana. We had never been especially close – I had always got along better with the other children in the village because I was the intruder who had come into my father's family from the outside. But now I was glad to see their familiar faces in these strange surroundings. Without them, I would have felt desperately alone and lost.

Everyone started pitching camp at daybreak, and we were sent off to collect firewood. We crawled on all fours through thick undergrowth, picking up branches and roots and breaking off dry twigs with our bare hands. We had no saws, knives or machetes to help us. We arrived back in the camp, proudly bearing our bundles of wood, hoping for words of praise and something to eat. But we were merely relieved of our bundles and sent off to gather more kindling.

We collected a second bundle, and were packed off again immediately to gather yet more firewood. I asked one of the boys who took the wood from us when we would get something to eat, and was given a resounding slap in reply. With growling stomachs and parched throats, we set off again. Although this area was not as bone dry as the mountain region around Asmara, there was still no water to be found unless you knew exactly where the water holes, springs or streams were. It had been farmland before, but now the fields were choked with weeds. The war had been especially fierce here, and the people had fled long ago.

That day, we had to go back and forth fetching firewood until darkness fell, when we were finally allowed to sit down with the others. We were bitterly disappointed to be rewarded with only a drink of water and a couple of pieces of dry *injera* bread. There was no gravy to eat the *injera* with, only a strange paste which tasted so horrible that we could hardly swallow it. But we were so hungry and tired that we forced ourselves to eat it.

Later on, I learned that the paste was made of dried powdered sardines, which were mixed with water or oil. I had never eaten fish before then, but this powder tasted so little of anything I had ever eaten that I didn't have to think about whether I was breaking my pledge never to eat animals. In fact, I was so hungry then that, had I been given it, I would have devoured a rare steak.

During my time with the army, I got to know not only hunger but thirst. Everything except weapons and munitions was in short supply in our unit, and water was strictly rationed. Everyone got one beakerful – often from a rusty old tin – which had to last until the next meal. The water was kept in a plastic canister guarded by a soldier. You handed the tin to him, he filled it, you drank up and handed the tin to the next person in the eager crowd around the precious canister. The water was drunk in a trice – there was no time to gargle, slurp and luxuriate in the feeling of it. Everyone pushed and shoved and urged whoever had the tin of water to drink up and pass it on.

Before, we had been used to eating two or three times a day, but now we were lucky to get one meal a day or even a meal every two or three days. For us, the hardest thing to understand in this strange new life was the lack of food. We woke with growling bellies, worked all day, and went to bed with hunger still gnawing at us. We were happy to get a few gulps of water out of a rusty tin. We led a miserable life in the wilderness, all in the name of freedom for Eritrea.

Enemies

In the school beneath the corrugated iron roof, we had learned a good deal about Eritrea's independence, and the high ideals of the revolution against the evil Ethiopian powers. Here, in the midst of all these lost souls, no one seemed to care for such talk. Survival was foremost in all our minds.

So many factors seemed to threaten survival that it was hard to pinpoint exactly where danger lay. Our unit had made camp near the front, and though we saw no action, we heard the noise of battle regularly, day and night. The sound of gunshots, exploding grenades and the rumble of artillery constituted a veritable orchestra of booms and blasts. At night, we sometimes saw flashes of light tearing the sky into uneven halves. Every day, a group of the older soldiers drove or walked to the front to join the battle. Some of them returned days later, but others came back after only a few hours, covered – often – with blood.

None of the children really understood what was going on, as nobody explained anything to us. All we were told was that the enemy was out there and that it was dangerous, so we were not to go there – *yet*. I had always been a curious child, wanting to see, try and learn about everything, but I had no desire to go to the place where the loud noises were coming from. I knew there would be nothing beautiful there, nothing worth striving for. I also knew there were things that I ought not to know about.

Though we knew there was an enemy, we did not know who the enemy was, what he wanted from us, nor what we wanted from him. We were sacrificing ourselves for the cause of the ELF, just as the other side were for the EPLF, but we didn't even know what the letters ELF stood for. All we knew was that we were the ELF, who were the right side, and they were the EPLF, who were the wrong side.

Politics was not important for us – other things took precedence. More and more people in our unit were falling sick. Barka is a malaria-infested region, and we all knew that mosquito bites brought fever and illness. But we had no choice; we spent all day and all night outdoors – sleeping without tents, nets or other protection – so it was impossible not to be bitten.

Apart from the EPLF, the army of mosquitoes was the second enemy we had to face, and the rats were the third. Rats were our constant companions. They scuttled between us as we slept at night, and when we woke, we could tell from their droppings where they had been. I used to wonder why there were so many rats in the camp when there was hardly anything to eat there.

While malaria was the big illness to fear, there was also '*chain-itschiwai*', which both Tzegehana and I fell victim to. When dusk fell, I lay down on a rag – it could not be called a blanket – on the rocky, sandy ground, hungry, thirsty, dusty and sweaty, but shivering, for it was often cold at night. Then my legs and feet began to itch. I scratched furiously, but the itching got worse – my skin felt as if it was on fire. I jumped up and tried to find out what was plaguing me, but could see nothing in the dark. Panic overwhelmed me – was there a swam of tiny insects I could not see? Frightened, I woke my sisters, but they could not see anything either. I started crying.

An older girl soldier came over to us, and Yaldiyan told her what was wrong with me.

'It will get better tomorrow,' the girl said comfortingly. 'But don't scratch, all right? Or it will only get worse.' She stood up and walked away.

I lay there, frozen, not daring to move. And it did get better, slowly. My legs were still itchy, but the burning sensation faded. It must have been caused by the scratching. That was all I managed to work out for myself. No one ever took the time to explain or show things to the younger ones like me.

'You had the "rats' eyes",' Yaldiyan said to me later. The condition was called *chainitschiwai* in our language because the sores on the skin looked liked rats' eyes.

I was horrified when I looked at my legs the next day. The other children laughed at me, but they all knew what I had. It was said that the disease came from being bitten by rats, but that was nonsense. It was really an infection spread by the rats in all that dirt and dust. We were bitten by rats as well, but those bites were different. The tiny bite marks on our skin were barely visible at first, but then gradually filled with pus and grew larger and larger until they were red and inflamed. I still have the scars on my legs from those bites.

The first deaths

Amid all the chaos, my foremost thoughts were of where to get something to eat and drink and how to avoid the toughest work.

We learned to live with the sickness. There was a doctor in our unit, but he could do very little for us. He did not have the medicines to treat minor conditions such as pus-filled rat bites, infected eyes, embedded thorns, inflamed mosquito bites or cases of flu. There were far worse things for him to deal with taking care of the heavily injured. Death was ever present.

Apart from the friend who had bled to death in the orphanage, I had never see a dead body before, but now I saw them every day. Dead men and women – or, more accurately, boys and girls, for most of the soldiers were much younger than my parents, let alone my grandfather, and twenty was old in that company.

The first dead body I saw in the camp was that of a young girl, lying face down on the ground where she had been offloaded on the return from battle. She had long frizzy hair sticking out in all directions, just like we all did at the time – it was the hair that marked her out as a girl. Sometimes the hair on the dead bodies stuck to their heads, smooth with dried blood. But I still remember standing there looking at that dead girl – no one else gave her a second glance. I did not know what to do. No one seemed to be doing anything about this girl. (It often took some time before the dead were buried – no easy task given the rocky ground and the overpowering heat of the day.)

So the dead girl lay there as the flies buzzed round her. I knelt down to look at her face. I didn't recognise her, but then I wouldn't have recognised anyone at the beginning. One of her eyes was half-open, showing its white, which seemed unnatural to me. I put my hands over my face, as I did whenever I could no longer bear to look at something, uttered a cry and ran off as fast as I could. I could not run very far. We were not allowed to leave the camp – it was dangerous, the enemy could be anywhere and there were landmines in the ground. But running away did no good; I could not get rid of the smell from the girl – the smell of death.

The smell of death is the most penetrating smell I know. I can hardly describe it – a sweet, fleshy stink of putrefaction, rot and decay. Anyone who has smelt it will recognise it instantly, even years later. It was a smell I was to come to know well.

The smell attracted the hyenas. The rats seemed harmless compared to the hyenas and lions who circled the camp from time to time. The hyenas began to sing their song of death, which I registered for the first time that evening. They sang to the dead girl, whose body had been covered with stones as temporary protection before she was buried the next day alongside the corpses of those who had been brought back to the camp that evening.

The hyenas' crooning broke into hysterical laughter over and over again, but no one seemed to take any notice of this macabre night time serenade. I lay on the ground with my hands pressed to my ears, humming and singing my own song to drown out the sound of the hyenas, only stopping when someone prodded me to be quiet. Then I tried to counter the hyenas with quieter sounds: drumming my hands against the ground, kicking my feet, and making sounds of life in the face of this concert of death. But my efforts were in vain. The singing and laughing of the carrion-eaters was overpowering, and I fell into an exhausted sleep.

The last contingent

I was woken by a kick, the usual morning greeting for sleepy-heads. Everyone had to be awake by daybreak at the latest. Although there was often work to be done in the night as well, if, for example, we had to pack up and decamp to a new location, if we had to unload lorries that had arrived in the night or if we had to fetch water under cover of darkness because it was too dangerous to do so by day.

Sometimes the enemy was so close that no one dared to leave camp in the daytime. There was no shortage of work to do in the camp itself on those days. We did the washing by hand, with small quantities of soap and even less water, or we kneaded the dough for *injera* bread, ground coffee beans and cleaned our superiors' uniforms.

We were also given military training. Yaldiyan and Tzegehana joined in the training immediately, while I started a few weeks later. Even by the standards of the time, I was too young to be a soldier. Both the ELF and the EPLF started training children at eleven years of age but only sent soldiers into action from the age of twelve or thirteen, when they were regarded as young adults in African culture. By the age of fourteen they were on the front line.

However, by the time we got there, the ELF was on its last legs and this system had completely broken down – as least in our unit, which our leaders called the Jebha al Tahrir or simply Jebha ('front') or Tahrir ('morning star' – the name, signifying youth, given to the younger brigades of the army). At its height, the ELF had had tens of thousands of soldiers, but now there were only about a thousand, or perhaps even fewer. We never saw all our fellow soldiers together because we were moving around so much, and had been divided up into different units, but one thing was clear: we were part of the last contingent.

Sometimes our leaders called our camp Che Guevara, in honour of the Cuban guerrilla fighter – for the Cubans had supported the ELF, largely with arms supplies. The name meant nothing to me at first, and I only registered a garbled Tigrinya version of the name. Child soldiers like us, the youngest in the history of the Eritrean fight for independence, were called Tegal-deties.

Both Eritrean guerrilla groups – the EPLF and the ELF – had started out with organisations dedicated to training young people: the Red Flowers in the EPLF and the Morning Stars in the ELF, which took in children between six and ten years of age, not as child soldiers yet but in preparation for fighting. Within these organisations, the children were given lessons in reading, writing and maths, alongside Eritrean history, Marxism and party propaganda. They were also given paramilitary training: drills in running, jumping, crawling and orienteering. When the children were older, they were given guns and sent off to the front. The Ethiopian army was almost always stronger, and the partisans needed every soldier they could get, even ill-trained ones.

As the ELF had declined, so the system of special youth troops, the Morning Stars, had broken down. The last Jebha contingent consisted of a motley collection of soldiers who were just about capable of holding a machine gun, and my unit was no exception. When my sisters and I arrived at Che Guevara, the Morning Stars were fighting alongside the grown-ups, and their training regime had long been abandoned. The only thing that remained of the old system was the song we all had to sing:

> The morning star never goes out,
> It burns brightly
> Through night and day
> The morning star lights up eternity

I loved that song – it gave me hope even when I no longer knew what to hope for.

By this time, the early 1980s, who fought for the ELF and what kind of training they received was of practically no consequence. We were no longer fighting for Eritrean independence; our fight was not one of political struggle but for pure survival. Eritrea had struggled against Ethiopia for over twenty years, but in that time had made no progress. Not only did the Ethiopian troops have greater numbers plus support from the Soviet Union, but the Eritreans lacked unity among themselves. The original freedom fighters, the ELF, were engaged in a ferocious battle with its splinter group, the EPLF, who were called Shabia, the Arabic word for 'people'.

By 1979, it was clear that the EPLF had the upper hand, and by 1981 the ELF had collapsed. My sisters and I had joined an army at the end of its tether in 1980 – my father had handed us over to the losing side.

Under fire

The Jebha unit trained newcomers constantly, and my two elder sisters were taught how to use guns in the Che Guevara camp immediately. Right after our arrival, Yaldiyan had a Kalashnikov – a large, heavy sub-machine gun – pressed into her arms. One of the older soldiers showed her how to load it and release the safety catch, and then told her to fire into the blank expanse of the desert. Yaldiyan found it difficult at first – the recoil from the gun jolted her to the ground. With practice, she realised that if she braced herself against a rock or a tree, she could resist the violent jerk from the gun a little better, though she still staggered from the recoil. It was a miracle that the soldier who trained her did not get shot in the process.

I had difficulty coming to terms with the thought of my eldest sister handling a gun, but soon Tzegehana, also, began to learn how to fire a Kalashnikov, which I found even more difficult to accept. That all this was a matter of life and death was difficult for me to grasp. I had seen my sisters in domestic environments: washing clothes, using household utensils like knives to peel vegetables, herding goats, feeding chickens or playing with cats and dogs. Now these same sisters were to go forth into the wilderness to shoot people and flee bullets themselves. I watched them at their machine-gun drills everyday – they were merely doing as they were told, for there was no question of resistance or doubt. We did not speak of fear or death at all.

The situation in Che Guevara grew more and more miserable. Often there was no food for two or three days. There was a lot of talk of hunting for it, but most of the animals had fled at the sounds of battle. Our camp was constantly on the move because it was either being threatened by the enemy or searching blindly for it. When we were unable to find a new site for the camp – something that happened more and more often – the few possessions we still had stayed on the lorries so that we could move on at a moment's notice. When it got too hot during the day, we lay in the shade of the vehicles or under trees, while at night we slept on top of or beneath the lorries. We had almost nothing to eat and very little to drink – we scrabbled for new water holes in every new place we moved on to.

Bihuk

The afternoon sun beat down relentlessly on the stretch of sand we had pitched camp on, near Bisha, a tiny village on the edge of the Dar plain in western Eritrea. This area, in the province of Barka, was one of the most remote and hottest regions of the country. The air shimmered with heat above the thorn bushes and the scraggy undergrowth on the rock faces that rose directly behind the plain. The landscape had grown even more colourless in the last few months – even the cacti looked bleached. The cacti, which were as tall as a man, were as hard as rock and covered in a thick layer of dust. The sky above us was no longer blue, as it had been in the winter and in late spring, but white with heat, melting away under the blurry glare of the sun. The air was still and heavy, disturbed not by birdsong but by a distant roar and rattle of guns on the front.

I lay in the shade of a tattered tarpaulin, trying to escape the darts of sunshine that came in through the many slits, but moving as little as possible in the process, for the slightest motion made me sweat. It was growing hotter and more humid, and everyone was drained and on edge.

I had just found a halfway comfortable spot for myself between the sharp stones and patches of sunlight when the older soldiers streamed into the camp.

'Get up, you lazy thing!' one of them screamed at me. 'Get up now! There's no water left.'

That was a disaster. For if there was no water left, not only was there nothing for us to drink, but we had to start digging. I emerged from the shade reluctantly, rubbing my eyes, for I had dozed off. Michael, the soldier who had shouted at me, was one of the most repellent of the group. The yellow teeth sticking out of his mouth in all directions frightened me, as did his red, streaming eyes, which darted back and forth all the time, and his stick-thin legs, which were always ready to kick someone. His foot jabbed me in the back again. 'Get up, Bihuk!' he screamed. 'Come on, get digging!'

'Bihuk' is what we call a kind of dough made out of flour, water and salt – an indefinable mixture of nothing much. The word has come to mean 'coward', and tears sprang to my eyes whenever I was called by that name. I did not want to be weak and useless; I longed to be strong and brave like everyone else.

I jumped up to run over to my sisters, who were sheltering under a tarpaulin at the other end of the camp with some of the older soldiers. But I seemed to slam into a solid wall with my very first step. The heat was indescribable. My feet were scorched by the ground – it was impossible to run barefoot. I lifted up the plastic mats beneath the tarpaulin sheet I had been lying under, looking for my rubber flip-flops. I pushed aside a few plastic bags, a blanket and a bundle of clothing, but still I could not find them.

Michael smirked and asked, 'Are you looking for something?' He kicked me again. 'What are you looking for?'

I said nothing but continued searching. Michael shook with laughter, sounding like a goat bleating hysterically. 'Might you be looking for these?' He dangled my flip-flops before me on the butt of his machine gun.

'You're so mean!' I screamed, hurling myself at him as he retreated. Tears sprang into my eyes and I ran over the burning hot ground littered with sharp stones.

'Look at the little coward crying!' Michael was doubled up with laughter, whistling through his crooked teeth to draw everyone's attention to me hopping painfully over the ground.

Some other soldiers hurried over and started clapping, shouting, 'Jump, coward, jump!' I hopped from one leg to the other, reaching desperately for my flip-flops. The ground was far too hot for me to stay on one surface for long. The machine gun, my flip-flops, Michael and the others who had formed a circle around me all blurred as my eyes swam with tears.

'Leave her alone, you idiots!'

Everyone fell silent immediately.

Agawegahta, one of the leaders, had arrived on the scene. 'Give them to me!' she ordered Michael, who did not dare to utter a word.

She yanked my flip-flops off his machine gun and put them on my feet. Not to have to stand on the hot stones brought immediate relief. Michael shrugged and sloped off. The others followed him, for there was nothing left to watch. I started to thank Agawegahta, but she dismissed me with a wave of her hand. 'Run along then, we need water!'

In that moment, Agawegahta seemed to me even greater and more powerful than she already was; a mighty woman who expected no reply or thanks. I nodded dumbly and ran off.

The last games

Agawegahta was one of the three or four most powerful people in our ELF unit, but I regarded her as the most important of them all, for she was the only woman among the leaders. I looked up to her, and she sometimes looked out for me. She was a strong woman, as powerfully built as any man. She had broad shoulders, muscular arms and sinewy legs, but still looked like a woman, for her face was feminine and she wore her hair long in the Afro style of the time, though she sometimes braided it. Agawe–gahta walked quickly and talked loudly, in a voice too deep for a woman but too high to be a man's. She seemed very mature, but in reality was only about eighteen or twenty. She could holler and kill like any brute soldier, but you would not have known that she was capable of such violence by just looking at her. She commanded respect, and I regarded her with a mixture of fear and wonder from the very start.

When I reached the shelter where my sisters had been, they were not there. Was I meant to set off by myself to dig a waterhole and carry the water back to camp? I looked around helplessly. The air was as still and heavy as before, but something had changed – the white sky was tinged with yellow in a way I had never seen before. I stepped out from beneath the shade of the tarpaulin to take a better look, and spied my sisters squatting between two rocks. They were hiding so as not to have to do any work, so were not best pleased to see me.

'What are you doing here, Senait?' Yaldiyan asked.

'We have to go and fetch water,' I whispered. 'I can't do it alone.'

'You'll have to,' Yaldiyan snapped. 'I don't have time to come with you. I have to go off to training,' she said, pointing at the Kalashnikov beside her.

My oldest sister had changed completely since she had been given the machine gun. She no longer wanted to have anything to do with the younger children, even with me, and refused to play any games with us. She did not want to tie a ball of rags to a tree and hit it with a stick. She refused to trace the outline of a palace on the ground with stones and furnish its rooms with yet more stones. Yaldiyan wanted to be a soldier.

'Will you come with me?' I asked Tzegehana. She had not got very far with her shooting. Her face, arms and legs still bore the scratches from the stones and thorns she had fallen on because of the recoil from the machine gun. As a result, Tzegehana preferred working in the 'hospital', which was a shelter with a couple of blankets, a few bandages and syringes, which she handed to whoever was acting as 'doctor'. The doctor could never do much: short of a miracle, the seriously injured could generally not be saved.

Tzegehana did not like working in the hospital that much either, but the blood, broken bones and other horrors she saw there were preferable to fighting on the front. She was not able to use her machine gun properly, did not like shooting and was also afraid of the enemy. Yet she too had lost her appetite for childish games. Although she moved the stones around with me to build palaces, she would pretend she was looking for something on the ground, not playing, the moment someone else came along.

'If you can't shoot, you have to fetch water!' Yaldiyan nagged. 'Go with her!'

Water

Tzegehana and I fetched a spade, a large old tin and two plastic canisters, then trudged down to the river. But the riverbed was dry. There had been hardly any rain for almost a year – a couple of light showers in this time had barely wet the surface of the ground, but evaporated from the hot stones and sand immediately. The riverbed was nothing but rock, sand, gravel and a few straggly bushes.

Despite this, it was our only hope of finding water. We had to dig in the spots where water was nearer to the surface of the ground, although every extra inch that we had to dig in that incredible heat was utterly exhausting.

We walked over the gravel like tracker dogs. The water holes we had dug before were completely dry – the water had taken another course. We pushed bushes aside and parted dried-up clumps of grass, prodding at the sandy ground, hoping to find a trace of moisture. We looked under rocky overhangs, lifted stones and scraped at the ground – in vain. There was no sign of water – no slightly green branch or stalk that indicated the presence of that precious liquid.

We went further and further upriver in our search of water, getting grumpier and grumpier with every step, for the further away from camp we went, the greater the distance we would have to carry the water back. As we walked on, more and more of the sky turned a pale yellow that I had never seen before. Now Tzegehana had also noticed it. 'Maybe it's going to rain,' she said.

I remembered dancing for joy in the soft, warm, wonderful rain in Asmara – was there rain here, too? 'If it rains, we won't have to go on looking for water, will we?'

Tzegehana hesitated and looked up at the sky. 'I'm not sure if the rain will really come,' she said. 'Sometimes it looks like it's going to rain, but then it doesn't.'

My flicker of hope was extinguished. 'We have to go on looking, then, do we?'

Tzegehana nodded. There was no hope of salvation from the skies. If we returned without water, we were sure to be beaten soundly. So we glued our eyes to the ground again, looking for the slightest hint of water.

I spied a couple of clumps of grass by the riverbank that did not look completely dry. We started digging like moles, taking turns to use the spade or claw stones out of the way with our bare hands. We had dug about half a metre into the ground and were drenched in sweat, but we were still only shovelling damp sand. Just as we were about to give up, a miracle happened. The sand became darker and a trickle of liquid could be seen. We scrabbled away in a frenzy until a muddy pool appeared, first as deep as a hand, then two, then finally as deep as our tin. We lowered the tin carefully into the water, filled it and poured the contents into the plastic canisters. This water was not for the camp – it was for us, for us only! We slurped from the neck of the canister greedily, letting the brown liquid trickle down our throats.

The water tasted horrible and wonderful at once. It looked like cloudy apple juice, and drinking it was like licking a mud wall – sandy and rotten tasting.

But it was water, and that was the main thing. We knew that we ought to let the worst sediment settle before drinking it, in order to minimise the risk of diarrhoea, but it was impossible to wait. Our throats were burning and our heads were bursting with heat. We were as parched as the desert, and it was heaven to drink that water. When we had drunk enough, we poured more water over our faces and heads and backs. It was wonderful.

Then I stopped and looked up at the sky. Was it evening already? If so, we ought to hurry to fill the canisters and carry them back to the camp. But this was no ordinary twilight. The sky had not darkened like it did on normal evenings, but instead had turned from a pale to a dark yellow. The air grew closer and closer, and the rumble of noise from the front seemed to be coming nearer. Was it going to rain after all, now that we had found water?

We couldn't count on it raining, so we continued bailing water into the canisters until they were full, then we bound them to our shoulders with the ropes we had brought along and started stumbling back to the camp with our loads of twenty litres each. Once we arrived back in the camp, the canisters would be grabbed from us and the water would be distributed. We would be shooed away immediately along with the other smaller children.

We felt very important as we made our way back from the water hole – we had found it, after all, and could lead the others to it. Just as we neared the camp, the growling sound grew louder – this was not the sound of gunfire, but something else. We looked up to see a sky that was no longer yellow, but grey. Suddenly, bolts of lightning shot crackled around us. We were just about to take shelter when the rain came down. And how it came down! At first there were a few fat drops, then more, then it poured down in a shower, then a torrent, until there was a wall of water standing before us. We were soaked through in seconds. It took us a split second to realise what was happening. It was raining! It was raining at last!

We danced with wild abandon in that rain, whirling around with arms outstretched on the riverbed, hugging each other, opening our mouths wide and tipping our heads back to drink it in. But we couldn't help thinking that we had slaved away earlier that day for nothing.

Rain collected in puddles and pools on the ground every-where: much better quality water than the brackish liquid we had dug out with our labour. But it was good that it was raining. In no time at all, we had refilled the canisters, and continued walking back to camp, feeling happy. That was the best evening we had had for a long time. We almost forgot that we were living through a war. Our enemies must have felt the same way, for there was no sound of fighting from the front. Or had the rain drowned out the sound?

Bodies

When the first rays of sun woke me the next morning, I was soaked to the skin. The sensation of thirst quenched filled me with a deep contentment. I could barely believe my eyes when I saw the water coursing through what had been the dried-up riverbed next to our camp – the river flowed so swiftly that even an adult would not have been able to cross it. I had seen brooks and streams before, but never a river like this, with so much water.

Along with the other children, I ran over to the river. We wanted to immerse ourselves in it, but when we waded knee-high into it, we found it was an effort even to stand still in the strong current which swirled around us, threatening to carry us off into the river's depths. Frightened by the force of the river, we retreated to the bank.

Mihret – a self-assured singer and soldier who was a little older than Tzegehana – and I were so mesmerised by the water that we walked all the way along the bank up to a bend in the river. Hardly anything could be seen of the wide riverbed of gravel and rock now – only the edges peeped out here and there. At the bend in the river, the water was not so deep and swift, but it lapped at the rocks gently, so I clambered up on to a rock and sprang into the river gleefully.

I wished I could have turned back mid-jump, but that was out of the question. I landed on something soft, and sprang up again with a blood-curdling scream. I continued screaming, and Mihret hurried over, thinking I had hurt myself. When she saw what lay behind the rock, she started screaming as well. Our happy game had turned into a vision of hell – two swollen, rotting corpses with bloody hair and clothes, skins purple and brown, feet slimy with decay. They had been washed downstream by the river.

When we were able to speak again, we noticed more bodies: one floating towards us, another caught in the branches of a thorn bush, and two more in the overhang of the riverbank where I had dug for water only the day before. We ventured a closer look at the last two bodies: the faces were an unrecognisable mess of blood and the bodies engorged and twisted – I could hardly bear to look at them. They were young men, so were certainly soldiers, as all young men in the area were. But it was impossible to tell whether they had been fighting for us or for the EPLF, for both sides wore the same motley mixture of T-shirts, shirts and jeans from the clothes distribution centres of the international aid organisations.

Our skins and hair were the same colour – black. Most of the people in Barka province were Tygrai, with a few Kunama, but all spoke the same language, Tigrinya. There was no difference in the appearance or the language of people in the ELF and people in the EPLF, among neither the living nor the dead. But whether they were on our side or the enemy's, I hated those men in that moment, for my dreams were haunted by the sight of their dead bodies from that day onwards.

We walked on to the next bend in the river, where we found another dozen or so bodies, then we ran back to the camp to tell everyone what we had seen. Nobody believed us at first, and no one wanted to come and see the bodies. But our distress made such an impression that people did eventually follow us to the river. Discussion raged over how the bodies had come to be in the water, and someone eventually identified two of the corpses as ELF soldiers who had deserted our unit a few weeks ago.

Agawegahta thought the men had probably crossed paths with the EPLF and been killed. She said this in a matter-of-fact manner, as if it were the most normal thing in the world. Her calmness was impressive. While others screamed and wailed, she walked from one body to the other trying to identify them. When a corpse lay face down, she turned it over, but some faces were too disfigured to identify.

Death is everywhere

The older soldiers soon lost interest in the corpses.

'We see this every day,' one of them said. 'Death is everywhere.'

I wondered if 'death' was a person lurking in every corner, but quelled the desire to ask this out loud in case I was laughed at.

The next day, Agawegahta summoned a few of us younger children – those who were not carrying machine guns yet – and told us to get the bodies out of the river. I stared at her, aghast at the thought of having to touch the corpses.

'It has to be done,' Agawegahta said sternly. 'If we let the corpses lie there, they will poison the water, and we will have nothing to drink.' She expressly forbade drinking directly from the river. All water had to be brought back to the camp in canisters and boiled before it was drunk. We were to carry the bodies out of the river and bury them in a place where they would not pollute any groundwater supplies.

It had rained again that morning, but the river was no longer a strong torrent of water, merely a pleasant stream which would have made a wonderful playground if not for the stinking corpses in it. We now had to dig them out of the riverbed and drag them up over the bushes and on to the rocky bank.

The sweetish, repellent smell of death and decay spread around the river and towards the camp, settling upon it like a film on the lungs. I longed for the traditional female headdress of a white cloth which could be pulled down to cover the face when necessary, something I had always thought laughably old-fashioned before. I found the remnant of a T-shirt which I tied over my nose and mouth, but this was no defence against the smell. When I went over to one of the corpses, the putrid wave that assaulted me was so strong that I had to tear the rag from my face and throw up.

I bent over a rock with my head pounding, silently cursing the ELF, this infernal war, the dead bodies and Agawegahta, whom I had previously looked up to. How could she have asked us to do this, the most ghastly of jobs? I yearned to be doing anything else – fetching water, making a fire or gathering kindling – rather than this. But nobody disobeyed Agawegahta.

In pairs or in groups of three, we set to pulling the bodies out of the water. Some of the corpses were so heavy that it took five of us to move them. After a while, I was able to glance quickly into the faces of the bodies. They did not look sad or tortured, but they were bruised, battered and swollen from fighting, from the rocks in the river and the time they had spent in the water.

We were still a long way from finishing our task when the sun began to set. We were being plagued by swarms of flies and the rats were scuttling so close to us that I could have reached down to my feet and grabbed one. The sound of jackals laughing grew louder and louder.

Getting the bodies out into the undergrowth was only the first step. We had to bury them quickly to keep them from the jackals, the rats and the flies, and also to bury the all-pervasive smell. No thought of any religious ceremony even crossed our minds.

We started digging on the same day. There were not enough spades to go round, so some of us had to dig with our hands. We also had to heave rocks out of the ground to create a grave large enough for all the bodies. While moving a gigantic rock with the others as darkness was falling, I was suddenly overcome by a wave of putrescence so strong that I fainted. It was night when I regained consciousness, and the stink of the corpses was still in the air.

It took us all of the following day to bury the corpses, but by then we were starting to have problems because of the polluted water. One of our group had been unable to resist drinking from the river the day before, and had started vomiting constantly, as well as suffering from fever, diarrhoea and stomach cramps. A friend of his prayed for his survival.

Diarrhoea and stomach pains were inevitable, given the conditions we were living in. A dozen or so of us ate with our hands from the same bowl, which was never washed, merely scoured with sand. Needless to say, we never washed our hands either. We kept our supplies in the open, with makeshift protection from the rats, the insects and the sun, and ate everything, from ground fish to cooking oil and flour, all mixed up together to stem our hunger.

But the boy who had fallen ill was suffering from more than

an ordinary attack of diarrhoea – he seemed to be eliminating his entire body weight. No one could do anything for him, and he died a few days later.

Drought

After the incident with the corpses in the river, we started to boil our water. However, this meant we had to gather even more firewood than usual, adding to the drudgery of camp work. The river had almost dried up again in the meantime – though we didn't have to dig half a metre into the ground to reach water, we did have to scoop out a bit of earth before the brackish liquid appeared. Everyone said that there really ought to have been a few more good spells of rain, and the older ones looked up at the sky in despair. But the sky was nothing but a great expanse of bright blue with a few flecks of white that did not look remotely like rain. It was the same every day: blue skies and non-stop sunshine. Listening to the others talk in the evenings, I learned a new word that everyone spoke with a worried look on their faces: drought.

There was still water, though. It was possible to find a stream of murky liquid without digging too hard. I hardly knew what fresh, clear water looked or tasted like any longer – for me, water was that warm, brown, sandy stuff that smelt of earth and mud. We were glad to have any water at all to drink and to cook with, but washing with it became a luxury that we could ill afford. The rains still did not come.

Mihret and Agawegahta

It would have been wonderful to pour even that brownish water over our bodies after the daily training we had, which was called 'school', but was different from any other school I had been to before. At the start of my time at Che Guevara camp, I had watched from afar as the younger children gathered every morning to carry out physical exercises under command. I had kept away instinctively, knowing that I would hate such training.

One day, Mihret told me I was 'allowed' to join the others, when she really meant that I *had* to join them. Perhaps she hoped to rouse some enthusiasm in me by making out it was an honour, but she was quite wrong.

Mihret was often wrong about things. When she told me to join the others in training, I decided that she was my enemy, and that I would no longer believe anything she said or, as far as possible, follow her orders. Mihret was about eleven or twelve years old and about a head taller than me – one and a half at most – but she behaved as if she were a grown-up. She would have liked to have been one of the leaders in the camp, but she was still too young. Instead, she ordered the younger children around and herded us to training and to our shooting practices, which were like the sessions the older soldiers had.

Mihret was stocky and fit, and proud of it. She wanted to be a fighting machine. She kept her hair short and wore a big T-shirt that hid her full breasts, along with a pair of camouflage trousers, of which she was very proud. She always carried a heavy Kalashnikov over her shoulder.

Mihret was also proud of behaving in a tough and crude manner. She burped loudly and slapped her thigh when she laughed, and liked telling extremely crude jokes as well as playing stupid tricks. Once, on a rare occasion when there were calves' livers for dinner, she took great pleasure in dangling a stinking, pale brown liver in front of me, knowing that I was repelled by it. I tried to run away, but she cuffed me around the ears and laughed loudly. All in all, Mihret appeared more like a boy than a girl – which was the impression she sought to give. But that illusion was shattered as soon as she opened her mouth to speak. Her voice was very high and, when she shouted, it rose to a hysterical pitch that no one could take seriously.

Boys were worth more than girls not only on the battle-field but in general. There were many females in our unit, but if women were given positions of responsibility it was mostly to do with looking after the children. Agawegahta was the only exception. Her position among us was equal to those of the men, and I worshipped her. What she said was taken as seriously as anything the men said, and was worth even more to me because she was the only female leader in Che Guevara. She proved to me that a woman could reach the top if she had the will to do it. But I knew that I was not the kind of girl who could do it, for I was much too cowardly and hated the military training and exercises.

Mihret too wanted to be like Agawegahta, but failed. Unlike Agawegahta, she always had to shout to make herself heard, and her confidence was feigned rather than real. She was nothing more than a girl striving to live up to her mother's expectations of her as a soldier. No one knew where Mihret's mother was, and though Mihret boasted of her mother's heroic deeds, I did not believe a word. Her mother had probably been killed in the war, otherwise she would have been with us in Barka fighting the enemy. We needed every man and woman on the front, after all. How could Mihret's mother be a hero if she was not here with us?

Exercises

'Sit down here!' Mihret ordered, pointing at the ground before her feet. A couple of dozen children were already sitting there, the morning stars, the youngest soldiers in Che Guevara. Most of them were only a little older than me, between eight and twelve years old, though a few of them looked older than that because of their height. I felt very self-conscious, knowing that I was the youngest and smallest of them all. I would have liked to just go on collecting wood, fetching water and doing other work in the camp, but there was no choice. From now on I had to join in both the daily drudgery of camp work and military training. I felt like crying, but I pulled myself together and listened to Mihret lecturing.

She talked about Eritrea, how we wanted to liberate it, and told us that the EPLF was our worst enemy. 'We will win,' Mihret said, 'because we are right and because we will never surrender.'

Surrender sounded appealing to me – wouldn't it be easier? How were we ever going to win when everyone was against us? I did not understand why Mihret was telling us these things that we had heard thousands of times already. We were the goodies and everyone else was evil.

Mihret's torrent of words was greeted with silence. She looked at us expectantly but, when there was no response, she leapt up from the rock she had been perched on and shouted, 'Come! Let's get started with our training!'

Everyone was relieved that she had finished hectoring, and jumped up in relief. Mihret pointed at me and said, 'You, you're coming too!' just as I had feared.

The training ground was right next to our camp, a stretch of flat ground that was scattered with rocks. 'Take cover!' Mihret shouted suddenly, and everyone instantly threw themselves on to the ground or behind rocks. Everyone except me, that is. I stood there, stunned, not knowing what to do. Mihret emerged from behind a rock and stared at me. I stared back. I did not understand how this girl was supposed to have any power over me.

Mihret was so astonished that it took her a few seconds to react. This had never happened to her before. Was it rebellion? Then she jumped up with a shrill cry and charged towards me with hatred in her eyes, striking me in the face with such force that I collapsed to the ground. She hit me on the head again, and kicked me in the back.

'Take cover, I said! Take cover!' She kicked me until I was crouched behind a rock. 'There, you piece of shit, get in there!' Then she shouted at the others, 'What are you looking at? You are supposed to be taking cover! On the ground, I say! The bullets are flying overhead, you idiots! Follow me!'

Everyone threw themselves to the ground again and crawled after Mihret.

I touched my face gingerly, and my fingers turned red with the blood streaming from my mouth and nose. It reminded me of the dead soldiers I had seen. But there was no time for self-pity

– Mihret was already looking threateningly in my direction. I started crawling towards the side of the mountain like the others. I made slow progress, for my shoulder hurt where I had fallen against a rock, and one of my legs was badly grazed. I trailed blood through the dust as I crawled.

There would have been no point asking to be let off training for the day. I tried to remain inconspicuous and duck behind rocks as far as possible in order to avoid Mihret's gaze.

Mihret seemed content that her little troop was under control again. We crawled a couple of hundred metres through thick undergrowth. When she shouted, 'Go!', we had to jump up and run, bent double and huddled together in a group. At the end of the session, we had to stand still looking straight ahead as Mihret walked up and down shouting at us to move forwards or backwards a little or to keep our hands to our sides. I could feel the dried crust of blood on my leg. I did not find standing still like this difficult, but I thought it was nonsense all the same.

When Mihret was satisfied, she dismissed everyone except me. I instantly feared that she was going to beat me again. Everyone else looked back at me curiously as they left, but Mihret shooed them away. Then she grabbed me by my T-shirt, shook me and hissed threateningly, 'If you ever dare to do that again, I'll get you to carry rocks the whole night through and beat the hell out of you! Is that clear?'

I nodded.

'Now go!'

As I turned to run off, relieved, she hit me on the head again, so hard that I stumbled and almost fell.

'Go, I said!' she shouted. That final blow from her was nothing out of the ordinary. Any child could be hit by someone older for no reason.

I hurried away, longing for a bit of peace and quiet. I wanted to lie down in the shade for a while before going out in the midday sun to fetch water.

Weapons

I lost all sense of the seasons after a couple of weeks with the ELF, and did not know whether it was summer, autumn or already winter. In Asmara, the seasons had always been distinct, for the city was high in the mountain regions. There, the nights were cool in autumn and winters were cold, about five or ten degrees celsius. On winter mornings, the mountain tops on the horizon were swathed in thick mist, which sometimes sank into the city. During the day, the winter skies were a clear, brilliant blue, not like the milky blue of summer skies, when the heat shimmered over the high plains. It was only really hot in the summer in Asmara.

In Barka, by contrast, it was always hot, all throughout the year. We broke out in beads of sweat at the slightest movement. The nights brought little relief, only a slight drop in temperature before the sun rose with the heat of the day again. Everything was dry and barren in that landscape, too, so it was no wonder that there was no sense of the seasons passing at all.

We had been at Che Guevara camp for a few months when Agawegahta came to me one morning just when I was getting up. 'Come with me,' she said brusquely. I jumped up and followed her immediately.

She led me to a large tent that I had often wondered about. The entrance to this tent was always closed, and I had never dared go in. I knew it was not Agawegahta's tent, and, as she pulled the tarpaulin flaps aside, I wondered what she wanted to show me in here.

She stepped into the dark tent and beckoned me to follow her. I hardly dared to take a breath. When my eyes grew used to the dimness, I saw piles and piles of chests, boxes and cartons. Every time we moved camp, we had to load and unload these boxes, but the younger children had never known where they were stored. Perhaps the older soldiers had been afraid we would get our hands on what was in them.

Agawegahta opened one of the wooden chests and took

something out. I only recognised the Kalashnikov when she pressed it into my arms. It was so heavy that I nearly fell. I looked up at her questioningly and she said, 'It's yours, look after it.'

I hardly needed to be told to look after my Kalashnikov. Everyone in the camp took their guns everywhere with them and slept clutching them. Nobody was allowed to touch anyone else's machine gun – guns were sacred.

The little soldier

So I was supposed to carry a sub-machine gun and be a soldier, and go to war like the others. I did not know whether to be proud or frightened, but then the fear won out. I did not dare to show Agawegahta my true feelings however. I turned to leave with my monstrous lump of metal, intending to show it to my sisters, but Agawegahta stopped me.

'You've forgotten something.'

I looked at her uncomprehendingly.

'What are you going to shoot with?' she retorted. She passed me a box of bullets and said, 'Now go!' in a stern but almost maternal tone. 'Ask someone to show you how to use it, and practise!'

I stumbled back to my shelter with the machine gun and the bullets. I had no idea how I was supposed to carry all this around with me constantly, let alone load and fire the machine gun. Everyone would probably laugh themselves silly when they saw me carrying this. But when I looked around, I saw that no one was staring at me at all as I staggered along with the gun. I was proud and close to tears at the same time.

I had no choice but to pitch in. I had often heard remarks like 'We have nothing more to lose', but I had not understood what that meant. I did not want to lose, and I thought that we could not possibly lose if I joined in with my own machine gun. They must need me urgently, I thought, for every day someone returned from the front and died from his or her wounds. Others simply never returned. There were fewer and fewer people in our unit.

From listening to the older ones talk, I learned that not everyone who had gone missing was necessarily dead or being held by the enemy. Many of them had simply deserted – let their guns drop when they thought no one was watching, and run for it. Every now and then, a machine gun would be found in the bush – a clear sign that yet another soldier had deserted.

Many deserters tried to escape to the Sudan so that they would not be pressed into service again by the ELF, the EPLF or even by the Ethiopian troops. Some of them made it, but desertion was never spoken of openly, least of all to someone like me, the baby of the company. Although desertion was strictly forbidden, I heard the word 'deserter' whispered in conversations I overheard, so I was sure it happened anyway.

Our leaders spoke of freedom, a homeland, Eritrea and the enemy – the EPLF and the Ethiopians. I could not have cared less who the enemy was. My personal enemies were hunger, thirst, the heat, the rats, the hyenas, the relentless military training and the heavy Kalashnikov that I now had to lug around with me all the time.

Hunger

I did not want to, and could not, carry my machine gun with me all the time. It was an awkward lump of metal far too large for me to hang from my shoulder as the older children did as they worked in the camp, marched around or took cover crawling over the ground. The gun was also much too heavy for me to be able to carry it as well as a canister of water, a bundle of firewood or a spade. If I carried the gun on my back, it pulled me backwards; if I cradled it to my chest, it yanked me forwards so I nearly stumbled into the riverbed. It was difficult to climb with the gun, and it knocked against my legs whenever I bent down to pick something up. It slid off my shoulder when I threw myself on the ground to take cover and crashed against my knees. It was an impossible thing to carry around – I didn't want to have it with me at all.

The gun quickly became a burden to me, a very clear sign of my physical weakness. Life was already hard enough with the heavy work I had to do in the camp and the daily military training, but the worst thing that I and everyone else had to bear was the hunger. Hunger gnawed at us constantly, not just intermittently in the mornings or the afternoons. All I cared about was how I could get something to eat.

Along with all the other children in Che Guevara camp, my sisters and I had given up waiting for the camp kitchens to serve up anything edible. There was no point in waiting for a lorry to arrive with a few sacks of grain or rice or a couple of boxes filled with tins of ground fishmeal. It was ages since we had last had any fruit or vegetables, and meat – which I did not eat anyway – was a distant memory. I did long for an egg to eat or a glass of milk to drink, though – but we had no goats, sheep or hens either. Even the plain fare of *injera* bread and fishmeal was no longer served regularly and there was often nothing to eat for days before fresh supplies arrived. Even when supplies did arrive, there was no guarantee that we would get any of them. We hung around the cooking fires for hours before any food might be ready so that we would not miss out.

Once, my sisters and I organised a rota to keep watch. When it was my turn, I stood right next to the makeshift stove of rocks behind which the women who did the cooking had barricaded themselves. I hoped one of them would pass me a mug of fishmeal or a lump of dough while they were cooking, or even ask me to help them cook.

'Get lost, brat!' one of the women screamed. I ducked when she threw a stone at me, and slunk round to the other side of the stove, where I hid behind a pile of boxes. I crouched there for hours with my tummy rumbling, watching every movement at the stove. Some of the women kneaded and patted the *injera* dough into shape before putting it on a tray to bake, while others mashed up and boiled pumpkins with salt. When the food was almost ready I was in two minds: should I fetch my sisters or should I get some food for myself first? Luckily, I did not have to put my conscience to the test, for my sisters soon turned up, lured by the smell of the food cooking.

People streamed from all corners of the camp and clustered round the cooking fires. I had to jump up and run forwards to make sure I got some food after my long wait, but the older soldiers pushed me to one side – it was every man for himself here. I tried crawling on all fours between the grown-ups' legs, but was kicked, pulled and pushed in all directions. The crowd was pressed so tightly together that it was almost impossible to get through it. When I had finally fought my way through to the first row, it was too late. The last piece of *injera* bread was being handed out and the last ladleful of pumpkin soup was being served. I was left with the few bits of *injera* that had stuck to the baking tray and the crust of pumpkin mash in the pot that the others had not noticed – much too little to fill me up and quell the growling of my stomach.

The crowd by the stove dispersed even more quickly than it had gathered. All I could hope for was better luck next time.

On the hunt

I decided not to rely on my luck any longer, but to try to look for food for myself. The other children and the grown-ups who had not had enough to eat went in search of anything remotely edible. They climbed trees and used nets or slings to catch birds, bats or beetles, crawled through the undergrowth in the riverbed in search of tortoises, shot at the rare gazelle or other game they saw or made traps to catch mice, moles and ground squirrels. They roasted and ate everything they caught, even if it was just a couple of grasshoppers or beetles. The charred remains of small birds were a pathetic sight.

I had never participated in these hunts for food before because I did not eat meat. I was just as hungry as everyone else, but I had never been able to bring myself to swallow a tough, half-raw mouthful of sinew or a piece of flesh ripped out from beneath the shell of a tortoise. Everyone else thought I was mad to go hungry, but I knew that one bite from the scrawny frame of a bat would make me throw up immediately.

I ate other things instead. I plucked the leaves that seemed slightly less thorny and hard, and cooked them in a rusty tin over a little fire. They did not taste good, but at least they dulled the hollow feeling in my stomach. Sometimes I found small beets or tubers in an abandoned field, which I boiled and ate even though I had no idea what they were. Sometimes I was lucky, and found a root that looked like an onion, which I had seen the grown-ups use in their cooking. I was most successful in my search for food in the late summer, when the cacti bore prickly but juicy fruit in abundance. The others also ate these fruits, which satisfied not only hunger but thirst, and were deliciously sweet as well. It was a pity that the fruit all ripened at the same time, so much of it rotted or dried up in a few weeks in the intense heat.

Sometimes I also found *gaba*, tiny wild nuts that not many people bothered with because they were so small, and seemed hardly worth the effort of cracking open for the little they contained. I picked them anyway and kept them in my trouser pockets, spending hours cracking them open and eating them.

When all else failed and the hunger seemed to have bored a huge hole all through me, I climbed down to the riverbed and ate handfuls of earth. I scraped away the sandy surface to get at the dried mud, which I crammed into my mouth. I chewed away at it until I could force myself to swallow it, and continued until I was sick. The moist, mossy taste of the mud was not a problem, but I got terrible stomach cramps from eating it, and either had to throw up or suffered from diarrhoea. But that was still better than the horrible empty feeling of hunger. It was also better to be called a 'dirt-eater' by the others than to have nothing to eat at all.

'You fool!' the others screamed at me. 'You're made of nothing but dirt, and you're eating it!'

'Human beings don't eat mud!'

'I do!' I said. And I felt proud of myself for it.

Thirst

Hunger was not the worst of our privations, however. I managed to take the edge of my hunger by some means or other most of the time, but it was not possible to do the same with thirst. Chewing or biting into something, anything, did not go any way towards satisfying thirst. Only water would do and we had far too little of it, apart from the one month in the year when the cacti bore fruit.

I often wondered how the camels we travelled with survived. They never seemed to search for water, but merely nibbled at dried-out clumps of grass, at leaves in the trees, or at the barren ground itself. They always looked content and peaceful, except when they had to go down on their knees for riders to mount their backs, when they groaned and cried as if in the throes of death.

Camels' milk is normally drunk, but our camels had no milk, probably because they got too little water. They tore thorns off the bushes and walked around the whole day chewing at them, jaws grinding and rubbery lips stretched as if they were about to start laughing any moment.

Unlike the camels, we could not survive without water. We were constantly on the look-out for it. Sometimes I felt as if we were jinxed when Tzegehana and I went in search of water only to find the water holes that we had dug the day before had completely dried out, so dry that it was as if there had never been a drop of water in them. Sometimes we dug so deep for water that I could barely look out over the hole we had dug when I stood in it.

We dug our way through dried mud, a mixture of sand and scree which got into our hair and eyes, stuck in our throats and rubbed our hands raw. The gravelly ground that crumbled at the touch meant that we always had to dig a much wider hole in order to get to the depth at which there might be some water. Sometimes, all we found was a patch of sand that looked a little moist – perhaps if we had dug a few metres deeper we might have struck water, but we were only a couple of small girls wielding spades. Even the bigger boys in our unit whom we once asked to help us found it difficult to dig in that constantly shifting ground.

Gods

Digging for water made us even more thirsty. We sweated under the burning sun and our eyes streamed as sand got into our clothes and mouths. Our noses hurt from being completely dried up.

There was no hope of rain – the sky was an unforgiving blue, and the air was still. It grew hotter and hotter and the animals had all crept into earth burrows or into the shade of the bushes. The time for rain had come and gone without a single drop of it. Everyone in our unit prayed to all sorts of gods for it to rain. I, too, had prayed when I was sure that no one could see or hear me. I knew of Jesus from my time in the orphanage, and from my grandmother. I also knew about Mary, his mother, so I prayed to her: 'Mother of God, please make it rain. Just a little.' Or, 'Please let there be water in one of the water holes, just enough so that I can fill a canister.' 'Please let there be enough water so that I can put my head in it and pour water over myself, just once.' 'Please, Mother of God, you don't have to bring us anything to eat. Just a bit of *injera* bread maybe. But please let there be water!'

Others in the camp prayed to a god called Allah. They turned themselves in a particular direction, laid a cloth down and threw themselves on to the ground four times a day: in the morning, the afternoon, the evening and at night. They did not say anything about water, but recited their special prayers. One of the older ones, Mohammed, told me that he only ever thought about water when he prayed, though.

There were other people who prayed to gods I did not know. These gods could be anywhere – in a rock, a tree, or under-ground. The soldiers who prayed to these invisible gods crawled on all fours through the camp – as they prayed, they tore at their hair, rolled round on the ground, and their cries ranged from those of anger to pleading to guilt. They screamed and swore and begged, but the only thing that seemed to happen was that it grew hotter than ever. I did not think that was the right way to get water. Perhaps my grandmother would have known how to pray for rain, but no one in the camp seemed to have any luck.

Mohammed, who prayed to Allah, told me that he had never seen his god, not even a picture of him. He told me that his god was not meant to be seen. But my god and his mother were meant to be seen – Jesus hung on a cross with nails in his hands and feet and Mary had a blue shawl over her head and wore a robe like the one women in Eritrea wore, only hers was in blue instead of white. Jesus and Mary were both white-skinned, like Mike'ele in the ELF.

Mike'ele

Mike'ele had pale skin and light brown hair that fell to his shoulders in gentle waves, quite unlike my frizzy hair. His father was Italian. He was a good soldier and was liked by all. He was always up for a laugh, the joker of the company. He could pick up a stone, hold it in one fist, and then open the other fist, where it had magically appeared. He said that it was not magic, merely a trick that anyone could learn. But he did not say how it was done. Once, a couple of boys threatened to beat him up unless he taught them the trick, but Mike'ele still refused. The boys did not beat him up after all, probably because they were secretly frightened of him, as many others in the camp were. I had heard someone say once that Mike'ele could cast spells on other people so that they lost all the colour from their faces. That was mere rumour, for no one had ever seen Mike'ele actually do it.

Mike'ele told me that he had never seen his Italian father, only a photograph of him that his mother had once showed him. His father had been wearing a uniform in the photograph. Mike'ele said his father must be dead, for otherwise he would have been there with Mike'ele. I did not dare to contradict him but merely thought to myself that it was possible for fathers to be alive but not be there, as was the case with mine. Although unlike Mike'ele, I did not want my father there with me. Mike'ele said that what he wished for more than anything else was to see his father, but if he was dead, he would never see him.

Mike'ele prayed to my god, but not very often. 'It's no use,' he said. 'God won't even send rain. He doesn't care whether it rains here or not. If it had been somewhere else he would have sent rain long ago.' Parched with thirst, I lay on my mat at night thinking about what he had said. Why did God not want to send rain to us? Had we done something bad?

Agawegahta hated the sight of people rolling around in the dirt praying to Jesus, Allah or other gods. 'There is god,' she said. 'People have made their gods themselves.'

I knew that people had painted the pictures of God in the orphanage and in the church – the nuns and my grandmother had always said that those were only paintings and that God had made Himself. But Agawegahta did not want to hear any of this. 'We are our own gods,' she said. 'We are fighting for ourselves, not for a god. You should get to work rather than waste time praying – there's no one listening up there!'

I did not believe her, but sometimes when I lay at night on my mat feeling hopeless and exhausted from the heat and the thirst, I wondered if she was right.

One night, Mike'ele shook me awake. 'Come and fetch water with me!' he whispered. I jumped up immediately at the thought of water.

'Where …?' I asked, but Mike'ele held his hand over my mouth. I started to resist, scratching and kicking at him, but then I realised he did not mean me any harm.

He clamped his hand over my mouth more firmly and whispered, 'We're going into the village to get water.'

The water caravan

I had no idea how we were meant to get water from the village, but all I cared about was getting water to drink. I knew where the village was – Tzegehana and I had seen it in the distance before when we had been collecting firewood. We had not dared to approach the village then, for we did not know whether friends or foes lived in it.

Mike'ele signalled to me to follow him and be quiet. Along with three others, we slipped out of the camp, bent so low that we were practically on all fours. No one was allowed to leave the camp without permission from one of the leaders, especially not at night. I would never have dared to leave the camp alone, but I trusted Mike'ele. I knew that if anything happened, he would see to it that we escaped in one piece. We just had to make sure that no one heard or saw us.

There were sentry points in the camp, but we knew where they were: down by the river, up on the rocky outcrop over-looking the camp, and up by the clump of trees through which the older soldiers went when they set off for the front. We took a roundabout route to avoid them – through the shallow ravine, along the top of the hills beside the camp and then behind the clump of trees towards the village. We had to be careful not to trip on stones, not to jump, and not to speak even though the questions were burning on my lips: who were we going to get water from? Whose idea was this?

We successfully avoided the sentries and stumbled down to the valley in which the village lay. The moon had not risen yet, so I could barely see anything. After a couple of hundred metres, the person behind me gave me a shove and I started. 'You can walk normally again,' he hissed. I straightened myself, a little embar-rassed that I had been the only one who had still been crouching down as we walked.

We walked on through the night for a while, but saw no sign of the village. Then, suddenly, we were standing between huts. It looked like a very poor place – the huts were flimsy constructions with roofs made of branches and leaves and there was no sign of life from the villagers, no fire or light anywhere.

Mike'ele opened one of the lean-tos and called softly into the hut. A hunched old woman hobbled out sleepily. She did not seem surprised to see us, but appeared to know what we wanted. She led us round her hut to a small hollow in which there were a couple of canisters of water. I could hardly believe my eyes. Every one of us was allowed to drink from them, including me. I felt the water trickling into me and spreading in my body and filling my stomach. A feeling of peace and contentment overcame me.

Mike'ele pressed something into the woman's hand. When she reached to put it away, I saw that it was a crumpled note. This was the first time I had seen anyone handle money in Barka. There were no shops or bars here, and there was nothing anyone had to pay for. But the novelty of seeing someone pay for something was nothing compared to my desire for water. I wanted to take another gulp from the canister, and was allowed to do so.

The walk back to the camp seemed much easier than the journey out. We brought with us a few small canisters which we had filled with water. Now we buried these canisters in the sand a couple of hundred metres outside the camp, and put a few stones on top of them. Mike'ele fixed a long stick upright over the spot so that we would be able to find it later. 'Only drink from here when no one is watching,' he warned us. 'And only a couple of mouthfuls a day. If you drink more than that, I'll beat the senses out of you.'

He seemed to consider me the least trustworthy of us all because I was the youngest. 'Don't tell anyone about this,' he said, looking at me fiercely. I hardly needed to be told to keep the secret of our treasure from everyone else. A few minutes later, I sank on to my sleeping mat exhausted, but happy.

I seemed to have slept for only a minute before I was woken again. The silhouette of the hills behind the camp was growing clearer and clearer against a brightening sky. I must have had only one or two hours of sleep and I knew that I would have a hard day ahead of me. But our night-time expedition had been worth it. During the day, I only had to stop for a moment to hear a little gurgle of water still in my stomach.

I was allowed to go on these expeditions to fetch water a few more times. We were afraid of punishment if anyone found us out, but we went anyway. I discovered later that there had always been a store of water in our camp. It was kept in a couple of yellow canisters half-buried in the hollow right next to the munitions tent, and watched over day and night. I had always thought the watchmen were guarding only the arms, until I saw a couple of soldiers handling the yellow canisters one day. This discovery strengthened my resolve to go on the night expeditions for water – if they could hide water from the younger ones and only give us so little, then we would have to get water for ourselves.

The old woman never seemed to run out of water, except for one time when we got some from her neighbour instead. Mike'ele paid them with the notes of which he seemed to have an inexhaustible supply. We got water even on the one occasion he did not pay for it, for the women in the village were frightened of us. Their husbands were all either dead or still at war, and so the women had been left in the village with a couple of scrawny goats and a well that was so deep that it still had a little water. They thought we were dangerous even though we were not carrying any weapons – which would turn out to be a mistake.

Bedouin

One night, we came across some Bedouin on our way back to the camp. The drought meant that the Bedouin had to drive their camels, goats and cows in widening circles through the parched steppes in order to find a few strands of grass and any water holes that still had any water in them for their livestock. They travelled by night to avoid the heat of the day.

They saw us first in the pitch darkness of the rocky steppe, a landscape interrupted only by a couple of trees here and there or some thorny bushes. We only noticed them once they had changed their direction to head towards us. At first we thought that they were enemy soldiers on night patrol. We walked as fast as we could, but we could not shake them off. Then we started to run, but they drew closer and closer. When we reached a little rise in the ground, we saw that they were Bedouin, not soldiers. They were wearing long robes and riding camels. What did they want from us?

There was nothing for it but to stop and wait, for they were much faster on their camels than we were on foot. As they approached us, they called out in a language that I did not understand. A couple of them were swinging their swords. They were a fearsome sight, with their long beards, skins darker than ours, and gaps in their teeth. These were Muslim Bedouin from Sudan. One of our party understood a little of what they were saying and translated for us: 'They think that we are out to steal their camels, goats or cows.'

They did not believe that we had only been fetching water. As far as I was concerned, they could think anything they wanted, for my belly was full with water which no one could take away from me. Suddenly, one of the men jumped off his camel and came threateningly close to us. The soldier who spoke some of their language pleaded that we had nothing of value with us. All we had were the ragged clothes on our backs. The Bedouin did not believe us. They pushed Mike'ele, forced him to take off his shirt and rifled through his trouser pockets. All they found was a couple of pieces of wood he had collected before and a few almost worthless notes.

'Guns? Guns?' the Bedouin shouted. But none of us had our guns with us.

Then Mike'ele had an idea, and told our translator what to say to them.

'If you continue shouting,' he said, 'our fellow soldiers will hear you. We are from the Jebha and our camp is just over the hill.'

Our camp was not actually that close and no one would have heard the Bedouin shouting. Even if they had, we would have got into trouble for stealing out of the camp at night. But the Bedouin decided not to risk it, especially as we really did not seem to have anything of value on us. They mounted their camels again and rode off, taking with them only the few notes Mike'ele had had in this pocket.

On our next night-time foray, we took a couple of guns with us in case we encountered the Bedouin again. This made our expedition even riskier, for to have been caught leaving the camp with our guns would have been an even more serious matter, as it would have looked like desertion. Deserters were normally shot immediately even though it must have been clear by then that the ELF was in a hopeless position.

I had overheard two camp commanders talking once. 'Let the children go where they want! The war is over, after all. Nothing more can be done,' one of them said.

The other commander disagreed. 'If we do that, they'll all end up with the EPLF and try to murder us. I'd rather fight to my last bullet than let myself be shot by them! I'll kill anyone who tries to run away myself.'

Dawit

One day, I heard shots fired in the middle of our camp. Had the enemy come to kill us? I had heard people say that the enemy would defeat us soon. I dropped the washing I was holding and threw myself on to the ground. Another round of shooting followed. I pulled the bundle of washing over my head and lay still.

Suddenly I heard someone laugh, and then another person join in. 'Look at that little coward,' the first person said. 'Look at her grovelling in the dirt!'

I got up in surprise. There was no one around apart from my two sniggering fellow soldiers. 'What were those shots?' I asked, but they just kept laughing at me.

I only discovered what the shots had been on the next day. There was a body covered in sand and blood lying on the ground next to the tarpaulin shelters we slept under. It was Dawit, who was about seventeen, one of the older soldiers whom I had got along well with. He used to tell me about his family. I had envied the easy way he had been able to talk about his father, his mother and his brothers and sisters, without hatred or fear that they would abandon him, as my family had so often done.

Later on, my sisters told me that Dawit had been executed because he had tried to run away. He had been caught not far from the camp in the morning with his gun, a sack full of *injera* bread and a few personal effects. Dawit had wanted to return to his parents, but he had been shot by a patrol out on the plain. The two ELF soldiers who had spotted him had thought at first that he was a Shabia soldier from the EPLF and followed him. When he had started running, they had shot him and wounded him. They had carried him back to the camp, where he was then executed with a volley of shots at the command of our leader. One of the soldiers who had been on patrol later said he had recognised Dawit from the start but had not said anything to the others. He said he wished he could have shot Dawit dead immediately rather than waste those miles of walking through the heat.

Dawit had been silly. He had had no chance of escaping alone, especially not when he set off only at daybreak instead of by night, when the patrols were sleeping. If only he had left with us when we had gone on one of our water expeditions. I felt sorry for him, but also frightened of what would happen if someone found out about our night-time journeys to get water.

Along with a few others, I dug a grave for Dawit in the stony earth, deep enough for his body not to be disturbed by hyenas or vultures, for we did not have a coffin to protect him from the carrion-eaters.

Execution

A few days later, we all had to gather in the space between the tarpaulin shelters we slept under and the makeshift kitchen to witness a kind of court martial. Facing us were four soldiers tied to posts in front of the rocky overhang behind the camp. I had hardly had any contact with these soldiers because they were much older than me – between sixteen and twenty years old – but I knew their names.

One of them had weals on his arms and upper body, another had a bloody face and a third had grazed legs. Three of them were writhing as if they were trying to escape but the fourth simply stood there with his head bowed and eyes closed, as if he was no longer present in his body.

One of the camp leaders gave a speech about the ELF and independence for Eritrea, all of which we had heard before. But this time he added something new: 'Our backs are against the wall now. The enemy is bearing down on us and we must fight back with everything we have. We will win. But we can only win if we keep together, if no one runs away and if we all fight together. We cannot afford any weaknesses. Anyone who betrays us and our cause is a weakness which we will not tolerate.'

He turned to the four accused soldiers. He walked up and down before them, so close that they could have touched him even though their hands were tied to the posts. 'You have betrayed us!' he screamed. 'You ran away from the Jebha and tried to go home, you cowards. You are ruining our morale! I will not allow this kind of behaviour!'

He fell silent and looked each of the four men in the eye, slowly. 'You are to be executed!'

Two of the accused broke down – they fell to the ground and started screaming and begging for their lives. The one who had seemed entirely absent started tugging at the rope binding him and the fourth man simply stood there weeping quietly to himself.

'You wanted to destroy the Jebha,' the leader said. 'You must die in order that we may live!'

The sobbing and begging of the condemned men was the only sound to be heard. Suddenly Mihret called 'Bravo!' and started clapping. All eyes turned to her and a few others gradually started clapping, too, including the soldier standing next to me. I stood rooted to the spot, amazed that everyone seemed to agree that the four men should be killed.

Any one of us could have been standing where those four men stood now, for almost all of us had thought about going home – how wonderful and easy it would be to simply run away through the desert. I was the only one who had never imagined running away because I had no home to go back to. I would not have gone back to live with my father for all the world, and though I would have liked to go to my grandparents', the thought of Mbrat, who lived with them, put me off. After all that I had seen and lived through since, I could not simply go back to playing the same games with the same children in those small streets in Asmara that I had known so well. I was a different person now, and I could not go back.

'Clap, for goodness' sake!' hissed the soldier standing next to me. I lifted my hands and brought them together mechanically. They made hardly any sound but at least it looked like I was clapping. This satisfied the soldier but I felt numb inside. Death was inevitable here. Killing someone because he wanted to go home seemed horribly unfair to me, and the realisation that I had no home myself was crushing.

I felt as if I was witnessing what happened through a glass screen. Four soldiers stepped forward with their Kalashnikovs and positioned themselves before each of the condemned men. At the leader's shout of 'Fire!' they shot the men. The men's bodies jerked with the impact of the bullets, so hard that one of the posts was pulled out of the ground and crashed into the next post.

I held my hands to my face, pressing my eyes closed. But I could not close my ears, so the screams of pain bored into my head – the most terrible cries I had ever heard. It took a few minutes before all was silent again.

'This is what will happen to any one of you who tries to run away,' the leader shouted. He stood quite still, but was shouting at the top of his voice. 'Everyone who tries to destroy the Jebha will be executed.' He turned on his heal and left.

We stood there lost for words. The dead bodies remained tied to the posts until the evening as a warning to us all. It was an unspeakable relief to us when they were taken away.

Punishment

When Mike'ele came to get me the next night, I pretended to be asleep. I was shivering with fear, for I was too afraid to go with the others to get water now that I had seen what had happened to those who had been taken for deserters. Mike'ele shook me, but I pressed my eyes together. He did not notice me shivering, but simply thought I was sound asleep, and crept away.

I breathed a sigh of relief. I did not fear death itself – on the contrary, I often thought death would solve all the suffering and drudgery I had to live through. God would surely come to take me, as the nuns had always told me. But I was afraid of the sensation of dying, which looked very painful indeed.

Despairing, I tossed and turned on my sleeping mat, throat burning and eyes stinging from the tears I had shed earlier. I finally fell asleep shortly before dawn, when the others had already returned from the village safely. I was woken soon afterwards, and another long day of work, brutal shouting, shooting, hunger and heat stretched before me.

A few weeks later, we were forced to witness another execution. This time, two boys had been condemned to death for selling their guns to the Bedouin. They had slipped away in the night and nobody had noticed them. But one of the tribe of Bedouin they had sold their guns to had betrayed them to the Jebha. When Agawegahta confronted the boys with this revelation, they denied everything but were unable to produce their guns. The money they had received from the Bedouin was found instead.

The boys had not wanted the money for themselves, but for their families. Perhaps they also hoped to use some of it to pay for their journey back to their families. There was certainly nothing to buy in the desolate wastes of western Eritrea where our camp was stationed. The old woman in the village who we paid for her water could not do anything with the money we gave her. Like everyone else in the region, she eked a living from the few animals she kept and from international aid supplies.

Money was worthless in those parts. Some of us had never encountered it before and did not even know what it was. But Agawegahta did not care about that – she ordered the execution of those two boys to set us an example. I stopped respecting her after that, and began to hate her. I realised that the woman I had admired for her supposed strength was actually a weak creature who exercised her power through a regime of terror. She punished anyone who committed a crime in her eyes, fearing that she would be punished herself one day.

Hiding places

My newfound hatred for Agawegahta was strengthened by her insistence that I joined the other smaller children at shooting practice. We were the last group of children who could not shoot yet, for there had been no new recruits since our arrival.

I dragged my Kalashnikov from my sleeping mat to the artillery range a few hundred metres from the camp. The range was merely a few boards and a couple of tree trunks resting against rocks to simulate human beings. They were riddled with holes.

I hated everything about shooting: the heavy guns, the sound of them and the jerky recoil. I could not bear the idea of killing anyone, even someone who wanted to kill me simply because I was fighting for the other side.

I paused on my way to the shooting range. What if I didn't go? I could go and do some other work that was much more important than shooting, like collect firewood, which we were short of.

'Come along,' one of the others said to me.

'I'm coming, I've just got to get something.'

'What do you have to get?' he asked. He knew that I had not been to shooting practice before.

'Ammunition,' I said quickly. 'I've forgotten to bring some.'

'Well, hurry up then!' he said. He walked on unsuspectingly.

I felt like running, but walked back to the camp at a normal pace so as not to arouse suspicion. I wondered where to put my gun. If I left it on my sleeping mat, everyone would know that I was not at shooting practice after all. I looked round desperately. It was hard to find a hiding place in this barren landscape, especially for something as unwieldy as a Kalashnikov.

Then I remembered how Mike'ele had hidden the water canisters, and realised that I could dig a hole to hide my machine gun in. I looked round for a suitable patch of loose gravel that I could dig up easily. I scrabbled at the ground with my bare hands until I had dug a shallow hole to lay my gun in.

Just as I was almost finished burying my gun, Tzegehana walked by. I knew that if she found out what I was doing, she would tell Yaldiyan, who could never keep anything to herself. I kicked a few more stones over the gun and pretended that I had just relieved myself. This patch of ground was used by people from the camp as a toilet so Tzegehana did not notice anything, much to my relief. I just had to try hard not to think about what would happen the next day.

I went off to collect firewood with Tzegehana. When I returned, carrying a heavy bundle of firewood, Mike'ele called to me, 'I have something to show you!'

I dropped my bundle immediately and ran over to him.

'Come with me,' he said, running ahead.

I suddenly realised that he was running towards the shooting range, and my heart lurched. Mike'ele was leading shooting practice that day – had he, of all people, found my gun?

When we arrived at the spot where I had buried my gun, I saw that the magazine was sticking out of the ground. I must have overlooked it before. I hung my head in shame.

'Do you know what will happen if I tell the others about this?' Mike'ele asked.

I knew only too well.

'Now get your gun out of there and go!' he said, walking off.

I was overcome with gratitude, and hastily uncovered my machine gun.

The next shooting practice I had to attend was led by Mihret. I wondered if I dared to try to escape it. Mike'ele was not going to be there, and I was sure that he had not betrayed me to anybody.

But Mihret made it easy for me to escape by leaving the shooting range – she had something more important to do. The others seemed to be absorbed in learning how to shoot and kill as well as the grown-ups did, and did not pay any attention to me.

I slipped away without anyone noticing and buried my gun once again, in the riverbed this time. Then I found a relatively shady place far away from the troop and lay down on the ground. Why should I go back to the camp now and do any work when they thought I was at shooting practice anyway? I relished this time alone without anyone ordering me to do anything, and felt so relaxed that I fell asleep.

When I woke, it was almost dark, which gave me a shock. I was supposed to have got a lot of work done by now. I jumped up and ran back to the camp as quickly as I could, rushing headlong into Agawegahta. I mumbled an excuse and tried to pass her, but she held me in an iron grip.

'I've been told that you keep hiding your gun because you don't want to fight and don't want to practise – is that right?'

Fear swept over me. How did she know? Had someone found my Kalashnikov? I stammered my excuses and apologies, but Agawegahta was impassive. I wondered if I was to be put to death.

'I'll let you off this time,' she said. 'Mihret will think of a punishment for you. But if you ever do it again, you'll be in for it!' She shook me hard and let me go so suddenly that I nearly fell to the ground.

That night, Mihret made me walk round the camp on my knees carrying a water canister on my back until my knees and shoulders bled. I was not allowed to drink a drop of the water I carried. The other soldiers watched, cat-calling and laughing. When they went to bed, I collapsed and fell asleep on the spot.

Later, I found out that Yaldiyan had betrayed me after she had overheard Mike'ele tell a friend that he had found my gun. Yaldiyan always liked feeling important, and she also did not like me much. She felt that I did not give her the respect an older sister deserved, but I had no desire to knuckle under to her.

Everyone shunned me after my public humiliation. Mike'ele and others who had been friendly to me stopped speaking to me, fearing that I would harm their standing in the unit.

Fear

As time passed I grew more and more frightened. I did not want to be executed or to be blown to pieces by a hand grenade or a mine – I had seen what horrific injuries and deaths they resulted in.

'Why are we killing them?' I asked Mihret when she was holding forth once again about the glory of fighting the enemies who wanted to destroy our homeland. 'They look exactly like us. They're from the same tribe as we are!'

I knew the people from other tribes looked different, for I had seen them when I lived in Asmara, where everyone lived together peacefully. There had been Eritreans with darker skins, thicker lips, larger builds, or wearing different traditional dress in Asmara. But the bodies of the enemy soldiers we saw over and over again all looked just like us.

'They look exactly like us!' I repeated stubbornly. I knew I was making Mihret angry, but I did not care. I was filled with anger, at the dead bodies, at the miserable life we were leading in the desert, at Mihret and Agawegahta, and at everything connected with them.

'They don't look like us, you fool! They are EPLF soldiers. They look different!' Mihret screamed.

'No! They look the same! Their hair, their skins ...'

Mihret flew at me. 'Don't you dare argue, you little coward! You're lying because you don't want to fight. You're talking nonsense simply because you're too scared to hold a gun!'

I held my arms over my head to protect myself from her blows. Deep inside, I knew that Mihret was partly right: I did not want to fight. I would have objected to people killing each other anyway, but it was the fact that I was expected to join in that had worked me up to this degree.

'You're lying!' I screamed, even though Mihret had pushed me to the ground by then, and my mouth was full of dirt.

After the confrontation with Mihret, it was clear to me that there was no way I could escape the war as long as I remained in the Jebha camp. I knew that I would have to learn how to use my machine gun. I no longer dared to hide it, but carried it with me constantly. I often took it with me even when I fetched water, though I could hardly carry it along with the water canister. I buried the ammunition, thinking that the gun would be a little lighter without it, but I hardly felt a difference.

Shooting practice

I was to regret burying that ammunition. One day, when Mihret and about a dozen children including myself were by a water hole, we saw four or five jackals tearing at an antelope carcass.

'Now you can show me what you can do,' Mihret hissed with relish, as if she were a jackal herself, thirsting for blood. 'Get under cover and crawl nearer. When a jackal seems as big as a rat right in front of you, take aim. Only shoot the creatures when I give the sign, not a moment before. Let's see if you hit them!'

I threw myself on the ground along with all the others, pulled the gun over my shoulder pointing forward and started crawling like we had learned to do in our training sessions. I found this crawling on all fours over stony ground ridiculous and humiliating – only animals move like this. No one else felt embarrassed, but they did not like crawling over the ground much either, though the excitement of stalking the jackals made it seem more exciting.

The animals soon sensed our presence. They raised their heads to try to pick up a scent, then returned to their spoils, but kept stopping to sniff the air. My view of them was blocked by a clump of bushes, and the air shimmered with heat, making objects in the distance blurry, like a collection of wavy lines. I found it hard to breathe so close to the ground, which was incredibly hot. I swore silently to myself, wishing that I had one of the head-cloths Eritrean women or Bedouin wore to protect their heads and faces from the sun.

The jackals were becoming more and more restless. They were standing next to the carcass looking around nervously as if they were about to run away at any moment.

'Now!' Mihret hissed. 'Fire!'

I raised my gun along with everyone else, released the safety catch and pressed my body to the ground as firmly as I could to brace myself for the recoil. But my gun only clicked quietly. Then I realised with a lightning jolt that I had no ammunition in my magazine.

To my left and my right, the others let off a volley of shots that tore through the air above the broad, arid valley. Most of the shots landed wide of their target, sending stones, dust and earth spraying through the air. There was a smell of burnt skin, and the jackals ran off howling. There were almost a dozen of them, clustered so tightly that they could have passed for one animal. Suddenly, one of them leapt into the air, its body grotesquely twisted, and crashed lengthways to the ground. It jumped up and crashed down again, and rose yet again. 'He's down!' Mihret shouted. 'Get him!'

The others stormed forward, shooting away. I was the only

one who stayed lying on the ground. I was overwhelmed by this explosion of violence and noise. Two of them continued shooting at the injured jackal until it stopped twitching altogether, then they all broke out in a cheer. When I finally joined them, wondering how I should react, Mihret hit me full in the face, grabbed my gun, tore the magazine from it and held it up accusingly in front of the others.

'Look at this idiot!' She waved my gun over her head like a trophy. 'She hadn't even loaded her gun. She's just play-acting. She's even more despicable than the jackal you've just killed!'

She hit me again and again across the face, but I said nothing. My face was burning and my nose was bleeding, but that was nothing compared to the scornful looks the others were giving me. Mihret's hatred was like a laser beam. 'You shitface! You're going to get it! You're really in for it!' She thrust the gun back in my arms and kicked me so hard that I nearly fell over. 'Get lost! Get her moving, come on!'

The others did not understand what Mihret meant until she gave me another kick. They ran after me, pushing me so that I stumbled and fell over and over again as they stepped on me and kicked me. I made no effort to defend myself.

Suddenly, a shadow fell across me. 'Stop,' an authoritative voice said. It was the leader of a slightly older group in our camp. My persecutors stopped immediately.

'What was that about? What did they want from you?'

'They hate me,' I sobbed, 'because I didn't shoot at the jackals with them. Someone must have stolen my ammunition last night, and I didn't dare to tell Mihret.' I was amazed at how easily I managed to tell a lie. I had made up the perfect excuse.

'Leave her alone,' the older girl said to the other children. 'Go away.'

She turned to me. 'If you are lying to me, I'll have you thrown to the jackals!'

I stood up, exhausted and grateful. The others walked away without a glance.

Accidents

I was too small to be a soldier – too young, too weak and too scared. And the guns were far too heavy for me. Almost all our guns were Kalashnikovs – gigantic, unwieldy sub-machine guns. Only leaders like Agawegahta had pistols as well. Pistols would have been more suitable for children like me, but there were not enough of them, thank God, or I would have been forced to shoot with them and kill someone. The jerky recoil from the Kalashnikov was so strong that I could barely fire it. None of the other smaller children could handle their Kalashnikovs either.

One day, I was busy sawing away at firewood with a knife when two boys only a year or two older than me walked past on their way to the shooting range, carrying their guns over their shoulders. The guns were so big that their butts practically reached the ground. Like all the younger children, they had to lift their guns when they climbed rocks, in order not to bang against them. There was nothing unusual in small children going off to practise shooting alone, so I did not take much notice of them.

Soon afterwards, I heard shots from the shooting range, and then one of the two children came running towards me, crying and shouting unintelligibly. His eyes were wide with horror. I dropped my knife and went up to him. His hand was wounded and bloody, and there was blood on his legs as well.

'He's dead!' he screamed. 'Dead!'

A few other people had arrived on the scene by then. They grabbed their guns and asked the boy who was dead, and where. He pointed towards the shooting range, where the rocky overhang behind the camp began. Thinking that the enemy had hidden among the rocks and killed one of our number, everyone released the safety catches on their guns in preparation for battle. Sometimes enemy soldiers had come close enough to the camp to be seen with the naked eye; there had been talk in the last few days of moving camp again soon. The problem we faced, however, was that the EPLF had already hemmed us in from two directions.

I took cover and watched what happened. The boy continued crying hysterically while the others stormed off to the shooting range with their guns at the ready. But no enemy awaited them when they got there. Puzzled, they called to each other and gradually let their guns fall.

We did not seem to be under attack after all, so I emerged from my hiding place and walked over to the shooting range as well, where I practically stumbled over the boy who lay dead next to a bush. His head had been blown apart, and his body was covered in blood. I screamed, and the others ran over to me, guns at the ready. But their help had come too late – the boy had been shot dead by his best friend, as we found out later. The heavy Kalashnikov had slipped out of his grasp as he was releasing the safety catch and he had mistakenly fired the gun at his friend.

The others shrugged when they saw the body and walked back to the camp. Two of them carried the small body to a grave we had dug the day before for two soldiers killed on the front. They lifted up the stones that were lying over the grave to keep the jackals away, and threw the body in with the others. It fell with a thump like a heavy sack – there was still blood running from the boy's wounds. I stood at the edge of the grave staring into it.

'Cover him up,' one of the soldiers said to me, pressing a spade into my hands. Mechanically I shovelled sand and gravel over the body, crying all the while.

When I had finished, I turned to go back to the camp, and saw that the boy who had killed his friend had been sitting behind me all this time, perfectly still.

'He's dead,' he said, when I looked at him. 'I killed him.' He buried his face in his hands and wept.

I took him in my arms and he leaned against my shoulder as he cried. I felt like his mother, and was filled with deep sorrow, but no anger. This boy had not wanted to do what he had done. None of us was responsible for all that happened as a result of the war.

The boy rested his head in my lap. My eyes were dry at first. I felt a sense of calm at the comfort the boy was drawing from me. I had never held someone close before or had someone lean against me. I had only nestled against my grandmother, but she had not turned to me for comfort. The thought made my eyes fill with tears, which flowed unchecked.

Trial and error

I knew that my fellow soldiers had been wounded or killed in shooting practice before, but this was the first time I had witnessed it. Accidents were almost inevitable, for everyone who joined the ELF was given a gun straight away, regardless of whether he or she had ever used one. On account of my age, I was the only one who was given a Kalashnikov a couple of months after my arrival rather than immediately.

The Jebha was on its last legs by that time, so most of its soldiers were not given basic military training with practice or dummy guns, but went straight to the real thing with real ammunition. Even the youngest soldiers were merely handed their guns and told to look after them. If the safety catch was released by mistake, a shot would be fired. I had done this myself by mistake but, luckily, had only fired at the ground, so the sole consequence of my action was sand spraying in my face.

Another time, I fired into the sky by mistake, but nothing happened, though I dropped to the ground screaming and holding my arms over my head, thinking that the bullets would fall back down on me. Instead, blows rained down on me for my clumsiness as soon as I dared to open my eyes. That was all the training I got – whenever I did something wrong, the others hit me rather than taking the trouble to explain anything to me or tell me the right way to do things. I was soon able to do more and more of my daily work without attracting blows – the result of this painful process of trial and error.

When I finally started shooting practice, I was unable to hit anything at all. None of the younger children had a good aim at all, for the recoil from the gun was too strong, once even flinging me a couple of metres backwards on to the ground and leaving me with grazed knees and elbows and a bruised back. Despite this, we were not allowed to lie on the ground when we first learned to shoot, but had to stand up or kneel.

Later on, I learned to control the recoil from the gun by bracing one knee against something solid, like a rock, or by leaning against a sturdy tree, which was rare in the desert. The landscape we were in was not strictly speaking desert, but after the long drought, the steppes and grasslands were endless stretches of barren land with only a few clumps of trees or scattered rocks to break the monotony.

Eventually the guns were taken away from the smaller children like me who were too young to be sent to the front. Things were getting worse and worse for the Jebha, and supplies were running low, so they could not afford to waste their guns on us. The guns were needed for battle instead of for shooting practice. Despite having no guns, we still had to continue with the military exercises.

'This war is hard, too hard for me'

I was into my second summer with the Jebha, and the war was taking its toll on every aspect of life. All that was left to us was hardly worthy of being called a life. We were constantly on the run, shivering, hungry, crawling in the dirt and fearing for our lives. We had to move camp every couple of weeks or even every couple of days, for we were being hunted like animals. We lived in fear.

One night, we arrived at a spot our camp leaders took to be reasonably safe because it was quite well hidden, yet had a good view of the surrounding area. We pitched camp in a small hollow between the crests of two hills, one of which was only a kilometre away. We only guessed at the distance, for it was a dark night and the stars only cast a faint light as we stumbled over the rocky ground and pricked ourselves constantly on thorns and thistles. There was no sign of water anywhere, which meant that we would spend the night with our throats rasping with thirst, and have to go in search for water the next morning. My feet were bleeding from the sharp pebbles that my flimsy rubber flip-flops were no protection against, and I did not relish the prospect of the tortuous search for water.

Utterly worn out, we lay down our mats and bundles with only one thing on our minds: sleep. I managed to summon up enough energy to push a sharp rock aside so as not to be scratched by it in the night, and then fell into a deep, dreamless sleep.

Whether the EPLF troop on the top of the hill nearby had already been there when we arrived or whether they had been sent after us, I do not know. It made no difference, in any case. As soon as the outlines of the rocks and our sleeping bodies became visible in the first grey light of dawn, they began firing at us.

Stillness exploded in a thunderous volley of shots, sounding as if the world was coming to an end. Clouds of dust rose up among us and gravel sprayed through the air. Woken from deep slumber, we leapt up and started running for our lives. Everyone grabbed what they could and the lorry engines started a few seconds later.

I had already run a couple of metres clutching a few blankets when I realised that I had left my gun behind. At that time, the gun had not been taken away from me yet. I kept running, but then I suddenly thought that I would have nothing to defend myself with when the enemy came to kill me. Or perhaps I feared that leaving my gun behind would be doing a disservice to my fellow soldiers. The thoughts skittered incoherently through my mind in a split second and I ran back to get my gun.

All was chaos, shouting, screaming and cursing. Mike'ele came up to me, panic-stricken, shouting and holding up his arm – blood was streaming down it and over his hand.

The air was filled with smoke, the smell of burnt flesh and of fear. I stood still for a moment, not knowing where I should go. Holding my blankets and my gun tight, I ran a couple of steps in the wrong direction, instinctively avoiding the growl of the lorry that I should have jumped on to the back of. Just then, a grenade landed in the spot I ought to have been standing in before climbing on to the lorry. I saw a light flash and heard an explosion. I was thrown back a few metres by its force. The lorry had been hit. It was burning. Some people were jumping off it while others lay injured amidst the wreckage and the smoke. I wondered where the shards of glass had come from.

I stood up and carried on running in the open field beyond, still holding the blankets and my gun. I nearly ran headlong into one of our smaller vehicles, a kind of pick-up that was already driving off. With difficulty, I caught hold of the tailgate, almost sliding off the slippery step. I tossed my bundle aside and clung on with all my might until someone pulled me up and into the back. I squeezed in, pushed and shoved from all sides by people covered in blood and sweat. I felt as if I had landed in the entrails of a large animal that was moving forwards in a juddering motion. Everyone was quiet apart from one man who was groaning. I wondered how the driver was managing to find his way, for it was still almost dark. I was no longer frightened, but numb with shock from what I had seen. This was my closest brush with the war so far.

Our convoy of about ten vehicles travelled on and on through the day, with the tallest soldier in each vehicle standing guard behind the driver's cab with a machine gun at the ready in case we were ambushed. Everyone else cowered silently in the back of the lorries. There was plenty to occupy our thoughts. We all knew someone who had been killed that morning. Even worse, some had been left behind injured, to face execution, imprisonment, torture or brainwashing by the enemy.

I wondered where Mike'ele was. Whenever the unsealed road through the mountains curved, I leaned out and looked at the other lorries, hoping to catch a glimpse of his blond hair in one of them. I could not see him anywhere – he must have been left behind, for he would not have been able to climb into any of the lorries with his wounded arm. He would probably bleed to death – he had been bleeding so profusely. Even if he had made it on to one of the lorries, no one could have done anything for him, for we had no bandages with us to make a tourniquet. We had left behind most of our things: pots and pans, blankets and even food. Every second longer we had stayed in that camp would have cost us our lives. Yet we did not feel that we had been saved yet, for we had no food or water with us, and there was scarce hope of finding any.

Someone started singing quietly, 'This war is hard, too hard for me.' The voice sounded from deep within the packed lorry. 'I've lost my brothers to the war, I've killed my brothers because of it …'

I suppose I ought to have started crying at the sound of that song, but I merely listened with my eyes closed, agreeing with every word I heard.

'I run out through the front door while my family is being slaughtered in the back …'

The singer was a girl called Eden. She was the best singer in the Jebha. I had not noticed her earlier in that crush of bodies. The girl and boy beside me started singing along and another voice behind me joined in.

'It is my brother who is killing my family. My enemy, my enemy, oh but why is he my enemy? He is my brother.'

Everyone in the lorry sang the chorus at the top of their voices: 'This war is too hard, too hard for me.' No one cried – everyone was caught up in the music. We rattled through the landscape, sweating and hungry, with not a shred of hope apart from the song we were singing.

The song lingered in my head long after it had ended, and its melancholy air stayed with us as we drove on through the rocky landscape. We had sung it often before when we had time to sit together for a while in the evenings. Mihret did not like the song. She had always made us sing military songs after our training sessions with her. I did not like those songs, which were always about heroic deeds, freedom and the fatherland. None of these concepts meant much to me – I was not a hero and I did not want to be one. And I hated my father, so why should I care about the fatherland? But I would have liked to have known about freedom – no one had ever showed me what it was before.

Eden was singing the right kind of song, I felt. I tried to catch a glimpse of her or to reach out to touch her, but I could not get through the massed bodies, which seemed to form a solid barrier between us. She had a wonderfully full, yet gentle voice when she sang, quite unlike Mihret's screeching or my twittering. I resolved there and then that I would one day try and sing as beautifully as Eden.

Eden was not only an amazing singer, but also wise, and she knew that she could not leave us in the melancholy mood lingering from her first song. She started singing another song: 'Oh, the EPLF, those shady characters, have grown big through lying and betrayal …' Everyone else joined in after a couple of syllables, for we all knew every word of this song, which condemned our enemies, and which many of us clung to in our despair. 'But don't worry, my people! Every evil person comes to an evil end. Don't worry, Eritrea! The Jebha will come and free you and open the way to independence …'

We sang loudly and with spirit. I don't know where we got our strength from in the midst of our hopelessness – singing, humming and clapping away as we drove on into an uncertain future.

The front

Two days and two nights after the dawn attack, we stumbled across two more convoys from our unit. We established that a couple of dozen of our troops had been killed or left behind. We had a lot of guns and ammunition still, which had been left in the lorries the night before the attack, but that was all. We had to scour every hut, every hamlet and every village on our way in our search for food. The inhabitants – half-starved themselves – fled screaming from us without offering any resistance. They had nothing apart from a couple of pots and pans and a few scrawny goats, which we took from them. We must have condemned countless families to certain death by taking their livestock away from them, for that meant that there would be no milk for the children and no meat for the parents. The few crops that they had managed to grow had practically all withered away in the fields, for there had been almost no rain since the early summer. All they could hope for was help from the international aid organisations. But aid convoys rarely made it to these parts, which were mined and scattered with bandits and troops like us, who had nothing to lose.

It broke my heart to watch our soldiers herding the frightened, bleating animals out of their sheds. Ragged village women tugged at the soldiers, crying, cursing and pleading, but to no avail. The soldiers pushed the women away and kicked them while the children clung to their mothers in fear. The men heaved the goats on to the lorries and drove on. The animals were slaughtered, cooked and eaten that same evening.

Driven by severe hunger pangs, I, too, chewed at some of this meat. I had grubbed around in the earth looking for roots or grass that I could eat instead, but there was almost nothing. I had my first proper meal for weeks when we stole a few sacks of flour from an aid delivery. I did not know what kind of flour it was, but it tasted wonderful. The dough we made from it was not *injera*, for it had a different consistency, but it formed tasty dumplings and I ate as many of them as I could get my hands on.

I could hardly believe my luck as I walked around with a full tummy, free of the gnawing hunger pangs. It was a tremendous relief not to have to wonder constantly where the next mouthful of food was coming from. But my conscience plagued me – I wondered who the sacks had been meant for, and who now would have to go hungry instead of us.

We were constantly on the run. Our leaders had no clear plans any longer – they themselves did not know where we were going from day to day. We retreated further and further into the west, from the area around Bisha in the Gash Berka province through low hill country and the Dar plain towards the border with Sudan. A couple of scouts went ahead in a small car or on foot to check out every road we took. We waited in the blistering heat for them to return, clustering in the shade of the lorries or under the isolated clumps of trees we encountered.

More and more trees appeared the further west we went. At first there were only lone baobab trees, tamarisks and tamarind trees, but then we came across groves of eucalyptus, acacia and palm trees. The landscape was not noticeably less arid, but there were more bushes and clumps of grass, some of them dried-up. Still no prospect of rain though. Day in, day out, the skies were unrelentingly blue.

During our flight, we had intermittent skirmishes with the EPLF troops pursuing us, whose aim it was to get rid of us altogether. Normally, a couple of dozen soldiers were sent out to cover our retreat while us children rode a little distance up the road in the vehicles, which were almost empty. Along with a couple of grown-ups, it fell to us to prevent the lorries from falling into enemy hands.

We were lucky that there was never an attack on the lorries. We squatted between them holding our guns, staring at the horizon in the shimmering heat. The trees, the grass and the sky all merged into a whitish-brown blur, impossible to see through with the naked eye. We jumped up from time to time, thinking that we had seen a convoy of vehicles or a group of people, but the shadows and the points in the distance faded away or metamorphosed into a group of trees standing on the horizon. I was not used to the wide vistas of this landscape – the immeasurable distances that disappeared into nothing after a couple of kilometres of greenish brown – a plain that kept its secrets to itself.

We heard volleys of shots fired from time to time, when our soldiers were defending themselves against the approaching enemy. Sometimes a black cloud rose into the air from a grenade explosion which set fire to a stretch of grass on the steppes. There were also sounds of vehicles moving and engines grinding, but so far in the distance that they were barely distinguishable from the sound of the wind through the tops of the trees.

Our journey gradually became less hectic: we no longer had to move on every few days, and we no longer heard frenzied shooting every day. Instead, sometimes there were planes flying overhead. We wondered if those were the Ethiopians, shelling the EPLF convoys, and therefore hindering the EPLF attack on us. It was strange to feel grateful to the common enemy for bombing our own countrymen.

In the middle of the arid steppeland, which was broken up only by a few isolated clumps of trees, deserted villages and dusty roads, we finally made a more permanent camp a couple of kilometres from the Sudanese border. Our camp was not built in caves or hollows in the earth this time, but in a stretch of brick buildings that had once served as animal stalls or barracks.

The buildings we moved into had been empty for a long time. In the war-stricken conditions we lived under, it made no difference whether animals or human beings had once been housed in them, for all shelters looked equally desolate. We tied dry brushwood together to make brooms, and swept animal dung, sand and earth out of the buildings, and patched up the holes in the corrugated iron roofs with palm leaves and branches so that we would have more protection from the sun. We also swept away countless scorpions from the nooks and crannies in the huts. I was bitten twice by a scorpion, which was excruciatingly painful. But I was lucky that the wounds did not get inflamed, for an infected wound would have killed me.

Malaria

We had a few months of relative peace in the new camp, as the EPLF were busy attacking the Ethiopian army.

But this brief respite from fighting did not mean that our lives got any better. We did not have any more to eat than usual, and it remained just as difficult to find water to drink. We also faced the continual threat of death from malaria. We had struck camp in a very dry area called Gash, named after a river that had almost completely dried up but which was still a breeding ground for the disease.

We children understood almost nothing about the dangers of malaria. I knew that it was considered bad to be bitten by mosquitoes at night, and I also knew that there was an illness called malaria which gave you high fevers and sickness and also that you could die from it. But I never made the connection between the two, and never realised that the only way to avoid the illness was to avoid being bitten in the first place.

We had no mosquito nets, no creams, no sprays or repellents to keep the persistent mosquitoes away. It was impossible to escape being bitten by them while we worked during the day. We were all bitten so often and so regularly that we barely noticed the bites or the itching any longer. At the start of my time with the ELF in Barka, I got more mosquito bites than I had ever had before in my years in Asmara. There are no mosquitoes or malaria in regions over 2000 metres above sea level, and Asmara was 2300 metres above the sea, so it was malaria-free.

Here, by contrast, there were swarms of mosquitoes. When there was no wind, they besieged us as soon as darkness fell, so that even the toughest boys in our unit found it impossible to fight them off. Within minutes we had been bitten a couple of dozen times, and even those who did not react as badly to insect bites as I did would start itching terribly. At night, in order to protect myself, I covered myself with ragged cloths, old clothes and any blankets I could find. The temperature was not much lower than in the daytime, so it was very uncomfortable under the blankets. Lying there in a itchy bundle of dirt, dust and sweat, I had always kicked off all the coverings by the time I finally fell asleep, so it was no surprise that I eventually got malaria.

At first I thought I was suffering from food poisoning. There had been no proper food for a few days, so I had been eating various grasses, roots and handfuls of clayey earth. This made me feel very sick, and I threw up several times. I also endured bouts of shivering and fever, when I could neither stand up nor drink any water. It was impossible for me to participate in any training sessions. I lay in my sleeping space bathed in sweat, all thought of food gone from my mind even though I had been so hungry the day before. Even the thought of the best *injera* bread in the world made by my grandmother in Asmara made me feel ill, let alone the thought of a clump of grassy earth. I had never felt like this before.

After two or three days, my fever dropped, and hunger gradually returned. I did not dare to eat any of the roots I had collected, but simply drank the brackish water that the others had collected from water holes in the nearby riverbed.

When I was finally able to get up again, I had a wonderful surprise. There was proper food to eat – *injera* bread dipped in tomato sauce. It seemed like a dream, a feast of happiness. The war had ground us down so much that a basic, everyday meal was enough to put us in celebratory mood.

My elation did not last long, though. That night, I realised that something was wrong. My temperature rose and rose and waves of nausea swept over me. It was still dark when I stumbled out of the barracks to throw up. I cursed my body for rejecting all the delicious food I had eaten earlier that day.

I felt even worse in the morning. I was so dizzy when I got up that it was all I could do to keep myself from falling over. Time and time again, I had to get up and feel my way along the wall to go outside to throw up. Fever coursed through my head and my swollen limbs, and my mouth was parched and stinking. Tzegehana brought me water and damp cloths, which I used to wipe away the sour sheen of sweat.

When I began speaking deliriously in the night, the unit's doctor was fetched to see me. He was a real barefoot doctor – with practically no medicines, instruments or knowledge. Despite this, he quickly pronounced that I had come down with malaria and that I would either recover after a few days or be dead, depending on the type of malaria I had. This statement worried my sisters greatly. He also said that even if I recovered, it did not mean that I would be well for ever. 'The malaria will return,' he said. 'There is no escaping it.'

The doctor gave me an injection, and the injected area swelled and grew very painful. That was all the effect I noticed from it. Unable to sleep, I tossed and turned in a dark corner of the room I shared with a couple of dozen other soldiers. My bed consisted of a few dirty blankets spread over a packed earth floor. There were heated arguments over who would get one of the precious blankets every night.

I got up often to go outside for a few minutes – to relieve myself or to breathe in the night air, which was slightly cooler. The air inside the barracks was sticky and stank of sweat and dirt. I sat in front of the door and leaned my head against the crumbling wall, looking up into the endless starry night. I did not dare venture further from the building in case one of the camp leaders saw me and deemed me well enough to work again. It was impossible to stay out there for very long because the building was infested with termites, and anyone sitting next to it would be surrounded by them and bitten within a few minutes.

When I stumbled back into the clammy atmosphere of the room, groggy with fever, the blankets had disappeared from the corner I had been sleeping in. Covered in sweat yet shivering with cold, I went down on to the dirt floor and crawled on all fours through the building to get hold of a new blanket, but every time I tugged at a piece of fabric, a hand or a foot shot out to push or kick me away. Finally I gave up and retreated to my corner, curled up in a shivering ball and longed for an end to everything.

This state of martyrdom lasted only a few more days before one of the two outcomes prophesied by the doctor came to pass: my illness disappeared as suddenly as it had come. The fever and the nausea abated, but returned a few months later, as he had predicted. This cycle happened eight or nine times until I was finally granted a respite for a few years.

Still a girl

During my first bout of fever, I lay shivering in a corner of the building when the clammy air suddenly grew warmer and thick with a strong odour. I felt someone approaching me. A hand reached out and pulled me round while another hand pressed me to the dirt floor and yet another hand – or was it the first? – tugged at my dress and pulled at my pants.

I curled myself into a tight, trembling ball and tried to scream, but a hand had been clamped over my mouth. I knew what was about to happen. I jerked upright, but my head was spinning and the ground seemed to be moving – like deep sand at the bottom of a stream.

The floor beneath me suddenly became as hard and as solid as a rock. One of the boys tried to penetrate me while the other one held me down. I managed to get one hand free, and pushed away the boy who was holding his hand over my mouth. I screamed so loudly that they let me go. They had not succeeded this time. But I was not always to be so lucky.

Boy or girl, we were all treated as equals in the unit, and we had the same rights. I was no better or worse than any of the other soldiers I fought alongside for Eritrea's independence – at least, that was what Agawegahta and the other leaders tried to drum into us. I wanted to be part of the whole venture and to join in everything except the fighting with guns. I did not want to murder in the name of Eritrea.

However, despite what we were taught, it was constantly made clear to me that girls were worth less than boys, and that we did not have the same rights. And although I tried my best to disguise it, I was still a girl. It was not only through sexual aggression that the boys tried to show me and the other girls where our place was. As a girl, I was to give way to them in everything and to submit to their every command whenever they wished.

I had understood this status quo for some time. There were shining exceptions like Agawegahta, but she had paid a price for the position she had achieved as a woman – she was just as cruel as the men, if not a touch crueller. I knew about the difference between boys' and girls' bodies; I also knew that there was a secret that the boys shared with each other, but not with the girls. This was something that the boys could take for themselves without asking, and we just had to put up with it, no matter how strenuously we defended ourselves.

Big bellies

Boys and girls were together all the time in our unit – there was no segregation of the sexes. It was taboo to talk about sex or rape. Girls fell pregnant all the time, but everyone behaved as if the pregnancies were not happening. I saw girl after girl growing large with child. In the beginning, I used to ask where they had got so much to eat that made them so fat – I thought they had secret sources of food that I did not know about. But as these girls' bellies stretched and stretched, I saw for myself that food had nothing to do with it.

'They are pregnant,' my older sister Yaldiyan whispered to me through a cupped hand. I must have looked baffled, for she added, 'They have been together with a boy, and now children are growing in their bellies.'

'Together with a boy?' I asked, bewildered. 'And children come from that?'

Yaldiyan did not go any further. She did not like explaining things, least of all to me. But I had so many questions, and she was the only one of the older children whom I could trust, for I felt that this was a special subject. I could not ask a boy about it, only a girl. That girl had to be older, but not be a superior like Agawegahta, so only Yaldiyan could be asked about it. Tzegehana could not help me, for she knew little more than I did on such subjects. She would have liked to have known more, but Yaldiyan did not tell Tzegehana anything more than the hints she had given me. Sometimes I even doubted that Yaldiyan herself knew all about how being together with a boy brought children, and the details of how everything worked.

I did not know anything about the female body. I did not know what was happening when one of the three boys who had attacked me the first time grabbed me one day, half-strangled me, tore at my clothing and thrust himself inside me. I felt pain, shame, hatred, revulsion and helplessness, but I had no idea what it was all supposed to mean. The three boys constantly warned me to keep my mouth shut. I knew that what had happened was a matter of great shame both for them and for me, which I had to bury deep inside me. So I never told anyone about it, and the pain and the shame writhed deep within me. I could not sleep and could hardly bear to touch myself. All I could do was press my arms to my stomach and lie still so that I would not attract attention.

I was not the only girl who had no idea of what was happening with her body. One girl soldier got a shock when she noticed blood running down her legs, and ran to see the doctor. The doctor slapped his thighs and laughed so heartily that a few people came to ask him what had happened. He pointed at the girl. 'Look at this stupid girl,' he said. 'She has become a woman, and thinks that she has a tummy ache from eating something wrong!'

The others saw the blood running down the girl's legs and started laughing too. So this blood clearly was not anything serious. But why should that girl have become a woman and what did the blood have to do with it? It was a mystery to me.

Eden

What was troubling me was that I had a tummy ache, too. And I also had a painful sore in my genital area that probably came from the attack by the three boys. I was frightened that I would start bleeding from the stomach like the other girl soldier. I wanted to ask Yaldiyan for advice, but she was out on a reconnaissance mission. When I was unable to find Tzegehana as well, I sat on the ground and started crying. The tears that I had held back for so long through the bouts of malaria and other horrors finally overcame me.

Eden the singer, who had never paid much attention to me before, knelt down beside me and took me in her arms. When I cried even harder at this, she pressed me to her even more tightly in a wordless embrace.

Eden was a very beautiful woman, tall, with incredibly long, wild hair and skin that was light coloured for an Eritrean. Her skin colour alone was one reason I had always admired Eden. To me, a light skin was always a sign of coming from a good family, and I, like most people, considered people with light skins were more beautiful. I was one of the darkest-skinned Eritreans in the Jebha, so I always felt that I was ugly.

Eden was not only fair-skinned but also good-tempered. She always started us off singing ELF songs after our training exercises. She also sang whenever there was something to celebrate in the evenings – on the rare occasions when one of our leaders managed to get hold of a crate of palm wine or the bottles of colourless liquid that smelt even more evil than the petrol in our lorries. She sang also when the leaders requested a song, but sometimes she sang simply because she felt like it.

Whenever she was singing nearby, I ran after her and listened to her, but though I longed to sing like her, I had never dared to speak to her or ask her to teach me anything. Eden had never seemed to notice me before – she had certainly never spoken to me – but now she was here holding me.

'What's wrong?' she asked. She was no more than ten years older than me, but I loved the way she spoke to me like a mother speaking to her child.

'I don't know,' I sobbed. 'My tummy hurts, and I'm scared I'll start bleeding like that girl everyone laughed at. They say she has become a woman, but they just laugh at her.'

Eden smiled, but I did not mind, for I knew it was a smile of understanding and encouragement, and that she was not laughing at me. 'It happens to every woman,' she said, settling down beside me on the ground as if she was about to tell me a long story. 'It happened to that girl very early. It is the secret we women share.'

Eden told me about periods and children and men, while I listened in rapt silence. I felt much calmer once she had explained everything; Eden always had a special place in my heart after that.

That was not when I started having periods, though – they only started many months later, once I was no longer with the Jebha.

After my talk with Eden, I was able to speak about periods with other girls, mostly my sisters. I learned that girls who got regular periods used rags to stop the blood from running down their legs. And I also found out that it was normal for the boys to take whatever they wanted from us. I hoped never to suddenly grow fat, and, indeed, I was lucky not to fall pregnant. Many other girls and women had to go to war while they were pregnant. A lot of them disappeared for a couple of weeks to give birth in some desolate area. These women almost always returned without their babies. There was no support for them so they either murdered their infants or put them in orphanages like the one I had spent the first few years of my life in.

Sisters

There was no such thing as unity in the Jebha. No one trusted anyone else. You constantly wondered if the person next to you would take away your portion of *injera* bread, pretend to be ill when it was his turn to go the front, or tell the leader stories about you to make himself look better. It was each for himself, and everyone against everyone else. Although nobody really had anything to lose, there were still scraps of food and respect from other people to be fought over to ensure survival from day to day.

My sisters and I were no exceptions. Yaldiyan liked bossing us about, but though Tzegehana accepted her leadership tacitly, I did not. I was the youngest, but I was much more spirited than

Tzegehana, and I did not like taking orders. As a result, Yaldiyan sought to exert her authority over me all the more.

When Yaldiyan was at her wits' end with me, she pelted me with small stones, pulled my hair or tried to tug my blanket away from me during the night. 'Let go!' I screamed. 'Hands off!'

'You little shit, don't you dare scream at me! You brat! Your mother is a whore!'

I did not understand her. What was a whore? I knew it was terrible for a woman to be called a whore: it was not respectable, not something I ever wanted to be. But I did not know what Mbrat had done to be called a whore.

'Liar!' I screamed back at Yaldiyan. 'Mbrat isn't a whore. You are!' This was not true, but I did not know what else to say.

'Mbrat is not your mother! Your mother is nothing but a dirty whore!'

That struck home, for I had already had my doubts about Mbrat. She had fetched me from the orphanage and she had never been mean to me or beaten me. But she had also brought me to my father against my will, to live with my stepmother and two sisters, one of whom hated me because she had to share her father and sister with me. It was clear that Mbrat had betrayed me, but she was still my mother, wasn't she?

Yaldiyan's words fed my doubts about Mbrat. After all, I remembered, why did Mbrat have another daughter also called Senait? Yaldiyan knew how to ask these and other questions that gnawed away at me.

Some children in our unit occasionally had their parents or other relatives visiting them. These visits were rare, but they made me think. It was clear enough that our father did not visit because he had wanted to get rid of us in the first place. But why did my mother, Mbrat, never come to visit? Did she not know where I was? Yaldiyan and Tzegehana's mother also never visited. Did she not know either? Did our mothers not care for us at all?

I was only able to talk about these things with Tzegehana, for nobody else in the camp knew who Mbrat was. But Yaldiyan did not allow Tzegehana and me to speak to each other.

'What do you have to speak to her for?' she asked Tzegehana.

'She's my sister!' I screamed.

'You're wrong! You're not her sister. I am! You're the child of a whore!'

Tzegehana was not strong enough to disobey Yaldiyan. I could feel that she wanted to talk to me and play with me but that she did not dare to, except when Yaldiyan was at the battle-front. As soon as Yaldiyan was gone, Tzegehana allowed herself to talk to me. At first I refused to talk to her, but then I gave in. It was better to have Tzegehana's company some of the time than not at all. In fact, Tzegehana and I spent a lot of time together, for Yaldiyan was often at the front for days.

The front was generally about five to fifteen kilometres way from our camp, but though we often heard shots and grenades exploding, we did not see any fighting as long as we kept to the camp and its surrounds. Getting to the front involved a long march, facing danger from mines, ambushes and snipers. I often overheard our leaders fighting over what was to be done because it was impossible to get an overview of what was happening in the battle. We had radio equipment, but it did not always work, and we did not have enough equipment to link up all our troops with each other. More often than not, one part of the unit did not know where the other was, and when our soldiers came back after days on the road, they were often astounded at the changes in the situation on the front, even though they had just returned from it themselves.

Action

Tzegehana and I were both frightened of fighting – she less so than me. Towards the end of our time with the ELF, Tzegehana often had to go to the front, but I was seldom asked to go into action.

Once, we were both sent out to the front together, for we were to be driven a good deal of the way instead of marching on foot.

I did not have a machine gun of my own by that point in the war, but it was normal for a few younger ones like me to go along to the front to help the others so that we would one day be able to fight as well.

We sat in the back of the lorry squashed up against everyone else, without the faintest idea of where we were going. Tzegehana had found two old batteries that someone had left lying in the lorry. These batteries were very precious to us. We gnawed at the top of them until a gummy black substance appeared, and we chewed at this pretending it was chewing gum, enjoying the strong, bitter taste. I had tried chewing gum in Asmara, and I knew that it was sweet and tasted good, but that it tasted of less and less the longer it stayed in your mouth. The batteries tasted horrible and their taste grew stronger and stronger instead of fading, but we loved chewing at them anyway. It was comforting to having something in our mouths.

Suddenly, the lorry stopped and we were rudely jolted out of our daydreams.

'Out! Get down and over there!' An arm pointed from the driver's cabin towards a little cluster of trees next to the track. 'Hide!'

We jumped off and ran into the bushes. We had barely taken cover between the trees when the shooting started – it was coming nearer and nearer. We saw our fellow soldiers running past, pursued by the enemy.

'Shoot!' someone shouted, as a couple of enemy soldiers passed. I had never been so close to the enemy before. The others raised their guns and started shooting. I was terrified that I would die or be burnt to death or that Tzegehana or the soldiers next to me or even the enemy soldiers would die. That did not make sense, for the enemy were trying to kill us, but I could not bear the thought of being surrounded by dead bodies in the midst of all this fighting and shooting.

We were lucky, for the enemy soldiers ran off after a few minutes. We were supposed to go after them, but that proved impossible in a landscape covered with tall grass, bushes and trees, and we soon lost sight of them. A whistle shrilled to call us back to the lorry and I trotted back very willingly, scratched and stung all over.

Just as we had finally climbed back on to the lorry, a couple of shots rang out nearby. I was rooted to the spot in the centre of the lorry, a warm liquid trickled down my legs – I was peeing in my pants. I heard harsh laughter from the bushes next to our lorry. It was impossible to see who was hiding there, for it was almost dark. Another shot rang out and I collapsed – I had not been hit, but the fear had made my legs buckle.

Someone started laughing, then others joined in. I did not notice that they were laughing at me. I raised my head carefully, but could not see anything. Then I sat up and saw that everyone was in a good mood. One of us had shot at an enemy soldier running past and had hit him on the second attempt. Now they were dragging the body round to the lorry's headlights to see if the man had anything on him worth taking. They found nothing, and let the body fall.

I stared at the corpse, completely forgetting that I had just wet myself. '*Senait bideva shenait!*' the others chanted, laughing. 'Senait's peed herself!' The children often chanted that at me back in the camp, and '*Senait bideva shenait*' became a second name for me.

Filled with shame, I squatted quietly in the lorry until we had reached the camp. Tzegehana stayed by my side, silent. She had not joined in with the others in taunting me, but she had not defended me either. I had not expected her to, for nobody was strong enough to stand up to a gang like that. Not even Yaldiyan would have dared to do so, let alone quiet Tzegehana.

The end in sight

By the time we made camp in the abandoned barracks by the river Gash next to the Sudanese border, we knew that the war against the EPLF was lost. We had always been the weaker force, or so I had heard from older soldiers' reports from the front. But there was no official acknowledgement of this fact. We were told that we were making progress when we had actually been forced into a corner and were on the verge of fleeing over the border to the Sudan, along with the entire ELF army. The enemy had herded us towards the Bisha region, then towards the Sudan, almost directly opposite Kassala, the first city over the border.

We were never told about any of these things while we were in the army. None of the child soldiers had the faintest idea what the war was about. The ELF and EPLF were only letters to us. Our political education consisted of a couple of songs which featured us as the good guys and the others as the bad guys. The ELF was brave and strong and the EPLF were all murderers and traitors – that was all we knew. The Jebha were the great victors, Eritrea's saviours, and the Shabia were the enemy.

In truth, the war against the EPLF had already been lost by the time my sisters and I joined the ELF. The ELF did not even have to fight the common enemy – the Ethiopian army – by that time, for it had its hands full defending itself against the EPLF and keeping its own army from disintegrating altogether. The ELF's courage sprang from despair: the hopelessness of our cause lent our battle a certain solemnity that had an almost religious quality to it. I often thought that the purpose of the Jebha was to pray, for many of the men oriented themselves in a certain direction to say prayers several times a day.

Later, I realised that the praying had nothing to do with the Jebha, but with the religion of Islam. Some of us, including Yaldiyan, Tzegehana and me, were Christian. We had no priests, church services or crucifixes, but we prayed secretly nevertheless. The official doctrine of the Jebha was secular: equality. We were constantly told that we were fighting for a more equal world, a world in which people were neither rich nor poor, where everyone had enough to eat, their own livestock and their own fields.

I had no conception of what a rich person was. I had only known poor people, who had never complained about their lot even though they lived from hand to mouth and possessed nothing. I wondered how we were supposed to change that. There was a grain shortage because there was too little rain, but the leaders of the ELF could not make it rain.

I asked Mihret about this one day, but she slapped me in the face and said that she would beat me to a pulp if I continued talking such nonsense. So I kept quiet. It didn't make much difference to me anyway, for the wider philosophy of the ELF made no difference to the problems I faced daily.

Asking too many questions had led me into trouble before, for example when we had political instruction. These were not proper lessons, but propaganda sessions that always followed the same pattern. Every few weeks, we were called to a meeting, mostly impromptu, for it was impossible to plan anything with the war situation changing every day. Adult or child, everyone who was not at the front or on guard duty had to attend these meetings. At them, we sat down on the ground and listened to one of the older soldiers talking about the war in a stilted, rhetorical fashion, quite unlike the way in which they ordinarily spoke.

Sometimes Agawegahta gave the talk. She lectured loudly, in strangely convoluted sentences that I never understood. At the end of each session, she raised her voice even more and shouted, 'The Shabia are traitors! The EPLF are betraying Eritrea – we must destroy them!'

These last sentences were simple enough on the surface, but I still did not understand them. When it was time to ask questions, I put my hand up. 'The Shabia soldiers look exactly like we do,' I said. 'Why do we have to shoot them?'

Agawegahta did not shout at me. She just laughed, and most of the others joined in. A huge swell of laughter rose, and the soldier sitting next to me hit me in the face, then someone kicked me from behind until I fell forwards into the sand. That was answer enough for me. From that time onwards, I knew there was no point in asking questions like these. But I also knew that the questions would remain in my head.

Bush fighters

The war became increasingly violent, and we suffered heavier and heavier losses. Hardly a day passed without corpses or seriously injured soldiers being brought back to camp. Only a few hundred people were left in our unit. Younger soldiers like me were being sent to the front more and more often. It was clear that we would soon be worn down or simply unable to carry on fighting any longer.

I was responsible for making sure that the others had enough supplies of ammunition. As I carried cardboard boxes of ammunition between each post on the front, I was constantly frightened of being ambushed by the enemy in the undergrowth, or of being blown to pieces by a mine, as a couple of my fellow soldiers had been a few days ago. I had a vague idea of what mines looked like, but had never actually seen one. Though I knew that it was impossible to detect mines when they had been properly planted deep in the ground, I still kept my eyes fixed on the earth when I walked. All I saw was roots, grass, bushes and undergrowth, behind which enemy soldiers could be lurking. It was hard to know which to be more frightened of – mines or enemy soldiers.

In the evenings, I lay down to sleep immediately after our meagre meal. I crept under the blanket and tried to shut myself off from the world – I did not want to see or hear anything more. One evening, I heard someone singing, 'Camel, oh camel, how pretty is your name.' This was a children's song, one of the first songs we had learned in the ELF, designed to make the war sound more appealing to us. I uncovered my head so that I could hear better. 'Stand by the soldier and carry his weapons. Stand by him in heat and cold, through hunger and thirst …'

I did not particularly like the camels that were our constant companions – they were large, frightening creatures, and you had to watch out not to be kicked by them if something disagreed with them. I did like looking at them from a distance, though, and I loved the idea of someone always being by my side.

I couldn't prevent myself from crying when I heard that song, and my tears kept flowing as the voice went on to sing the Jebha's worn-out song of war.

'Oh, the EPLF, those shady characters, have grown big through lying and betrayal … But don't worry, my people! Every evil person comes to an evil end. Don't worry, Eritrea! The Jebha will come and free you and open the way to independence …'

The soldier singing was called Genet. She did not sing as beautifully as Eden, but I liked her because she often sang with the children. With us, she sang songs like the one about the camel, or the song about the start of a new day, bringing us luck and a good harvest: 'We stand before the dawning light …'

I gradually fell into a deep, dreamless sleep, and heard no more about the visions of a wonderful future for me and for Eritrea.

7

Flight

Signs of the imminent disintegration of the Jebha increased from day to day. One evening, two girls did not return from gathering firewood. Some other children went in search of them the next morning, but they did not find even the slightest trace of them. It was only on the following day that the girls were found – dead. We thought they had probably been stabbed to death by the Bedouin – whether this was over firewood, or because of some other dispute, we never found out.

Another time, a group of soldiers set out for the front late in the evening. They wanted to make the journey by night because it was slightly cooler then, and safer as well. They planned to rest a little early in the morning and then lay an ambush for the enemy. There were thirty or forty soldiers in this group, many of them mere boys. None of them ever came back. At first, our leader suspected that the group had been ambushed by the enemy, but we could not find any sign of them, no matter how hard we searched. Then we suspected our soldiers had probably deserted and fled over the border to Sudan. Though none of us dared to say it out loud, some of us had already begun to think that our battle was a lost cause – why should we continue risking our necks when there was an alternative?

A few days later, my sisters and I went to the nearby river to fetch water. The riverbed was dry, but we knew that there was a spot further down where a few scraggy trees stood – a sure sign of water. We had often been lucky there. It was only a question of how deep we dug before we would find water.

We clambered through the undergrowth and down the steep, sandy riverbank, carrying a spade, a bucket and a couple of plastic canisters. Once we had found the right spot, we took turns digging, which was relatively easy. The ground was very sandy and it soon darkened with liquid. We just had to be careful that the sides of the hole we had dug did not collapse in on themselves, for the earth was very loose.

One of us hummed a tune as we dug, feeling quite peaceful. Suddenly, we heard sounds from the opposite bank of the river. A few Bedouin were setting up camp there with their camels, and two of them were climbing down into the riverbed. We did not meet Bedouin that often, but it was also not unusual to bump into them as they travelled through the borderland between Sudan and Eritrea searching for grazing ground for their animals and conducting all manner of trade. As we had neither money nor possessions to trade with the Bedouin, our contact with them was limited to chance. They normally left us alone because they knew that we had nothing, but we still had to be careful, because there had been a few unpleasant encounters.

The two Bedouin who had climbed down in the riverbed were heading towards us. We wondered what to do – should we run off?

If we left, we would be leaving our water hole, which would have been reasonably deep by now if not for the sand constantly crumbling into it. And the thought of going back to camp empty-handed was not an appealing one. We whispered agitatedly about what we ought to do. Yaldiyan thought the Bedouin would leave us alone as long as the three of us kept together, so we kept on digging, hoping to hit water any moment. We concentrated on our work as if we had nothing else on our minds – easy to do, as we were very thirsty.

'Psst … psst!' One of the Bedouin was trying to attract our attention. We looked over, and he pushed his headscarf back – he looked different from his companion, much lighter-skinned, with more defined features. He was also taller, and looked less rough than most of the Bedouin. In fact, the man looked very much like us.

Almost all the Bedouin only spoke Arabic, but this man suddenly called out a greeting in Tigrinya, our language. We couldn't understand him at first because he was so far way, and was speaking so softly. But then he raised his voice, and we heard the words clearly: 'Yaldiyan! Yaldiyan! Come here!'

Yaldiyan started and stared at the man in shock. Then she whispered to us. 'That's Haile, our uncle!'

I had never met Haile, and Tzegehana could no longer remember him because she had been so little the last time he had visited. But Yaldiyan was quite sure it was him. She murmured, 'Haile! It's Uncle Haile!' over and over again, staring at the man as if she could read from his face what he intended to do.

Haile did not seem happy to see us, or perhaps he just did not dare to show it. Some way behind us, a couple of children from our unit were climbing down to the riverbed with buckets and canisters to help us fetch water. Haile kept about twenty metres away from us, but he said in a low voice, 'I'm here to help you. I have a message from your father.'

'We don't want to have anything to do with him!' I burst out, while my sisters nodded, though not as vigorously as I did. 'We don't want to go to him!' I said decidedly. I could survive here, I thought, while death was a certainty if I went to my father.

Haile remained where he was, undisturbed by the children from our camp, who were almost within earshot, or by our movements to leave. I picked up my canister, Yaldiyan took the spade and Tzegehana the bucket. 'Come again tomorrow!' he said to us. 'I have to speak to you alone.'

We had no idea what to think about this – was it a trap? An ambush laid by my father? But Haile's tone was so urgent that we nodded. 'All right,' Yaldiyan replied. 'We'll be here to fetch water again tomorrow.'

Haile seemed satisfied with our response, and turned to go. The other children reached us shortly after. 'What did he want from you?' they asked.

We shrugged. 'We didn't understand a word!' I replied.

'Of course not, stupid,' one of them said. 'You can't understand Arabic!' They asked no more questions after that.

That evening, we lay awake for hours wondering what was going to happen. Yaldiyan was absolutely certain that the Bedouin man was Haile – our father's youngest brother. She remembered him to be an honest and friendly man. We decided we could trust him, but that we would on no account let ourselves be taken to our father.

The next day, we went to the water hole again. No one else from our camp was around this time. Haile appeared, once again dressed as a Bedouin, but he had come alone this time. He told us that he had come to take us away – there was no hope for Che Guevara, our unit, and either the EPLF or the Ethiopian army was going to win the war.

'You will be in great danger if you don't come with me. A lot of you are going to be killed. The ELF is on its last legs.' He was stating what we knew already. 'Come here again the day after tomorrow, and I will take you with me to Sudan. I promise you that you will live with me in Khartoum, the capital city there, and that you will not be taken to your father. Your father left long ago for Europe, where the white people live.'

We hesitated, but agreed. He had spoken so urgently yet so warmly that we could not refuse.

'We shouldn't meet at the same spot again,' Haile said. 'Pretend you are looking for water on the other side of the river. I'll wait for you there.'

Hope

We were filled with doubts and fears, but also with hope. Were we to be free of the fighting at last? Free of the hard work of digging for water? Free of hunger and constant uncertainty about what the next day held for us? We could hardly believe that we were really going to escape.

That day and the day after, we managed to avoid being assigned to any of the look-out or patrol groups sent to the front. These duties lasted a couple of days, and we did not want to be killed by an enemy bullet or fail to keep our appointment with our uncle for any other reason.

When the time came to meet him, we hurried to gather our equipment to fetch water and were on our way out of the camp when Mihret shouted at us, 'Hey, come back! You have to come with me on patrol!'

My heart almost stopped. What were we to do now?

'We're coming!' I said. 'We just have to fetch a couple of buckets of water that we've left down by the water hole!'

'All right, but hurry!' she said.

We needed no encouragement, and ran as quickly as we could.

Panting for breath, we arrived at the riverbed and crossed to the other bank. No one was watching, so we did not bother to pretend that we were fetching water. Suddenly, Haile and another man whom we did not know appeared from behind a bush, and gave us some robes so that we could disguise ourselves as Bedouin children. I tugged at my robe awkwardly, and my sister had to help me put it on, for I had never worn anything like it before. The strange man looked sinister and I did not trust him, but this was no time for doubt or hesitation.

'Come,' said Haile, once we were disguised. 'You're leaving this place for good!'

We set off, not exchanging a word until we met another man, who was waiting some way away with a donkey. Haile's companions seemed to be real Bedouin – or at least they looked like it. All three of us were told to get on to the donkey. When we climbed up on its back, it gave a deep sigh, like a human being. I felt sorry for that donkey, but Haile merely said, 'Don't be silly! We have to travel a long distance quickly, and you should thank God that you have a donkey to carry you!'

We *were* thankful. We travelled the whole of that day without pause, and without meeting a single soul. We passed a couple of Bedouin with their camels in the distance and saw a motor vehicle as well, probably packed with soldiers. No one took any notice of us – with three children and a donkey, our little group looked like the poorest of the poor who could not even afford a camel, so were surely not worth bothering with.

The march

As we travelled on, the plain became more and more barren. There were no trees, just dried-up clumps of grass and a straggly plant here and there. It was the most monotonous landscape I had ever seen. The sun beat down on us mercilessly, but we had to keep the headscarves wrapped round us for disguise. Although it was very hot and sweaty with them on, at least the sun did not burn our heads and faces.

We stared into the horizon with our eyes screwed up, trying to make out our destination. But all that lay before us was a light blue, almost white mist that formed and re-formed itself into strange shapes. One moment the shimmering heat took on the outline of a huge city, then a lake, then a range of mountains. Everything seemed to be in constant movement, but everything we saw was just a mirage. Every time we came to a tiny hillock, all that greeted us was the solid line between earth and sky, an immovable line that held no secrets.

In the evening, when the sun had long disappeared from the horizon, we stopped. The men put up a tent and they gave us dry bread and water, which we gulped down. During the day, we had been burning with questions to ask Uncle Haile – he had not wanted to speak while we were travelling in the heat – but now all we wanted to do was sleep. The inside of the tent was warm with the heat of the day, but it was cold outside. We huddled up against each other and I fell asleep with the wonderful feeling that my life was entering a new and better phase.

The next day, we started off on foot in order to give the donkey a rest. That was fine by me until around noon, by which time my feet were burning, my throat was parched and the Bedouin robe I was wearing was soaked through with sweat.

All of a sudden, we came up against a couple of soldiers in uniform. I had been looking down at the ground all this time, concentrating on my tatty flip-flops and the sharp stones to avoid stepping on them, and I hadn't noticed the soldiers at all. They spoke to us in Arabic. Haile said something to them and they looked us up and down thoroughly. Then one of them jerked his head towards the horizon to signal that we were allowed to go on. Haile thanked them profusely and bowed, but the soldiers merely waved him away. Disguised as Bedouin, we were clearly of no importance to them, which was all the better for us.

Uncle Haile had played the poor fool to the soldiers perfectly. I liked his calm and friendly manner more and more. If this was the man whose family we were to live in from now on, nothing would make me return to the Jebha, not even a couple of snooty Sudanese border guards.

The third day of our journey was very tough. We had hardly any water, so were only allowed a tiny sip of the lukewarm water that the men had brought with them in a length of carburettor hose carried by the donkey. My eyes were rimmed red from the glare of the sunlight and from the sand that constantly blew in our faces. My head was whirring from the heat and with questions about where we were going to live and what Haile was going to do with us. Was our father behind this after all?

I did not have much time to brood, though, for we encountered border guards over and over again. Haile said that Sudan was trying to seal off its borders because there were too many refugees trying to come in from Eritrea. So we were told not to say anything at all when the soldiers asked us questions, in order not to betray the fact that we were Eritrean. But the soldiers only ever asked Haile and the other two men questions, never casting us a second look. Later I learned that men in the Sudan never spoke to women when they wanted to ask for information.

Lights

It was an incredible relief when the relentless sun sank over the horizon at night. The sky flared red, only to turn a deep blue minutes later, as if a magic wand had been waved over it. Gradually, the stars began to shine. I have never seen the change from day to night as dramatic as the one you get in the desert.

As we travelled on, longing for Haile's signal to stop and set up camp for the night, we suddenly saw two stars rise over the horizon. In fact, they were actually *on* the horizon itself, and looked different from the stars in the sky. We squinted into the night. 'What's that over there?' I asked Haile. I thought it was yet another mirage.

'That's where we are heading for,' he murmured. 'Kassala.'

We felt like screaming with joy, but did not dare to do so, so we merely hugged each other. All desire to stop for the night had gone – the only thing we wanted to do now was press on to the wonderful place on the horizon.

It was amazing to watch the lights on the horizon multiply – lights from windows, streetlamps and the lamps that hung from market stalls. I felt like crying with happiness, not only because we had finally reached our destination and had some prospect of water to drink and food to eat, but also because I had not seen a town or a city for months, and barely believed in their existence any longer. Were there really collections of lighted houses with people who walked about without killing each other?

My life over the last few years had been filled with war, destruction and hatred. The more I thought about it, the gladder I was to have left it behind me. For a moment I forgot my thirst and hunger and simply took a few deep breaths. Tears rolled down my cheeks, but I tried to hide them from my sisters because I was embarrassed. I need not have feared, for they were not taking any notice of me at all, but staring at the lights, too, transfixed.

The lights grew larger and larger and we could see the outlines of houses and the minarets of mosques against the horizon. No one paid any attention to our pathetic caravan when we entered the city late that night. The streets were full of life: camel herders with their camels, traders squatting next to piles of fruit and vegetables on the ground, men sitting on the steps of cafés, women carrying canisters of water, firewood or shopping bags and children skipping about between the grown-ups.

Food, I thought, there would be real food here! Before me were the familiar things I had longed for: fruit, vegetables, bags of groceries, sacks of beans, grain and coffee, dried fruit and spices. The people here were not starving, but simply went into a shop to buy what they wanted whenever they wanted. I was over-whelmed, and my mouth watered at the sight.

We felt embarrassed, knowing how starved, dirty and bedrag-gled we looked. Kassala was nothing special as a city, nothing compared with Asmara. It was the last stop for people travelling to and from Eritrea, an outpost in the desert in which the highest buildings had only two storeys. Yet this collection of tiny grey and white houses lined up next to each other in the dust in a crude grid, interrupted only by a market or a mosque or two, seemed like paradise to us.

In paradise

Uncle Haile and his two friends seemed as unimpressed by the scene as the donkey was. They walked on determinedly through the city, stopping finally in front of a house that looked exactly like all the others. We stepped inside, and found ourselves in a dark room lit only by a single bulb. This was the home of one of Haile's friends, whose wife set about immediately to make us a meal. We sat down on the floor and a girl brought us a jug of water, which we drank glass after glass of. We could not drink enough of it. It was wonderful to be drinking water from a jug, to have water without searching for it, digging for it or carrying it.

The girl passed us a bowl with a small piece of soap in it, held out another jug and poured water over the bowl for us to wash our hands in. Just as in Eritrea, it was the custom here to greet guests in this way – offering them the chance to wash their hands before a meal – for we all ate with our hands. I was touched to be served in this way, for at my grandmother's or my father's house, I had always been the one who had poured the water for guests and handed them the towels to dry their hands with. It had been years since anyone had bothered whether my hands were washed or not.

We ate a simple meal of *injera* bread with a tomato and onion sauce. It was the best meal we had ever had. We tore chunks of *injera* off and dipped them in the sauce, eating contentedly. It was indescribably wonderful to sit there and eat without thought of imminent danger, a command to obey or the horrors of the night to come.

Our nights would no longer be nights of fighting, hunger and thirst, and we would no longer have to sleep in the same room as dozens of other people. Yaldiyan, Tzegehana and I stretched out on a couple of mats in the kitchen instead and, while the adults drank tea and chatted, we fell into an exhausted slumber.

The next morning, we bade farewell to Haile's friends and to the donkey, which had spent the night in the yard. We walked to the largest square in the city. All was chaos. Thousands of people loaded with suitcases, bundles and sacks were milling about among dozens of buses, camels, donkeys, bicycles and hand-pulled carts. Miraculously, Haile immediately found the right bus to take us to Port Sudan, a city on the Red Sea. The bus was packed, but we managed to get seats near the door. All manner of boxes, suitcases and sacks were tied to the roof, along with two goats, which settled down to chew calmly among the luggage.

The oppressive heat in the bus lifted a little when it starting moving. It edged slowly through the crowd, but picked up speed once we were out of the city. The bus travelled along a straight track into a wall of heat, trailing a huge cloud of dust. I sank into my seat contentedly – although it was narrow, it seemed incredibly comfortable to me – and snuggled up against my sisters. It seemed like heaven in comparison to walking next to a donkey.

After several hours, we arrived in Port Sudan, where we changed for another bus to Khartoum, the capital of Sudan, where Uncle Haile lived. The journey took a whole day, which we passed in a haze of sleep or half wakefulness – the exertions of the last few days and weeks and years had taken their toll. Our bus journey through the expanse of Sudan did not seem like escape to us – it was more like much-needed rest. The other passengers sighed and grunted about the heat, the dust and how cramped the bus was, but we found the journey entirely relaxing, having spent the last few years working hard under the heat of the sun, not sitting comfortably on a bus.

My eyelids drooped over and over again. Vivid images from my last three years spent with the ELF flickered wildly in my head, but all I had to do was open my eyes to chase away the suffering and the misery of those years. When I looked out of the window, I saw nothing but sun, rocks and sand, and the occasional hut with a couple of people dozing in the shade beside it – all images of freedom.

8

Khartoum

We arrived in Khartoum late in the evening. An infernal noise woke me from my dazed slumber. The people on the bus were shouting madly, and I instinctively took cover, thinking that we were under fire. The horrors of the last few years were still very fresh in my mind. When I raised my head, I saw that nothing terrible had happened. The passengers were only causing a commotion because we were about to arrive at our destination. Everyone was tugging at their bundles and packages, pointing out this or that happening outside on the street or talking loudly about what they were going to do next. I did not understand a word of the babble around me, which was all taking place in Arabic or other African languages that I did not speak. Haile sat up, too, and tapped Yaldiyan and Tzegehana gently on the shoulders to wake them up.

I gazed out of the window with my mouth wide open. There were so many things I had never seen before: buildings as high as the cathedral spires in Asmara, roads with several lanes of cars, mosques with minarets towering so high up into the sky that I could not see the tops of them from the window of the bus. And people everywhere. Asmara was a well-populated city, but there were so many more people here that there was no comparison. I pressed my face to the window, transfixed by the mass of people, the traffic and the buildings.

Haile took us to his house. He unlocked an iron gate in a high wall behind which there was an elegant garden and a house with several floors. When he saw our looks of amazement, he smiled and said, 'We will live here.'

I could not believe that we were really going to live in this palatial home. There was a separate room for everything here – a room to eat in, a room to cook in, one to do the washing in and one to sleep in – eight rooms in all. I had only ever dreamed of such a home. Water flowed from the taps, and there was a lavatory you could flush. I had only encountered this once before, when I had lived at the orphanage run by the Italian nuns in Asmara, though the children often had to use the earth closet in the garden, which I had thought a luxury at the time.

After looking round the house, we went outside and met the three gigantic dogs who lived in the garden. This was the first time I had come across dogs who were fed and treated like members of the family. All the dogs I had encountered before were street strays who were abused by everyone. No one I knew would ever have dreamt of letting a dog into his own garden.

We soon found out that the house did not actually belong to Haile, but to one of our relatives, a rich half-Eritrean, half-Egyptian woman who had in fact given it to her daughter. This woman was very beautiful: she had very fair skin, almost European, and pitch-black hair. I was staggered by her looks the first time I saw her – though I did not know what was generally held to be beautiful or not, I just felt that she was an extraordinary beauty. My wide-eyed amazement seemed to delight her, for she stroked my hair and spoke affectionately to me.

The woman's daughter, Sanaa, was a spoilt young woman who possessed everything except a husband. She had a house of her own, a car, servants, dogs, and all manner of gorgeous clothes. She wore Arabic style clothing, but without the headscarf – she let her hair flow free. I had only seen women leave their hair loose in the ELF before, but they had worn faded camouflage trousers and torn T-shirts and shirts, not beautiful clothes like Sanaa's.

Sanaa's mother grew to like me more and more, and eventually wanted me to move in with her and her daughter. So I lived for weeks at a time in an even grander and more beautiful house in a part of Khartoum filled with such houses, each with its own garden. Life there was a joy – I did not have to do any heavy housework like fetching water or firewood, but just help a little here and there. The cooking in this house was done not over a wood fire, but on a stove to which a gas cylinder was attached – fire magically appeared when you struck a match and held it to the hob. A mere twist of one of the many taps in the house brought running water in an instant.

All I had to do was go to the market to buy food and help the old woman servant with the cooking. I did not even have to help clean the house, for two young women servants did that. It was like living in paradise from which I was only cast out periodically for a few hours whenever there were visitors, when I had to stay in the kitchen along with the servants. I found that hurtful, for even though I had only learned a few broken phrases of Arabic and would have understood almost nothing of the conversation, I would still have liked to see the visitors and listen to them talk.

When I stayed at Sanaa's mother's house, I missed my sisters and Haile, who came now and then to visit, but carried on living at Sanaa's house. Once, when Haile was visiting, I got the feeling that he and Sanaa's mother were not getting along so well, and another time, they seemed to be fighting. I was sent out of the room, and heard them raise their voices with each other. Suddenly, the door flew open and Haile came out and took me by the arm. He pushed me towards the door and said, 'We're going. You won't be coming back here again.'

I was shocked but also a little relieved. 'What about my things?'

'Go and get them,' Haile said before letting me go. I rushed into the room which I shared with one of the cleaning girls and gathered up the few things I had – a dress that Sanaa had given me, a couple of towels and my flip-flops. The dress was my prized possession – I had never owned anything so gorgeous before. It wasn't just a few pieces of fabric sewn together, but was made of embroidered material which I thought suited me beautifully.

I hurried back to Haile, and he drove me back to Sanaa's house, where I had a warm reunion with my sisters. That evening, Haile told us what had happened between him and Sanaa's mother. I thought it was very kind of him to tell us, for nobody had ever taken the trouble to explain things to my sisters and me before.

Sanaa's mother had got to know our father when he, my stepmother and their children had come to stay with her after they had fled Eritrea. She liked my father a lot, and always spoke very warmly of him, but did not care for Haile. Haile said this was because he did not agree with everything she said, unlike our father. Nevertheless, she had allowed Haile and my two sisters to continue living in her daughter's house, on condition that I went to live with her and help out in her house. She did this because she was especially fond of me.

'I wasn't too keen on the idea,' Haile said, finally coming to why he had been so angry with Sanaa's mother. 'I didn't think you should be separated from your sisters. But when she decided she wanted to adopt you, I lost all patience with her. She called you her favourite, yet you had to sit in the kitchen with the servants whenever there were visitors, because you were too dark-skinned. I told her that was unacceptable, so she decided to throw us out of this house.'

I was very grateful to Haile, for no one I knew had ever taken my part so strongly before.

Uncle Haile

Haile took us to a photo studio one day. I had seen photos before, but never met a photographer or stepped into a studio. We had to put on our best clothes – each of us only had one set in any case – and stand next to each other in the studio. Behind us was a wonderful curtain with a picture on it, which we were not allowed to look at, for we had to face the photographer instead. The man disappeared behind a small box and

Uncle Haile had this photo of Tzegehana (centre), Yaldiyan (right) and me (left) taken after our arrival in Khartoum.

then a light flashed. Haile had warned us about this, so we were not frightened.

We went to collect the photo the next day. We could hardly believe that we were the girls in the photo – we looked pretty, well dressed and well cared for, as if we had never known any hardship. We looked so innocent, as if we had just come from the schoolroom or from a comfortable family home, not that we had lived through the longest and bloodiest civil war in recent African history.

It was only now that we had escaped the war that we began to learn what it was really about. Haile explained the ELF and the EPLF to us, and told us about the senseless slaughter that these two rebel armies were carrying out against each other even though they both wanted the same thing: Eritrea's freedom and independence from Ethiopia. He told us that there was no difference in the ethos of both organisations apart from the fact that the ELF, which had been founded in Cairo, was dominated by Muslims, while the majority of the EPLF were Christian. This should not have mattered, for both parties had no religious affiliation and were both ultimately Marxist, though the EPLF emphasised the importance of social revolution more than the ELF did. The reason the two parties were at war was because their leaders both wanted to hold power over the country after independence. They wanted to divide up the cake before it was even baked.

Haile had heard from friends who were still in Eritrea that the ELF was at the very end of its tether. In the face of starvation and war in Eritrea, he himself had fled to Sudan long before us. He did not want to die in a pointless civil war, and it had been easy for him to leave, as he had neither wife nor children. I did not understand why he was still not married, for he was an intelligent, good-looking man of thirty-five who had a job and was a good, kind person – what else did a man need to find a wife? But my sisters and I benefited from Haile being single, for his attention was entirely focused on us. We did not have to go through the same experience as we had with my father's family, in which his new wife had dominated everything.

Haile told us that our father now lived with his third wife, Werhid, and their daughter in Europe – in Germany. We did not know where that was, but I was happy to know that the country he was in was very far away at the other end of an ocean, so we would never see him again. Yet it was our father who had brought about our rescue. In Europe, he had heard about the desperate situation the ELF was in from Eritrean friends, and had asked Haile to get us out. At least this was what Haile told us.

Refugees were streaming over the border from Eritrea into Sudan every day at this time. From friends and acquaintances, Haile heard that the last few troops of the Jebha were engaged in battle near the Sudanese border. And when he was told that the very last Jebha unit would soon be wiped out, he had started organising to rescue us. Though he wore western clothes in daily life, he disguised himself in the long white robes of the Bedouin, and spent a few days with them in the desert in order to study their behaviour. He found a Bedouin he could trust, who led him to us in exchange for payment. Haile would never have found the way through the desert himself, for there were no signs, maps or proper roads through this desolate landscape. Only the Bedouin knew where it was possible to cross the border between Sudan and Eritrea without running into too many border patrols.

A fresh start

So Haile had saved us just in time. I was nine or ten at the time, Tzegehana was eleven and Yaldiyan was fourteen, and we were about to start anew. It was what we wanted more than anything else, and there was nothing in our way.

There was very little to keep us in Khartoum, where, now that we had no contact any longer with Sanaa and her mother, we had no relatives apart from Haile. Nor did we understand a word of the African languages spoken in the Sudan, for they were not related to Tigrinya. And we only knew the odd phrase or two of Arabic which we had learned from Muslim soldiers in the Jebha, who did not speak Arabic well themselves as it was not their mother tongue.

We picked up a bit more Arabic from other children in the street, and learned how to abide by the Muslim way of life. Girls always wore headscarves in public, while some of the women wore veils. I did not see the sense in covering the face and the head all the time, though – we only wore headscarves as protection against the sun when it was too hot.

After Sanaa's mother threw us out, Haile found another house in another part of Khartoum. The city was so huge that I could not imagine walking from one end of it to the other. It was an endless parade of streets and markets, houses, squares, mosques and large official buildings, schools, more houses, store-houses and factories, and yet more houses. It was impossible to see the horizon, the mountains or the shimmer of heat on the plain. It was an impenetrable city.

The part of the city that we now lived in reminded me of Asmara. The roads were stony dirt tracks, and the houses were clustered close to each other. Some of them had gardens or small yards, but these were behind high walls, so all that could be seen of them from the street were walls with iron gates set in them. This area was not as lovely as the one in which Sanaa lived, but at least there were no homeless people, and no one here had to live in a tent or in huts cobbled together from pieces of corrugated iron and other scrap.

Haile was able to afford to live in this area because he had a regular income, which was something quite unusual in Khartoum at the time. He worked for the Red Cross in a very grand part of the city, where there were lots of houses as smart as Sanaa's. He looked after the garden, the kitchen and all maintenance and repairs in the Red Cross building. Europeans worked in that building, so Haile was well placed to have good contacts with the outside world.

The houses in our area were very simply built. Power lines stretched between wooden masts, bringing electricity to every house, which had at least one or two bulbs hanging from its ceiling as well as a socket for a radio and a television. We, too, had a television, and we would sit for hours watching Sudanese singers perform love songs in Arabic. Sometimes there were dance programmes or documentaries about the desert or about new factories, but these did not interest us so much.

American television programmes were our favourites. We liked watching the white men and women driving through huge cities in enormous cars – everyone smiled and wore beautiful clothes. Sometimes the men got into fights and shot each other, which I did not understand. Everything looked so lovely and perfect in their world – they had enough to eat, they had homes and children, yet they killed each other. These films were mostly shown in English, with Arabic subtitles. I could understand a little Arabic but I could not read it, and I could not understand English at all, yet I was transfixed by the television.

But all the films, concerts and programmes about new factories on television soon lost their appeal – they began to seem the same after a while. We took to hanging around on the street instead. Apart from the few hours of school in the morning, most children were left to themselves all day. Not everyone went to school, though, and we were among those.

In the beginning, my sisters and I almost always left the house together. We felt safer that way in the new neighbour-hood – and we had no way of communicating with the other children, anyway. Our caution was well founded, for we had a few run-ins with children who had grown up in the area. Once, we went out to a shop nearby and were pelted with stones that struck our heads and our backs. We ducked immediately and ran like hunted prey to take shelter behind the shop. Our instinct for flight was still as well honed as if we had only left the Jebha yesterday. Once we were safe, we looked around to see who had thrown the stones, and saw a few children, some younger than us, shouting gibberish. Later on, we made out that they were cursing at us for being foreigners and for not wearing headscarves. Even the youngest girl child wore a headscarf here. We tried to say something, but suddenly two boys came from the other direction, throwing yet more stones and handfuls of earth at us. When the owner of the shop rushed out and started shouting angrily, we all ran off at the same time.

Even though we would wear headscarves more often in the future so as not to stand out, we still remained 'Havesh', which is what the Arabs call the Ethiopians and Eritreans, who all look the same to them. We were lighter-skinned and taller than the Sudanese, and our hair was not as frizzy as theirs, nor our lips as thick; all in all, we did not look especially African. The term 'Havesh' is related to the word 'Abyssinian', which is what the Italian occupiers had called the Ethiopians.

Lessons

Haile taught us at home because he did not have enough money to send three of us to school. Most of our lessons were in English, which Haile used daily in his work at the Red Cross. He also taught us maths and the Coptic script in which Tigrinya and Arabic are written. He liked teaching us as much as we liked learning from him.

We were unruly children, but we sat quietly when it was time for lessons, and also worked our way diligently through the books Haile brought back for us. When he came home at the end of the day and asked us where we had stopped the previous day, we would always have finished the book already, even if he had only started on a new topic the evening before and left off at page two or three. We learned lots of sentences off by heart, and Haile was delighted.

When Haile was pleased with us, he said, 'Oh, that *anjal*!' He was referring to my father. '*Anjal*' meant 'idiot' or 'fool', and Haile thought my father was a fool to have given away children like us. Haile could not understand how my father could have delivered us as cannon fodder to a rebel army on its last legs. But Haile never complained seriously about our father or used bad language about him.

Haile really treated us like his own children. The wonderful thing about him was that he loved us for what we were: he did not try to change us, but to teach us and expand our horizons. He regarded Tzegehana as the wise one and Yaldiyan, my eldest sister, as the dull one, while I was as unruly and stubborn as a boy. This was how he described us to any visitors. I felt proud to be described in this way, but felt that he was a little unfair on Yaldiyan – she was not stupid, just quiet and obstinate; a little dreamy and aimless, but not dull.

It was lucky for us that Haile did not follow my father's instructions for our care. Our father had written to Haile: 'Give Yaldiyan a good beating to get anything into her. Senait also constantly needs to be beaten. Only Tzegehana can be spared a beating.'

Haile read my father's words aloud and said to us, 'Your

father is mad.' He wrote to my father saying he thought it was nonsense to beat anyone without reason. To us, Haile said that everyone had to bear the consequences of their actions. Haile was as strict with us as our father, but he only slapped us when we gave him good reason. To him, smacking was an inextricable part of bringing up children – he had never known any different. But he never just lashed out in a temper like our father did, and only hit us when one of us had done something wrong. This happened from time to time: when we were sent to the market do some shopping and forgot to buy half of what we were meant to because we had got distracted; when we did not tidy up when we were asked to; when we came home later than expected. Many occasions warranted a slap from Haile. Once, I got a blood clot in my eye from one of Haile's slaps, which took four years to disappear. It made me look as if I had two pupils. When Haile was angry, he hit us not only with his bare hands but with a short length of hose, which he whipped us with until we developed sores.

Despite all this, Haile was different from my father. I was afraid of him when he was angry, but he had principles and he never beat us so hard that our lives were in danger – which is more than could be said for our father. Haile was also honest with us – he always told us why he was beating us and, once the beating was over, the matter was closed, and he was affectionate to us once again.

When Haile returned home from work, he checked to see that we had done our work in the house. We cooked lunch and dinner for ourselves, washed up, did the shopping, tidied up and cleaned the place. We also read a great deal. When Haile was satisfied with what we had done, he said things like, 'How could anyone throw these children away?' or, 'What have I done to deserve you treasures?'

Haile was a Christian, like the rest of our family. The many Islamic influences in Khartoum – the call of the muezzins from the mosques ringing through the city every morning and evening and the many Muslim friends we met – did not change this. We appreciated Arabic culture, but we did not embrace it.

I loved Arabic music, which could be heard on every street corner in Khartoum, from every café and shop. It was played on all festive occasions, and was constantly on the radio or television. My favourite star was a famous Egyptian singer called Mahmud. He had a daughter, Ranja, whom he sang many songs for, and she sometimes sang with him. I was moved to tears by their duets and, in quiet moments, I dreamed of that wonderfully harmonious relationship between father and daughter, in which they sang and made music together and became famous for it. Everyone knew who Mahmud and Ranja were at the time, and was familiar with their songs. Apart from the war songs of the Jebha, those songs were the first music that I consciously listened to and loved. I drank them in like a sponge soaking up water.

Refugees

One day, Haile said he had a surprise for me. 'Guess who has come to Sudan?'

I started, wondering whether my father was here. But surely if that were so, Haile would be telling all three of us at the same time, not just me.

'It's Mbrat!' he said, looking at me expectantly.

I hesitated. Mbrat had betrayed me in the worst way possible. She had taken me away from my grandmother and brought me to my father, who had given me to the army. She was not my real mother anyway, but my aunt, as I now knew. She was Haile's and my father's cousin, so she could not be my mother, unless my father had had a child with his cousin (which could be ruled out).

Haile was waiting anxiously for my reaction, so for his sake I said, 'That's nice.' I spoke automatically, but without real feeling. I had stopped loving Mbrat the day she had left me. So much had died within me that day, including any feeling for my mother, whom I had taken Mbrat for.

I was happy when I actually saw Mbrat, but I grew completely indifferent to her over the next three days. She had once been everything to me, but when she sat beside me by the round platter from which we ate the *injera* bread that I and my sisters had made, I spoke to her as if she was any other guest.

Mbrat brought news from Eritrea – she told us that the Jebha, including the Che Guevara unit, had been wiped out by the EPLF and the Ethiopians. The Ethiopian army had conducted bombing raids by night and killed hundreds of people, many of them children. The rest of the unit had dispersed all over the place – some of them had fled to the Sudan and some had jumped ship to the EPLF, while others had gone into hiding or back to their families, where they had been hunted down by EPLF pressgangs and made to go back into battle against the Ethiopians.

Chaos and starvation ruled in Eritrea. Mbrat did not know how our family was doing – to save her own skin, she had been travelling for weeks through Eritrea and Sudan. She made no secret of the fact that Khartoum was not the last stop on her journey. Less than a year later, she moved to Saudi Arabia, where she found a job which paid her an incredibly high salary compared to what she could have got in Sudan or Eritrea.

Mbrat was not the last refugee to seek refuge with Haile. A few weeks after she came, he asked me again if I could guess who else had arrived. This time, I guess correctly: 'Nazreth.'

Haile smiled as I held my hands to my face and screamed excitedly, 'Ahhh! Nazreth! My sister!'

Nazreth was actually Mbrat's sister, but we had grown up together as siblings in Asmara. She was older than Yaldiyan, Tzegehana and me, but we got on very well. She was just as cheeky as I was, just as unruly and full of crazy ideas.

Nazreth had run away not only from war, hunger and suffering in Eritrea, but also from her family, which she had found too restrictive. She wanted to have a boyfriend, but my grandparents had not allowed her to, so she had run away from home with a friend of hers. The two girls had saved some money and taken a bus west to Barka. The war had been in full swing there and there were no buses travelling to Sudan, for the border was officially closed. So the two girls had made their way on foot and risked their lives hitchhiking on trucks and lorries, alongside soldiers, until they had finally arrived in Khartoum. I was very impressed by their feat.

The friend Nazreth had brought with her soon went her own way, for she also had family in Khartoum, whom she moved in with. Nazreth had big plans – she wanted to see the world. First of all, though, she said she wanted a man, and not just any man, but someone with money. 'He must be able to offer me something,' she said. 'Not like the losers in Maitermenai, that lousy suburb of Asmara where nothing ever happens. I had to get away from there.'

I had never heard her speak like that before. Here was a woman who wanted something just for herself – not for the family, not for her parents, not for Eritrea, but for herself alone. And her only justification for this was her own will. This was such a new concept to me that I could barely grasp it. I had never thought of wanting something for myself before. I decided to stay close to Nazreth, which was easy, for she had come to live with us.

Nazreth

Nazreth proved to be every bit as interesting as I had hoped she would be. She was sexy in a way that no other girl I had ever met was. The way she moved and the way she talked were all designed to attract attention, especially from boys and men. Though she could not dress in a provocative manner – unthinkable in Sudan – she still managed to create the same effect with glances, gestures and comments. When she saw someone on the street who interested her, she murmured a quiet 'Oh …' or 'Uhh …', which always caught my attention, as well as that of the boys, who heard and reacted to Nazreth even with the noisiest traffic roaring around them.

Nazreth was only sixteen years old, and was not allowed to go out alone on the street – Haile was very insistent on this point – but we girls attracted even more attention from the boys when we went out together in a group. My sisters used to screech 'Ee …' as if they were trying to ward off the boys or protect Nazreth from them, but this had no effect either on Nazreth or on her admirers.

Nazreth was very outspoken – she was a wild child, a teenager whose hormones were running amok. 'He's cool!' she would say as a boy approached us, or, 'Ah – that one must have a big willy!' She was also very open about her feelings, much more so than any other girl I knew. When men looked at her, she looked them back boldly in the face rather than lower her eyes immediately, as other girls did.

Haile was Nazreth's cousin, but he soon slipped into playing a paternal role with her, which came about naturally because of the age difference between them. Nazreth's flirting did not escape his notice, and he was quick to take action – he beat her whenever he discovered that she had looked back at a boy or had spoken about a boy. Nazreth was beaten far more severely than I ever was by Haile – he beat her until the blood ran down her back and over her arms, but she stood firm. She said nothing – she did not scream or cry, but gritted her teeth and went on behaving exactly the same the next day. I was amazed – here was someone who was determined to do exactly as she pleased, and I wanted to be like her.

Haile could not keep watch on Nazreth all day while he was at work at the Red Cross, so my sisters and I were given the task. We were given strict instructions to follow Nazreth wherever she went, and to tell him everything about what she did and who she spoke to. We could not disobey Haile, but the notion of us younger girls supervising Nazreth was preposterous.

I loved following Nazreth around in any case, for I liked watching her, especially the way she attracted the attention of so many men. I never told Haile anything of what I observed, for I did not want Nazreth to be punished. I felt very much on Nazreth's side, and I also did not see that what she did was any of Haile's business. Yaldiyan also did not snitch on Nazreth – not because of the same conviction, but because she was afraid that Nazreth would take revenge on her for doing so. Only Tzegehana lived up to the role of detective – she told Haile every detail of what she had observed of Nazreth. Nazreth pleaded with her constantly not to tell Haile, but Tzegehana was unmoved. 'What am I supposed to do when I see you go up to boys? Am I supposed to keep quiet? If I do, he'll beat *me*.'

Nazreth soon started lying to us. She would say that she was just going to buy something in a shop round the corner, so we did not have to come with her, when really she was going for a walk in the city. We were not so easily shaken off, though. We trailed her from a distance, but Nazreth caught us over and over again – she was not stupid – and we would pretend that we had not been following her. Despite this, she continued to meet up with boys, stringing several of them along at once. Tzegehana reported all this to Haile and he beat Nazreth over and over again.

The situation only got worse. Nazreth was constantly getting marriage proposals from men. In a Muslim country, men do not make ambiguous gestures – if they want something from a woman, they are quite straightforward about it. They tend to come right out and ask for her hand in marriage from her parents, or, in this case, her cousin, who will only agree if the man in question is a good match.

The good match came from an unexpected quarter. Through his international contacts, Haile had met an Eritrean man who lived in Washington.

Through Haile, this man wrote to Nazreth regularly saying that he was doing well there – he worked in an office and had a car – and that he wanted Nazreth to join him. When Haile showed Nazreth the photographs that her suitor had enclosed with his letters, Nazreth was won over. She thought the man looked sweet, and she liked what she saw in the photos – his car and the sofas and built-in wardrobes in his flat. She agreed to marry him, and matters progressed quickly from there.

After all the fights and difficulties over her admirers in Sudan, I found this swift and straightforward resolution a disappointment. But Nazreth stood by her decision, and Haile granted his approval. He wrote to my grandparents, who immediately agreed to the marriage. There could hardly have been a better fate for an Eritrean woman than getting married to someone living in America – especially to a fellow Eritrean. After a few formalities had been settled, Nazreth departed for the United States to be married. Soon she wrote to say that it was love at first sight and that she was very happy living a wonderful new life.

Meanwhile I sat brooding in Khartoum, the city that had seemed like paradise to me a few months before, a place of salvation from everything bad. Nazreth had struck lucky – she had gone to live a luxurious life in the wide world out there – but I had to stay here with my sisters. Was the life we lived not one of ultimate fulfilment after all? Was it not the wonderful life I had always dreamed of?

Nazreth had changed my view of the world, and I lay awake at night after she had left, thinking about how I could make my way into the wider world. I had to take a different route from Nazreth, for I did not feel like getting married – I was still far too young and anyway no one had asked me. Even Nazreth had been young for marriage, but she was a stunning girl, so the offers of marriage had flooded in.

In Khartoum girls married when they were between sixteen and twenty years of age, unlike in Eritrea, where the girls married much earlier, especially in the villages. Marriages in Eritrea were almost always against the girl's will – her parents arranged the marriage in the hope of a dowry that would improve their lives, and also of having one less mouth in the house to feed.

Female matters

Nazreth had been the star among the Eritrean girls in Khartoum because of her light-coloured skin and smooth hair. We called women who looked like her 'frengi', and to be frengi was extremely desirable. Nazreth was so beautiful that men felt compelled to pursue her. My uncle Haile knew this, for he was a man himself. But he would never have allowed his cousin to be dragged into the dirt — she was not to have any sexual relations with a man until she was married to him. The scandal this would have caused would have affected not only Nazreth and the man, but the standing of our entire family.

To make doubly sure that such scandal is avoided, most fathers in Africa, especially in Muslim families, insist that their daughters are circumcised. Circumcision was a taboo subject for us — it was simply never mentioned by any of the grown-ups. It was Nazreth who first told me about circumcision when she lived with us in Khartoum. She told me that it would be easier for her to have sex with a man than for a Sudanese girl, because she had not been stitched up down there. I did not understand her at first, and she laughed at my ignorance. After I had pestered her a few times with questions, she finally explained that Sudanese girls traditionally underwent a type of circumcision called infibulation — the clitoris and the labia minora were removed, after which the labia majora were sewn together. If the girl did not die as a result of infection, the wound eventually healed, and the sewn-together labia majora were 'opened' like a present by the girl's husband on her wedding night. This was the proof of whether the girl was a virgin or not, and God help her if she was not.

Nazreth told me that hardly any infibulations were carried out on girls in Eritrea, who tended to undergo a type of circumcision called clitoridectomy instead, which involved the removal of part or all of the clitoris. There was no bitterness in Nazreth's voice as she explained all this to me.

I did not fully understand what Nazreth was talking about, but I felt my guts wrench at the thought of someone cutting off parts of my genitals with a blade. When she first started explaining circumcision, I was not even sure if I had been circumcised or not, as I could not remember anything of the kind. Only when Nazreth described the full details of circumcision was I certain that I had not been circumcised. It was probably because no one had bothered to do it. I had been too young for it in the state orphanage and the Catholic nuns would not have done it, while my father wouldn't have cared one way or another and in the Jebha, no one had felt responsible for the children.

After Nazreth told me about circumcision, I walked through the streets of Khartoum looking at the women with different eyes. I stared into their faces and eyed them up and down, thinking constantly that they were sewn up below. Urinating must be very painful for them, and the disfigurement a source of great shame. I could not detect any sign of it in their faces, but women in Sudan would never have let their feelings about circumcision show, let alone talk about it or complain about it.

'Women are only against circumcision if they have grown up in a country where it is not done,' Nazreth said. 'They're used to it here.'

It was not until a couple of days after this conversation with Nazreth that it occurred to me to ask my sisters if they had been circumcised. I found it difficult to approach the subject, for we had never spoken of it before. Now I felt it stood between us like a barrier to complete openness. I tried to imagine what their reaction would be: they might be horrified at my asking and frightened to answer or they might be relieved to be finally able to talk about it. Or perhaps they might be angry with me because they did not want to tell me.

It was unusual for me not to blurt out whatever was on my mind without pause for thought. But this time I waited for the right opportunity, as I did not want to ask my sister about circumcision when Haile was at home. I finally seized the chance when we were on our way to the market.

'I've always wanted to ask you – are you circumcised?'

My sisters were horrified. Yaldiyan looked as though I had just

The main road in Adi Keyh, where my father bought my mother a small shop.

tried to strangle her while Tzegehana burst into tears and turned her back on me. They found the subject deeply embarrassing. It was embarrassing for every woman, but especially taboo for men – if Haile had heard me, he would have started beating me immediately, for he would not have known how to express his shock and embarrassment in any other way.

I did not mention the subject again, but buried it deep in my innermost recesses. I did not want it to jeopardise the relationship I had with my sisters, which was better than it had ever been before. We had been getting on very well in Sudan and our time together was full of laughter. Togetherness with my sisters was most important to me.

In my yearning for normality, the only thing that jarred now was that we were not allowed to play with boys, as I had done in Asmara. In Khartoum, the boys played football together and the girls ran through the streets playing games that the boys were not allowed to join in.

I liked one boy in our street in particular, even though he was Sudanese. His name was Mohammed, and my heart raced whenever I saw him – which was every day, though only from a distance. He, meanwhile, was perfectly indifferent to me.

The only person I could speak to about Mohammed was Tzegehana. When I told her I liked him, she said, 'I'll tell Haile!'

but I knew deep down that she would not betray me. My sisters and I kept together – it was only Yaldiyan who occasionally told on me. She was still nagged by the suspicion that our father had left his family for my mother, even though she was wrong – quite the opposite was the case. Haile did not want to speak about what had really happened, but Mbrat and Nazreth, especially, had told me the truth. After he and my mother had split up, my father had got married again, to a woman called Abrehet, and had had two daughters by her – Yaldiyan and Tzegehana. Years later, my parents had bumped into each other at a friend's wedding, discovered that they still had feelings for each other and ended up in bed together. So my mother fell pregnant at almost the same time as Abrehet.

My father handled the situation by lying to both women: he swore eternal fidelity to Abrehet and promised my mother that he would leave Abrehet and marry her again. To make things easier, he bought my mother a small shop in Adi Keyh, where he and Abrehet lived, so that she would be nearby. This cannot have been a good solution, because my father then bought my mother a house in Addis Ababa instead, and told her to wait there for him. She believed him – and in this time she gave birth to me.

Soon after that, my father changed his mind again – or seemed to do so. He told my mother that he would not be coming to Addis Ababa after all, but that she should move to Asmara to be with him there. My mother apparently still believed him, for she sold her shop and moved to Asmara, where she discovered that my father had left the town and that his new plans did not include her. My father, Ghebrehiwet Mehari, had indeed left his second wife Abrehet, but not in order to marry my mother. Instead, he had married his new lover, Werhid.

Werhid brought her own children into the marriage, and she and my father wanted to live together with his and her children. My father wanted his ex-wife Abrehet to hand over their children, Yaldiyan and Tzegehana, but when she resisted, he hit her with a frying pan until she lost consciousness and then took my sisters with him. Soon after that, Yaldiyan and Tzegehana became less and less important to him and when Mbrat brought me to join his family, it became all too much for him, so he handed the three of us over to the Jebha.

There was nothing very pleasant in this knowledge about my parents, but at least I now knew how everything that had happened in my life had come about.

Off to Germany

In Khartoum, we lived a family life that was happy for the most part: Haile was our father figure and for a time, Nazreth was a young mother figure, with us as the three precocious daughters. As far as I was concerned, life could have continued this way indefinitely, but our idyll ended one evening a few months after Nazreth had left for America.

After dinner, we normally sat together for a while drinking coffee and chatting idly. All of a sudden, Haile's face took on a serious expression and he said, 'Your father wants you in Germany with him – you have to go.'

Our chatter died in our throats – it was deathly still in the room.

Then Yaldiyan burst out with, 'No! Never!'

Tzegehana also shook her head vigorously, while I said, 'Haile, we want to stay with you!'

Haile ignored us and went on with a speech that he had obviously prepared. 'You don't know what it's like in Europe. You have no idea about Germany – everyone has a good standard of living there, a comfortable life. No one suffers from hunger there. You can go to school there, learn languages, get a proper education that will set you up for life. In the end it doesn't matter what I teach you here – you need certificates, and you'll get those in Germany. You can go to university and you will find good husbands. Later on, you can settle down wherever you want. This is the best opportunity you could have in life. If your father manages to bring you to Germany, you will be safe and you will all have a good life.'

We did not believe a word of this. We did not know what awaited us in Germany, but we did know how our father compared with Haile, and it was very clear to us who we preferred to live with.

'We learn enough with you,' I said.

'We don't want to live all over the world,' Yaldiyan added.

'Your father wants you to go because he wants to see you again and because he wants to help you get on in life. I would love to keep you here with me but I can't go against your father's will. Anyway, I agree with him that going to Europe is the best thing for you. I would go, too, if I could. I don't know why you don't want to go – what do you expect?'

Yaldiyan, who was normally quite quiet, piped up again. 'We'll only go if he leaves our stepmother. We don't want to live with her – we don't want to be her slaves again.'

We all stared at Yaldiyan. Werhid had always been nice to me, but my sisters could remember only too well how they had been ill-treated by Werhid. It seemed that the thought of her, not my father, was what my sisters feared most.

Haile was stumped. He had not expected such a clear reason for not going to join my father, and could come up with nothing in reply to the statement that living with my father had been an unhappy experience before. 'I'll write to your father and tell him what you said, but you must still join him if he wants you to go.' Haile looked serious again, and signalled that the conversation was over.

We went out of the house to feed the leftovers from our meal to the cat and tidy up the cooking area in the yard, moving around in silence with our pots and pans as Haile lay resting on the bed in the living room. My head was filled with questions about what was going to happen to us.

A few weeks later, Haile showed us a letter from our father. We had thought that our father would have found our request preposterous and replied that it was out of the question for him to leave Werhid, whom he loved, and with whom he had a small daughter. Instead, he wrote to say that he had started divorce proceedings.

We could hardly believe it. Yaldiyan burst into tears and I started brooding over the real reasons for my father's behaviour. I knew that Haile had told him that he was spoken ill of by friends and relatives for not caring for his three elder daughters, so perhaps my father was only doing this to salvage his reputation.

Was he more concerned with his reputation than with anything else? Or did he really want to see us again – so much that he was prepared to change his life?

Whatever his reasons, it was clear that there was now no question of us not going. Haile started preparing us for our departure immediately. We spent hours going through all sorts of procedures at the German embassy, the Ethiopian embassy (there was no Eritrean embassy yet) and at various Sudanese authorities. The process seemed never-ending – a signature or a photocopy would be missing, or we might need just one more passport photograph than we had brought along. Our uncle had to dig deep in his pockets more than once to get us the documents we required, for many of the Sudanese officials were lethargic, greedy and corrupt.

We often had to join a queue at one of these offices even before dawn broke. We stood in a tight huddle before the closed door while more and more people pushed into the clammy corridor behind us. Families with small children and babies stood for hours until the officials arrived and unlocked the doors. Then the crowd swarmed into the offices like water bursting through a dam. The survival of the fittest was the law that governed everyone's behaviour. It was another couple of hours before we found ourselves finally sitting opposite an official, who was mostly completely uninterested in our problems. The official merely stamped or signed our documents and directed us to another

Yaldiyan, me and Tzegehana (from left to right) before we left for Germany.

office, where we had to go through the queuing and pushing all over again.

As the day that we were to leave for Germany drew closer and closer, Haile became more and more troubled, for he had grown very fond of us. But he wanted us to go to Germany to get an education, so he put aside his desire to keep us with him. We will never forget his generosity of spirit in doing this. Haile showed us principles to live by which we had never known before. He taught us what was important in life, and what was not, albeit by being strict with us and by beating us. Yet he never beat us for the sake of causing us pain – he only hit us when we had done something he did not approve of.

It was much more difficult to get us entry permits to Germany than either Haile or my father had imagined. Our visa applications were turned down over and over again. It was only after months of trying that the German embassy granted us entry permits on condition that we got German passports which included passport photographs and our birth dates. This was not as simple as it sounded, for we had no documents to prove our dates of birth – neither birth nor christening certificates – and no one could say exactly when we had been born. Our father did not know, and my mother had disappeared – no one had any contact with her. Yaldiyan's and Tzegehana's mother lived in a remote mountain village in Eritrea, cut off from all communication during the civil war. The German officials shook their heads and put four noughts in place of our birth dates in the small green booklets that were our passports, saying that we had to have the dates put in once we were in Germany. We had no idea how we were going to do this.

We had to change our names for these precious passports that we had spent months jumping through bureaucratic hoops for. The German officials did not recognise the Eritrean system of naming, with its never-ending sequence of first names that were passed on from father to sons and daughters, and from sons to their sons and daughters again. My father's name is Ghebrehiwet Mehari, and the official who processed my passport application simply decided to use Ghebrehiwet as the surname for all of us although it was really just my paternal grandfather's name. Mehari, my father's name, was used as my second surname. My first name, Senait, remained.

But this problem of names was the least of the bureaucratic hurdles we had to face. By the end of the process, we just wanted to leave for Germany, for Europe, for the wide world out there. Haile had encouraged us in this. 'If you get the opportunity to go to America, Germany, or Europe, grab it! You can go to university there,' he had always said. Our uncle's opinion was important to us – everything he said made sense to us, and it was impossible for us to go against him even if we had not agreed with him to begin with. He had given us so much, and now his advice helped prepare us for our new lives in Germany. 'Take care of yourselves and work with the flow, never go against it. Take everything you can get,' he said over and over again. He did not mean money or material possessions, but knowledge. 'You don't know when you will have to return to Africa, and that's when you will need all the knowledge you can get.'

Everything happened very quickly after we finally got our entry permits for Germany. The embassy paid for our flights, which my uncle did not have the money for, and which my father probably could not afford either. There it stood in black and white on these paper sheets covered with words we could not read: we were leaving in a week. We had seven more days of home and our old life before we would be thrown in the deep end to live a new life about which we knew nothing. It had all gone so quickly, and I was not ready to leave everything behind me for good – Haile, Khartoum, Africa and the life I knew.

When the time came to part from Haile at the airport, I was paralysed with sadness and could barely speak or move. As we went through the departure gate, Yaldiyan wanted to turn back once more and hug Haile, but he simply said, 'Come, come. Go on in, go.' Then he turned and walked to the exit. Haile was a proud man – he did not want to cry in front of us. He was a good, kind person.

9

Germany

Everything on the plane seemed strangely familiar to me. I had seen the insides of planes before on television, so did not find the sight of people sitting comfortably in rows with friendly white women walking up and down between them odd. I fastened my seatbelt and sat back as the huge plane set off slowly at first and then faster and faster until it suddenly rose into the air.

This journey from Khartoum to Zurich was the first flight I had ever been on. Until then, for me, passenger planes had been mere pinpricks in the sky above the desert. I knew that they contained people travelling from one place to another, and used to imagine what they looked like and what the people on board these planes did. Consumed by hunger and thirst when I had lived in the desert, I had never considered that they would mostly be occupied with eating and drinking.

Now here I was, sitting in a plane myself, looking down on endless steppes and the desert below, imagining lots of tiny people down there – standing or sitting in the shade of a bush – looking up at the tiny dot in the sky and wondering what was in it. I was too excited to eat any of the food that was served on board the plane. It all looked like meat anyway, which I did not eat, and smelt quite horrible. I wrapped myself up in my blanket, curled up in my seat and fell into a deep, exhausted sleep. My sisters had to shake me awake when the plane began its descent.

Still drunk with sleep, I stumbled through a tunnel in the

airport and out through another tunnel into a plane to Hanover in Germany. I did not get an impression of where I was at all. Before I fell asleep again, all I registered was that the plane was full of white people. None of them paid any attention to us.

At Hanover, I was shocked into full wakefulness when we left the plane and walked down the steps into the open. It was winter there, colder than I had ever experienced before. The biting cold almost took my breath away. I could hardly believe that I had come to live in this climate. Haile had told us that it would be colder in Germany, and bought us coats to wear. But all that he could buy in Africa were flimsy unlined coats, which were far too thin for these temperatures. I was paralysed by the cold, and thought I would never make it down to the bus that waited at the bottom of the steps.

Once we were in the airport, it was impossible to stop staring at the white people everywhere. They all walked very quickly, and were wearing a great many clothes, which I could see the sense of – the more clothes the better in these temperatures. Everyone was carrying bags and cases, and seemed to know exactly where they were going.

I had seen white people before as a child – the Italian nuns and the Red Cross workers who had come to the village – but to see *only* white people around us, and such a mass of them, was quite overwhelming. There had been some white people in Sudan, but they had been almost all dark-haired Italians or Egyptians. Here in the airport, the people were almost all fair-haired – there seemed to be thousands of blondes milling around. My sisters and I tried to joke about it at first. 'Look at all the albinos!' they said. Where we came from, pale-skinned people with blonde hair were albinos – I imagined that these people's hair would fall out and their skin dissolve at the merest touch. My sisters got the giggles at the sight of so many white people. 'Where on earth have we come to? Yuck! I hope they don't come near us!'

We stood staring round us, not knowing where to go until a

friendly white woman in a smart uniform starting speaking to us in English. I was happy that I could understand what she said, and immediately felt a little less lost. She pointed us to the baggage reclaim belt on which our bags were circling. The bags were packed with clothes that were totally unsuitable for this climate, I thought, shivering.

The next shock came when the gigantic glass doors we walked towards opened mysteriously to reveal our father. We stopped in our tracks and stared at him. He had aged considerably – his hair was grey and white and his shoulders were stooped. He was wearing strange thick clothes, like everyone else around here. It had been seven years since our father had brought us to the Jebha, and in that time he had become such a distant figure for us that he seemed to belong to a previous life. I could hardly believe that it was really him standing in front of us waving uncertainly: Ghebrehiwet Mehari, German citizen, resident in Hamburg-Stellingen, dressed in a thick, bulky coat with lots of buttons, feet clad in leather shoes.

A train of totally absurd thoughts flitted through my head. I realised that I had never seen my father wearing shoes before, only flip-flops or sandals. And I noted that he was the only black person standing in the crowd before the glass door. He had always seemed gigantic to me before, but here, in the crowd of white people, he seemed to be only of average height, perhaps a little short, even, for some of the women there were taller than him.

Our greetings were muted, for we felt as embarrassed as my father clearly did. He told us that we had to hurry, which surprised me, for I had never thought of him as someone who hurried. But there was scarcely time to give this further thought, as new impressions were coming thick and fast. The buildings here were very high, and there were so many cars on the roads, which were all tarmacked over. I wondered, too, at all the grass and trees around despite it being winter.

The inside of the train that took us to Hamburg looked like the inside of the plane. The sun had set by now, and the dark landscape around us raced by at breathtaking speed – it seemed as if the train was about to take off into the air any minute. I marvelled at the innumerable lights glimmering outside, and we finally drew into a huge cavern of light full of people and countless trains arriving and leaving. Our father picked up our bags and told us that we had arrived in Hamburg. 'Home,' he said, but he didn't sound very believable.

We continued our journey underground by U-Bahn through countless stations until we finally emerged above ground again between even taller buildings. This was Stellingen, a suburb of Hamburg full of identical blocks. I wondered how anyone found their way around here, for each street looked like the next. We were not the only Africans here, though – later, I learned that the Germans called areas like this 'foreigners' ghettoes'.

We followed our father silently, and were disappointed when he led us to a row of low houses next to the tower blocks. 'Here is your home,' he said, pointing to one of a series of doors. The small houses were part of a long terrace built in a straight line. They were huge inside – they had three floors, with a living room with lovely soft sofas and a television, a kitchen with a cooker and a fridge, and lots of other, smaller rooms. We would have been over the moon if not for the questions that nagged at us. What were we going to do here? And how were we going to live together with our father?

Our new home

I was thirteen or fourteen years old when I arrived in Germany, and had already lived through a great deal. Yet the most basic things presented me with difficulties, while I found what others would have found difficult simple – making friends in the neighbourhood, for instance, although I understood not one word of their language. On our first morning in Germany, I went straight out after breakfast to see if there were any other children living near us.

My sisters could barely believe what I was doing. 'What? Are you going out?' they asked when I announced my intention at the breakfast table.

My father shrugged and said nothing. I found my sisters' astonishment strange. 'Of course. How else can I find out if there are other children living here?' I put on every piece of warm clothing I had and went out.

I had a piece of paper and a pen with me to write things down on so I would not get lost. I had learned the alphabet in my English lessons, so I copied the letters on all the signs I saw carefully. PRIVATE ROAD from the sign on our house, and HERMANNS from the sign above the window in which repellent-looking joints of meat hung, and PRIMA from the lit signboard above the supermarket.

I worked my way through the estate until I finally found a playground full of wonderful things: wooden climbing frames, slides, swings, see-saws and a funny contraption which you could stand on while someone else pushed you round and round. The only other person in the playground was a girl with long blonde hair, who was sitting on a swing. I sat down on the swing next to her and smiled. She looked at me with wide eyes and smiled back. 'Hello,' I said, and smiled again.

The girl started speaking to me, but I did not understand a word of what she was saying, apart from 'hello'. She seemed to be asking me a question, but I could only shake my head in reply. She repeated her question over and over again until I was able to break down her stream of speech into syllables – 'What's your name?' – which I still did not understand. I said 'What?' constantly and she said, 'What's your name?' over and over again, to which I replied 'What?' again.

She said, 'Yeah, yeah, what.'

'What' was the only word I knew in German. I had heard it the day before in the airport, and had asked my father what it meant.

After the girl had understood that I did not speak German, she bravely switched to English and asked haltingly, 'Your name?'

I sighed with relief. 'Senait,' I said. 'And yours?'

'Bianca!'

The ice had been broken and we continued our conversation with hand gestures, playing at touching each other's skins. Bianca wanted to see if the colour of my skin rubbed off and I wanted to see if her skin stayed on if I touched her, or if it would peel off like the skin of a peach. After an hour or so of this mimed conversation, I thought I had better go home in case my father and sisters started worrying about me, so I said goodbye to Bianca.

Bianca looked sad, but I promised her that I would come again, and said, 'Bye, bye' as I left. I walked back home following the signs that I had copied so painstakingly on my way out: PRIMA, HERMANNS and PRIVATE ROAD.

My sisters couldn't believe their ears when I told them about my encounter with the white girl with blonde hair. We had only arrived late last night, and I had already gone to the playground and made a new friend. My father laughed when he heard my story. From his experience of me before, he was used to me doing things that other people did not understand or expect.

In the ghetto

My new friend Bianca was an exception among the people I met at the start of my life in Germany. Not long after my sisters and I arrived, we had to leave the wonderful three-storey house and move to a much smaller flat in Eidelstedt, another suburb of Hamburg, which was even more of a 'foreigners' ghetto'. There were hardly any Germans living there, but lots of Arabs, Africans and Turkish people. The streets were dirty, the parks were grotty, the walls were smeared with graffiti, the telephone boxes had all been vandalised and the shopping centres were grimy. Lots of young people hung around on the street aimlessly. Apart from the vandalism, much of the area looked not unlike Africa. Africa was a lot poorer and the buildings looked older and shabbier, but at least there was no vandalism there. There was a lot of theft in

A photo of Yaldiyan, Tzegehana and me (from left to right) taken by my father in his flat in Hamburg.

Africa – anything that was not locked up and put away safely could be stolen – but no one smashed windows and streetlights or pushed motorbikes over just for the pleasure of destroying something.

We left the ghetto every day, but only to take the U-Bahn to another ghetto at the other end of Hamburg, where we went to the only school in Hamburg that accepted asylum seekers and immigrants who had just arrived in Germany. The curriculum focused on German language instruction.

We sat in a classroom together with people from Turkey, Iran and Afghanistan. The only thing we had in common was that we were all foreigners. We did not understand them, and most of them – especially the girls – treated us with contempt. *Nutte*, the German word for 'slut', was one of the first words I learned at the school, because the other girls called us that all the time, despising us for not wearing headscarves, shawls and long skirts as they did.

I soon began to feel more out of place in this mish-mash of disparate foreigners than I did in the rest of the city, where normal people lived everyday lives. I did not feel at home in Hamburg, but I did not find the city incomprehensible or uncomfortable to live in. I was constantly surprised by the wealth I saw, and how busy and discontented everyone seemed. The variety of wares on offer in the shopping centres, from the magnificent fridges to the mountains of clothing, all amazed me. I marvelled at the knowledge that the people around me had fridges like those at home, and wardrobes full of clothes, but could not believe that there were beggars sitting outside the entrances to these over-flowing department stores. The beggars hardly got anything from the crowds streaming past.

The sexual freedoms of this society also surprised me. Girls wore tight tops and very short skirts – they wore a lot of make-up and cast boys come-hither looks. It took me a while to realise that it was all really for show, a game called 'flirting' that had little to do with the way real relationships were conducted here.

Gradually, it dawned on me that a lot that we had been told about Germany before was wrong. In Sudan, we had been told that the rubbish bins in Germany were filled with sweets and that the streets were paved with gold – all you had to do was pick it up. But all that was in the streets and the bins were wads of chewing gum, cigarette butts and other rubbish. We had been sceptical about coming to Germany, but the fairytale about the streets being paved with gold had achieved its purpose of making us look forward to going there – we had been excited by the thought of all the things we believed we could pick up for free in this strange new country. Though that had not turned out to be the case, I was still thrilled by the sight of all the clothes. Clothes had always interested me more than sweets, even from early childhood in Asmara or in the village I had lived in with my father. Every time a Red Cross lorry had turned up to distribute aid packages, the other children had always run towards the cries of 'Sweets here!', while I had run towards whoever was shouting 'Clothes here!' in order to get hold of an old T-shirt with words on it that I did not understand, gaily printed trousers or a jacket that I hardly had the chance to wear because the weather was too hot for it.

Old fears

It was not what happened out on the streets of Hamburg that caused me difficulty, but life within the four walls of our home in Stellingen. My father's mild manner had quickly disappeared soon after our arrival, and he had turned once more into the man that my sisters and I remembered only too well – lashing out with blows at the slightest provocation. It was not long before my old fears of my father returned.

The beatings started when we wanted to write to Uncle Haile to tell him how we were and what we had seen. Haile was still the only person we could talk to. Our father objected to our writing to Haile because he was afraid that Haile would find out something negative about him. He must also have been jealous of our relationship with Haile, so he wanted to cut off contact with our uncle.

He lashed out again and again whenever we forgot something small or asked for something he did not want to give us, or even when we accidentally knocked over a glass at the dinner table. As had been the case in Africa, I was the one who got beaten the most.

We insisted on writing to Haile, but our father vetted every word that we wrote so we had no chance to tell our uncle how badly we were being treated. Our father found something to displease him in every letter, whereupon he slapped us all soundly and either tore up the letters or took them away. Later, I found out from Haile that he had not received any of our letters, for my father had not sent them on. Little wonder that there had never been a reply from Haile.

The struggle with our father to allow us to write to Haile made even Yaldiyan lose her temper. 'Haile is our father – you will never be that!' she screamed at him.

Our father gave Yaldiyan a brutal beating and locked her in her room for the rest of the day. He seemed exhausted after that. 'I brought you all here because I wanted the best for you,' he whined.

We were unmoved. 'We didn't want to come in the first place,' Tzegehana retorted.

'We're only here because Haile said we had to come, because he thinks it's better for us to live in Germany than in Africa,' I said. 'But we would have preferred to stay in Khartoum.'

Amazingly, our father did not beat Tzegehana and me for retorting in this way. We went to bed unharmed that night. He had spent all his energies on beating Yaldiyan.

But he was back on form the next day, when he beat all three of us. I was so afraid of him that I often peed in my pants the moment I heard him opening the front door. Whether I was doing my homework, having something to eat in the kitchen or standing elsewhere in the flat, I found it impossible to control my bladder when I heard my father coming home. Even before he had opened the door, I shot to the bathroom, where I waited until he had gone into the living room or the kitchen.

As soon as I was sure of not bumping into him, I washed and changed my clothing and crept into my room like a hunted animal, where I tried to concentrate on my homework, on reading a book or on distracting myself with other thoughts. But most of the time I spent simply waiting for something to happen. Sometimes, I emerged from my room to get something to eat but, to avoid having to talk to my father, I pretended I was exhausted and was going to bed even at the early hour of seven o'clock. It was safest not to speak to him or have any contact with him at all, but even that did not always work. When he got into a rage about something, he used to knock and kick the door of my room until I was forced to open it.

My sisters adopted different strategies. Yaldiyan tried her best to do as my father wished, and only raised her voice when she was at the end of her tether and felt really strongly about something.

Tzegehana showed my father the most respect – she was very diplomatic with him, but not obsequious. She got beaten now and then, too, but less often than Yaldiyan, and much less than me.

My father knew the differences between how he felt about each of us very well, even though he pretended that all three of us got on his nerves equally. Shortly after we had arrived in Germany, he had given us a colouring book each. I had to laugh at his choice of cover for each of us: Yaldiyan's book had Goofy on the front, Tzegehana's had Mickey Mouse and mine had Donald Duck. I thought this spoke volumes.

I was familiar with these Disney cartoon characters from seeing them on television in Sudan, and my father had chosen exactly the right characters for each of us. Yaldiyan was clumsy like Goofy, but also small and delicate. Tzegehana was the clever one who knew exactly what was going on all the time and how to manoeuvre through it. And the brazen, quacking demeanour of Donald, who almost always ended up in trouble, was most similar to mine. Even today, we three still retain our similarities to these characters. Yaldiyan always means well, but behaves awkwardly. My father always put her down as the stupid one, but she is not stupid, merely very sensitive. Tzegehana is calm and clever – she was the only one of us who had any influence on our father. Sometimes when my father hit me she spoke sharply to him – 'Let her go!' – and he would let me go immediately. Unlike Tzegehana, I have always been quick to lose my temper and not particularly good at negotiating my way through matters.

My father found the responsibility of three children just too much to cope with. He was not used to it, and it was beyond him to care about matters relating to school, to take interest in our problems or to give us support from day to day. He never attended parents' days at our school, and did not bother to make sure that we had clean clothes to wear or food to eat. We had to take care of all that ourselves. We often had to do the shopping on our way back from school so that we would have something to make a meal with.

Sometimes, my father simply gave us ten deutschmarks and disappeared for a few days. We found those periods very difficult, especially in the beginning when we had not started going to school yet, so could hardly speak any German. We had no idea where to go to buy food to eat, or even what kind of food could be bought. So we used to go to the nearest paper shop and buy as many sweets as we could for ten deutschmarks. We sucked at the sweets until we were faint with hunger and an overdose of sugar. At that time, we hardly washed, and our clothes were as dirty and neglected as the house. We must have been a sorry sight, but no one cared.

Our stepmother

Later on, we learned that whenever our father disappeared for a few days, he was with our stepmother, Werhid. She lived with her daughter about an hour away from Hamburg. She was still in the flat he had shared with her before they had got divorced. They had lived in Hamburg at first, but my father had wanted them to move to a place in which there were hardly any African people and no Eritreans at all.

My father did not want to have anything to do with other people from Eritrea. He was the last, and most steadfast, supporter of the ELF – his loyalty was unwavering despite the Jebha's total defeat. He had fallen out with almost all his former friends and companions over politics. Apart from this, he had also told everyone that he did not know where his children were. Eritrean refugees had been arriving in Hamburg, including those who had fought in the Jebha and in the Che Guevara unit, and they brought news that we were still living and fighting alongside the last troop of soldiers. This news spread quickly.

Eritrean refugees are scattered all over Germany and all over the world, but they keep a tight network of contacts, like other diaspora communities. When my father's friends and relations heard that we were still alive in Eritrea, they started criticising him for being an irresponsible father. When my father had had enough of this, he wrote to Haile to say that he was being attacked for not looking after his daughters, and asked Haile to arrange for us to come to Germany. To escape gossip in the Eritrean community, in the meantime, he moved out of Hamburg with his family.

Once, when my father returned from one of his trips to see Werhid, he told us that she had suggested that he bring us to visit her the next time he went. Perhaps she was worried that we were left alone for too long. In any case, she said she wanted to see us again. Soon after that, we went to stay at Werhid's for a three-week stretch. We stuffed ourselves with the *injera* bread she baked every day and played with Flora, the half-sister we had never met before, who had just turned four. It felt good to be part of a complete family again.

Werhid and I had a very good relationship during that period. I was also happy because Werhid distracted my father's attention from me a little. However, my sisters did not get on so well with her. This was not only because she had treated them badly before, but also because they knew that our father had left their mother, Abrehet, for her. They blamed Werhid for the fact that my father had knocked their mother – who had been six months pregnant at the time – unconscious with a frying pan so that he could take them away with him. The scars from this experience ran very deep in Yaldiyan and Tzegehana. Yaldiyan had begged our father to let her stay to help her mother, but he had ignored her. I wondered how my father lived with his conscience, and perfectly understood my sisters' mistrust of Werhid.

But my antipathy was still directed towards my father. Over and over again, I relived the scene when he had taken me to the hollow and tried to kill me. It was Werhid who had saved my life. In Germany, he often said that he ought to have killed me there and then, but I never knew whether he meant it seriously or not.

He used to threaten me in a dramatic voice with statements like, 'I can promise you one thing, Senait. You won't be dying a natural death, but a death by my hand!' or, 'I never wanted to have you.'

When I replied, 'I'm sorry – just pretend I don't exist', he fell silent.

My father again

It was my father's unpredictability that made dealing with him so difficult. I never knew if what he said one day still held the next. He did not seem to live by any rules or follow any rational patterns of behaviour. He appeared to be content only when he had succeeded in getting everyone around him off balance.

Yet he had lovable qualities, too. The moments in which I witnessed them were especially sweet for their rareness; I particularly remember those times because I constantly hoped for more. I watched my father closely and hung on to his every word when his better side made an appearance. Tzegehana used to say that neither she nor Yaldiyan would ever love him as much as I did.

My father's more appealing aspects did not display themselves in consistent actions or qualities, but in fleeting moments, such as when he laughed or told a joke. I liked the way he wound up annoying neighbours or did impressions of people that he found ridiculous. For example, when we passed two women on the street – neighbours who never seemed to have much to do with themselves – gossiping animatedly, my father stuck his head between both of them and went 'Gagagagagagagaa!' I fell about laughing because I, too, took the mickey out of neighbours who I thought talked total nonsense.

My sisters thought my father's sense of humour banal, but I loved it whenever he played the fool, and constantly asked him for more – which he loved. Sometimes we sat in the living room bantering and complaining about people we knew, laughing ourselves silly until the early hours of the morning. My sisters would get up and go to their rooms to read because they found our fooling around so tedious.

At times like these, my father treated me affectionately –

though only to a certain extent. Sometimes he called me 'Senu', the diminutive for Senait, and once he said, 'If you were a boy, you would be my favourite child.' I swallowed a sob at that statement, which stayed in my mind for years afterwards.

I was very interested in music by then, and longed to have a piano. We had no room for one in the flat, and we could not have afforded it anyway. But my father did not give up – he took me to a flea market and bought an old electronic keyboard. It was completely out of tune and half the keys were broken, but I did not mind. What counted was that he had bought it for me, and I practised on it until my fingers ached.

But the father who had bought me the keyboard one day was the same father whose hand shot out to hit me the day after, so I could never trust him. I thought of him and referred to him as 'the Hand', and used to say to Yaldiyan and Tzegehana, 'I don't know if the Hand is going to hit me or caress me today.' They understood only too well what I meant – it was impossible to tell how he would treat us from one moment to the next. Yet I could not detect any real evil in his eyes or expression when he was angry – he seemed to be wearing a mask.

My father's dual nature affected other people apart from us. A certain group of Eritreans constantly sought out his company and attention despite the cold, condescending way he treated them. He had the air of a pasha surrounded by a grovelling crowd – there were about five or six people constantly hanging around him, either bringing food, inviting him out or helping him with paperwork and bureaucratic tangles. All this was thanks to my father's charisma, which nobody could take away from him. I soon realised that, apart from physical similarities such as the shape of my head, ears and bottom, my jagged teeth and my ugly feet, I had also inherited this from him, along with a quick intelligence.

Neither of my sisters looked like him or acted like him in any way. My father knew that I was very like him. The way I look when I am angry, or behave when I am excited about something, the way I negotiate my way around things, are all similar to him.

Like him, I do not like wearing people down with talk, but prefer to convince them through my behaviour. My voice and musical ability also come from my father – he had always been a singer, mostly of political songs. He had sung in Africa, and he sang at ELF rallies in Germany as well, when I stood in the row directly before the stage bursting with pride that he was up there singing in front of all these people.

Punch-ups

Eventually the ELF splinter group in Germany collapsed, so my father took us to EPLF rallies instead. Sometimes he stormed on to the stage in the middle of an event and started singing anti-EPLF songs from years ago. Most of the time, he would be summarily thrown out by a couple of activists, but they respected him too much to really beat him up properly – they merely bundled him to the door and shoved him out. We trailed after him, horrified, yet pleased at the same time that someone had finally dared to stand up to him.

My father was never particularly bothered by these incidents – he simply took us to the next EPLF meeting, where he got up to sing again. These gatherings often went on late, and we became so sleepy that we could barely stay upright, but my father paid us no heed, especially as he himself could often hardly stand straight after all the drink he had had. He babbled complete nonsense when he was drunk, and the other guests would look at us pityingly or tell us how sorry they were for us.

Sometimes my father's drunken behaviour at these events would lead to punch-ups, such as after he ran on to the stage screaming things like, 'You're all bloody losers!' or 'You shitfaces! Just you wait! The ELF will win again!' or 'You're all terror-ists! Sneaky and underhand! Look me in the eye and strike me down if you can! But you don't dare! You'll blow my house up while I'm sleeping! You cowards! Come on, let your fists do the talking!'

On a couple of occasions, we felt so ashamed of our father's loutish behaviour that we simply left him behind and took the night bus home. I sometimes wondered how a man of his age could have such childish tantrums instead of behaving in a mature manner. But my father was not a grown-up – he was completely unpredictable and a rebel through and through. If something did not suit him, he just totally ignored it.

Once, he took us to an Eritrean festival at Sternschanze in Hamburg. At the entrance, he bumped into Hagoss, a fervent EPLF member who had lost a hand in the war. We knew then that the evening would not go well – my father and Hagoss could not stand each other.

A disagreement ensued almost immediately. Hagoss was one of the Eritreans who had accused my father of not having taken care of his children, so when he saw us, he said, 'Are they yours, then? You can see in their eyes that they are frightened of you. You're lucky that your children are smart.'

My father did not take this well. 'That may be, but at least I can clap with both hands at my daughters' weddings!' he retorted, clapping wildly in front of Hagoss. The other man rushed at my father, who struck back, and it was only seconds before some more people rushed to the scene. Whether they were trying to separate out the two or wanted a part in the brawl was unclear – all we saw was a knot of bodies writhing on the ground.

Incidents like this happened again and again. One day, when we were at the train station in Hamburg on our way to Frankfurt to visit an Eritrean friend there, another man whom my father did not like came up to us. They had still been pretending to be good friends when my sisters and I had arrived in Germany, but had fallen out spectacularly soon afterwards. Now their animosity flared up again – in front of the lockers in the station, they started having a heated argument over some incomprehensible political issue, and began to exchange blows.

My sisters and I looked on not knowing what to do and feeling deeply embarrassed by the enquiring looks from the people around us. Luckily, two German passers-by came and separated the men. We thanked them and were relieved when we finally boarded the train with our father, who had been unharmed by the fight. But he was angry with us for not helping him.

'Why didn't you just pick up a suitcase and bash him on the head with it?' he asked us. I gave silent thanks that the other people in our compartment did not understand a word of Tigrinya.

My father could work himself up for hours at a time over politics, and I gained the impression that this actually gave him pleasure. He just would not accept that the ELF had lost the war. He did not speak about the war or explain anything to us, and he never apologised for having given us to the Jebha or for how it had treated us – that seemed to be nothing to him in comparison to the humiliation of the ELF's defeat.

I never really found out how genuinely he believed in what he said. My father was actually a very reserved person, and he hated talking about his feelings. Nevertheless, I could feel when he was unwell. Sometimes he had attacks of nausea even when he had not drunk anything, and there were a couple of times when he could not make it to the bathroom in time before throwing up. When he was in pain, I sat by him through the night, holding his hand. I had to go to school the next day, and I knew I would feel terrible with no sleep, but I still stayed by him, saying, 'You're going to be fine', and stroking his head. At the same time, I knew that when he recovered the following day, he would beat me for some reason or other as soon as I returned from school. Yet I treasured these times with my father.

I don't know where the strength to put up with my father's abuse came from. My sisters were not so strong, but, without this remarkable power, I would not have survived. My father must have had the same strength, too, for he had lived through five times as much abuse as I had. His stepmother had branded him with iron tongs and forced him to gnaw walls when he had said he was hungry. This is no excuse for his behaviour, but at least it explains it.

Stretching my wings

The longer I stayed in Germany, the more my father receded into the background of my life. He still ordered me around, beat me up and dominated the family, but I was slipping out of his hands as my life outside home expanded. I had made friends in school and my German was improving, so I could move around the city more easily. I had also begun going out, for the more confident I became, the more my hesitant interest in the opposite sex – which I had suppressed fearfully before – grew.

The turning point came when I was out with two friends one day. Martin was my age and Boris was a little older – both of them were simply good friends of mine, nothing more. They had suggested visiting Stefan, a friend of theirs they had not seen for some time. After a long journey to a very smart suburb of Hamburg, my jaw dropped when we finally arrived at a grand house set on a gigantic piece of land.

In the entrance hall was a boy standing in front of a big mirror trying out several different poses. He looked like Brad Pitt – sleek, smooth, glowing and very sweet. I couldn't stop staring at him. He radiated self-satisfaction, his body language was theatrical and uninhibited. Without knowing it, I fell in love with him on the spot. When we left the house, I realised that I felt different – there was a funny feeling in my belly that I had never known before. I felt strangely dizzy and heavy at the same time, and talked a stream of nonsense. Martin and Boris must have thought I was out of my mind.

I thought Martin was cool, but I did not fancy him, certainly not at all once I had got to know Stefan. Boris had been a good friend for some time, but after he had taken me to Stefan's house, I wanted to see him even more often than before, because I knew he was my link to Stefan. A few days later, Boris took me with him again to visit Stefan.

This time, everything happened very quickly. Stefan was very happy to see me again, and a couple of hours later, we were kissing and cuddling. We were a couple from that time onwards.

But sex was a wasteland for me – I associated it with pain and humiliation; I did not regard it as something worthwhile.

Many people who saw me in bars or clubs thought I was the kind of girl who had someone new every day because I appeared so lively and confident, and managed to dress in a way that attracted attention, even with my limited means. This was all for show – I had to act confident to feel it, otherwise I would have hidden in a corner whimpering. There were certainly boys who wanted to make passes at me, but there was no sex in my life, if only because of the rapes I had had to endure before.

Nor was I out partying all the time. Most of my time was spent working hard to do well at school. I made great progress learning German, especially after I realised that no one around me understood English. German was the only language I could use to communicate with my classmates, who spoke Turkish, Russian, Romanian or other languages. I could only talk to a few students in my broken Arabic.

I had to start in one of the lower years at school. My sisters and I had tried to lie about our ages at our entrance interview with the teacher, hoping to skip a few years, but to no avail. As there were no birthdates in our passports, our ages were estimated based on our height and physical frame, and birth certificates were issued with these approximate dates. Since then, my official birthdate has been 3 December 1976. In Germany, everything requires official documentation: birth certificate, identity card, social security card, local registration papers, bank account, mobile phone contract, everything.

With our thirst for knowledge, we had studied so hard in Sudan that we were one or two years ahead of the others in our year. Sometimes this caused friction with the other students, many of whom could not believe that a black person could be well educated or have a good general knowledge. Those who were victims of racist behaviour themselves were often the worst.

There was a Turkish girl in my class who constantly asserted that she was more 'German' than I was, saying, 'You may have a German passport, but you will never be white.' When I had finally had enough of this, I lashed out at her. I had not lost my temper so badly since arriving in Hamburg. As I pummelled her with my fists in a blind rage, I reminded myself of my father. The girl defended herself vigorously, scratching at me and biting until she drew blood. I don't know how much worse the fight would have got if we had not been separated by other students.

That was a time when I was fighting for my place in society, so I was quite aggressive, but I fought mostly with words – screaming and cursing – not with my hands. My violence did take a physical form with Yaldiyan however, whom I used to push to the floor or throw against the wall when she annoyed me.

Yaldiyan and I had always taken our negative feelings out on each other. She blamed me for a lot of what had disappointed her in life. Although neither she nor I had ever met my mother, she claimed that I was as nasty and as mean as my mother, and never gave me the chance to prove otherwise. It was only much later – too late for us to live peacefully together in our childhood – that we realised that we actually had many things in common.

Although Yaldiyan constantly picked fights with me, she couldn't stand it when Tzegehana and I fought. She marched up to us like a school principal and waved her hands wildly, shouting, 'Stop fighting! Stop fighting!'

What I say about my sisters may not sound particularly warm, but I love them more than anything else in the world. We hardly have any contact with each other today, but that does not change their place in my affections.

Running away

My ties to my sisters made me hesitate to make a decision that was long overdue – complete separation from my father. My father being the person he was, it was not possible to do this in small, deliberate steps. The separation had to be sudden, without warning. My father would never have let me leave home, and I did not want to – and could not – wait until I was of the legal age to do so. I was not quite fifteen when I ran away – I knew that I would not survive the pressures and humiliations of life with my father for another three years.

In the end, it was all quite simple, and to me seemed perfectly natural. I packed a few clothes in the rucksack I carried to school, added a hunk of bread and a few apples, rolled up a woollen blanket under the top of the rucksack and set off. My sisters had gone shopping and my father was out in the city somewhere. I picked up the rucksack just as I did every day, pulled the door of the flat closed behind me and disappeared into the U-Bahn between the tower blocks. There was only one difference: I was taking this journey for the last time. It felt amazing to be the only person who knew this while the hundreds and thousands of people who saw me in the U-Bahn and S-Bahn remained oblivious: I never wanted to return to that ugly flat in Hamburg Eidelstedt ever again.

In fact, I have returned to the flat twice since then, but I regret both occasions. At least I never spent another night in the flat my father lived in.

When I ran away, I had only a hazy idea of where I might stay the night. I had no money to rent a room or a flat. I had saved 400 deutschmarks from my paper round over the previous four weeks, but I would need that for food. I was determined that I would not run back home simply because I had run out of money. I knew that my father would certainly beat me to death if I did, or almost to death, leaving me lying injured and bleeding on the floor. These were not the wild imaginings of an adolescent girl – it was the truth. I knew my father well enough to know that he would be totally unable to control himself if I returned.

I went to Stefan first, and spent the day with him. We slept in his car that night, because we did not dare tell his parents that I had run away. The next day, I lied and told him I was going to stay with a friend. It was not concern about his parents finding out that made me do this, more that I did not want to exchange dependence on my father for dependence on Stefan. I actually got along very well with his parents, especially his father, who would certainly have taken me in. I was too proud to go to them, though.

After I had left Stefan, I made my way into the city. I had no clear destination in mind, but quite definite ideas about where I did *not* want to end up. My journey to a new life seemed to take on a momentum of its own, and I got out of the train automatically at Jungfernstieg, in the centre of Hamburg, which I was always drawn to whenever I did not know where to go. There were always lots of people milling about here who did not care what you looked like or what your problems were. And there were also lots of homeless people here – people who did not know where they belonged, where they would sleep that night or what they would be eating the next day – people who I would join only for the moment, for I did not want to live like them for long. I knew that much before I slept rough for the first time. I knew I had to start a new life and fend for myself.

I strolled down Mönckebergstrasse in a good mood, bought myself an ice-cream and savoured my freedom. I did not have to watch the clock and worry about how I was going to slip past my father unnoticed that evening or what my sisters and I were going to cook for dinner to keep him happy. The thought of my sisters made me start. I wondered if they were worrying about me, but then I pushed the thought aside. My sisters had each other.

As the windows and signs of the shops and department stores began to shine brighter beneath the darkening sky, I felt less carefree. I was not hungry, for the question of what to do next had put all other thoughts out of my mind. I longed for a room to lie down in but I knew that that was out of the question.

I walked towards the river Alster, to an area where a number of bridges span the many channels through which the river flows at this point. I imagined that homeless people stayed beneath bridges, where they were protected from the rain and could light small fires without being seen. After searching for a while, I found a bridge under which a couple of people were already settled by a campfire. They had mattresses, blankets, stools and what seemed like half the contents of a flat piled in several shopping trolleys beside them.

Beneath bridges

The men by the fire did not seem in the least surprised to see a teenage African girl come up and sit next to them, while I did my best to pretend that it was the most natural thing in the world to seek refuge under a bridge at night. No one asked where I was from, why I was there, or where I wanted to go. They chatted about this and that, told stories, made jokes and offered me a bottle of schnapps. The schnapps tasted dreadful, but it warmed my stomach and made me feel leaden with exhaustion. When I started to roll myself up in the thin blanket I had brought, one of the men offered me a mattress and a pillow. I can't have stared into the flames of the fire for very long before I sank into a deep sleep.

It was wonderful to wake up the next morning with no walls around me and only the arch of the bridge above me. Not having to ask or tell anyone anything, but to be able to just walk into the nearest bakery to get a coffee and croissant before taking the U-Bahn to school was also a marvellous feeling.

Sleeping rough had its downsides, though: my mood soon deflated when it started raining. My clothes got damp and felt uncomfortable. They were still damp and were even more uncomfortable after I had sat in a café for an hour with a cup of tea. I started worrying seriously about what to do next. One of the men living below the bridge had also begun to bother me – he seemed to think that lending me a mattress gave him the right to share it with me. I could think of nothing more repellent.

I did not miss a single day of school while I was homeless. As soon as I sat down in class, I checked my clothes and looked round at the others to see if they were staring at me. But everything seemed normal, so I leaned back, relieved, and unpacked my books. No one seemed to have the slightest suspicion of where I had spent the night. I rejoiced silently, filled with the conviction that I would succeed in building a new life for myself.

After school, I met my sisters, who had been going to a different school for some time. They bombarded me with questions. Our father had raged and threatened them with beatings if they did not tell him where I was, but he had finally had to accept that they really did not know. I did not tell my sisters where I was sleeping, for they would have told my father, who would have called the police immediately. I merely told them that I was well, staying with friends, and that I would soon have my own place.

Yaldiyan and Tzegehana did not believe a word of what I told them, and pleaded with me to go back home with them, but I refused, and made sure that no one was following me when I left school.

I had underestimated my sisters' stubbornness, however. Yaldiyan rang Stefan's mother and asked her to tell me to go home, otherwise I would be in terrible trouble. Once Stefan's parents learned of my predicament, they offered me a place to stay for as long as I wanted. They wanted to be kind to me, and perhaps they also thought that if I lived with Stefan, he would stop hanging around with his wayward friends and going clubbing so often. This was indeed the case temporarily. Stefan soon started going out every night again, only returning in the early hours of the morning. I did not stop him, but, at first anyway, I did not join him, for I would not have made it to school on time in the mornings if I had. Later on, I got drawn into going out with him, and we went all round the town together. But in principle I did not mind being alone at home. I loved the luxury of having a loo, a bathroom and a warm, soft, dry bed, which I appreciated all the more for not having had them for a couple of weeks.

Beatings

This idyll did not last long. Exactly three months into our relationship Stefan struck me for the first time. It was as if a dam had broken, as if Stefan had always wanted to hit me and had been unaccountably held back before.

It was summer, and we were at a beach party by the Baltic Sea with a couple of dozen people. Stefan and I got into a petty argument which escalated until we were the centre of attention. In front of everyone else, he raised his hand – half-serious, half-joking – to strike me. He hit me once, then twice, before I lost control as well and screamed, 'Hit me, then! You're just like my father! Do you want my blood?'

Our fights were mostly over small things, only rarely over anything serious. He would hit me, and I would kick and bite him. Sometimes I noticed that my shirt had blood on it even before I really felt his blows. He went crazy because he wanted to sleep with me but I was wrapped up in the protective layers that had built up from my past, and could feel neither pain nor desire. I was silent, cold, still and unreceptive to his advances. When this numbness got too much for me, I cut my legs with a knife when I was alone, in order to feel something.

At his holiday flat by the Baltic, Stefan hit me so hard that blood streamed from my nose and roared in my ears. I was so frightened that instinctively I ran to the house where his parents were – not to tell on Stefan, but to seek safety. Stefan's father immediately realised what had happened and he took me back to Stefan's flat to give his son a talking-to. He liked me, and he knew that Stefan was hot-tempered and undisciplined.

'Look for yourself!' he shouted at Stefan, pointing at my blood-smeared face. 'Are you out of your mind? How dare you hit her?' He was beside himself with anger.

Stefan looked sorry and kept silent. He sat on his bed like a naughty boy, staring straight ahead until his father's lecture was over. He seemed so forlorn that I soon began to feel sorry for him. Although I must say that I was not completely innocent, for I often provoked Stefan into losing his temper. I refused to listen to him, and I often lied to him. Indeed, I had lied to him about myself from the start of our relationship. I lied because I was ashamed of myself, of my background, my family, my father and all that had happened in my life. All I could see was how perfect Stefan's parents and home seemed compared to mine.

But I really had no home – no security and no family who could help me. All I had was myself. Against Stefan's will, and especially against his parents' will, I left them after several months to live on the streets again.

A friend

One of the men I had got to know when I had slept rough under the bridge was different from the others. He did not drink, he merely smoked and looked melancholy, keeping silent most of the time. This man told me that he came from a good family and had studied law. He had last worked as a judge. He had become a depressive when he found no meaning in his work or fulfilment in his relationship and, after many warnings, had been sacked after repeatedly failing to appear in court. After that, his wife had left him and filed for divorce. He had had to sell his flat to pay the divorce settlement, and did not have the energy to look for a new home or a new job – that was how he had ended up under the bridge.

Though I could hardly imagine how someone could sink to these depths from such apparently secure circumstances, I understood him. I, too, thought it was more honest to sleep rough than to live a lie in a beautiful house and a well-paid job. We struck up a friendship there and then, and he was the first person I told my story to.

Now, I remember what he said to me one night when he had taken me aside for a serious talk.

'Senait, you don't belong here,' he said. 'You have your life before you. You're clever and beautiful, and you can make something of yourself, but not if you hang around with people like me. You won't achieve anything if you go on living on the streets.'

I gulped. He had refrained from making hints of this sort before because he had been happy to have me as a companion, but it was clear to me, too, that I could not go on sleeping rough. I had to think of something else by the end of the summer, for I was not one of the hardy souls who could sleep outside through the winter months. It would have been possible in Africa, where it was never colder than ten degrees celsius, but not in the wintry grime of Hamburg.

'Senait,' the judge said sternly, 'you will be lost here. You have to do something. Go to the Youth Office and tell them how you have come to be homeless, and you will get accommodation. I know you will.'

I took his advice, and everything was exactly as he said it would be. I was allocated accommodation immediately, and was able to pack my few things and move into a sort of young people's home the next day. We did not live under lock and key, but in a normal tower block with tiny flats in it, each consisting of a kitchen, a bathroom and two bedrooms, one for each person in the flat. Everyone was responsible for their own food and for tidying up, and there were social workers employed to check up on us. Those who failed to take care of their flat, or who just hung around at home without going to school or to work were not thrown out but nor were they given an allowance either – which was severe enough punishment for most people.

When I finally sat down on a bed of my own in a room of my own for the first time, I was so happy that I had to share my feelings with someone immediately. I rang my sisters up and, full of pride, gave them my new address and told them what a wonderful flat I was living in. That was a silly thing to do, for my father rang the next day, screamed and shouted like a lunatic and ordered me to go home. The social worker who I had spoken to when I moved in had already prepared me for a conversation like this – many parents who beat their children rang them or came to try to take them home.

I tried to talk to my father exactly as the social worker had instructed me to do. I told him that I was well taken care of here and that it was all perfectly legal for me to make my own decisions and for the state to be responsible for me. But my father hardly let me get a word in. He carried on screaming until all I could do was hang up. He rang a few more times to tell me to go home, but I stayed firm. After a couple of weeks, he stopped calling. Perhaps a part of him thought that it was no bad thing I no longer lived with him. What surprised me, though, was that he never tried to gain access to the home or to my flat. Perhaps he thought that if he caused trouble he would lose his own social security payments, which were his main source of income.

Injustice

All in all, I was lucky to be in the young people's home. The only minor disappointment came when I found out on the my first day there that I would not get my first allowance immediately, but a few weeks later. I did not know what I would do for money in that time.

After a couple of days in the home, I realised why this rule had been set. Most of the young people in the block were drug addicts and petty criminals. They had completed a vocational training course at school at best. They shoplifted at Aldi, begged at train stations and took every opportunity to swindle each other and the directors of the home. It was clear that if they had been given money as soon as they moved in, it would have been spent immediately.

I had run out of money. When I had only one ten mark note left in my wallet, my stomach began to flutter with anxiety. Living independently was one thing, but begging was another. I did not want to even attempt it, because I knew I could not sit humbly outside a department store waiting for one out of a thousand passers-by to let a one mark coin fall. Neither did I want to steal, for the former judge had painted a vivid picture of what happened to young offenders. I wanted to work for my money, but I would not be able to find a job immediately, and no one would pay me in advance. I had not been able to look for a job before because employers offering even appallingly paid casual work required a permanent address or at least a telephone number.

Asking the former judge for help was out of the question, for he had hardly any money either, and I was too proud to ask anyway. I saw us as equals, and I did not want to be dependent on him in any way. I felt the same about Stefan, who I was now in touch with again. It was also impossible to ask any of the young people in my block for a loan, for not merely did they have even less money than I did, they were heavily in debt.

The only choice left to me was to turn to my sisters for money. It was not easy for me to do this, and I really had to force myself to get on the U-Bahn to Eidelstedt. I would not have been able to ask them for money at school in front of all those people we knew.

I still had the key to the flat, but in my time on the streets, I had never once been tempted to return to take a shower or bath there, to take food from the kitchen or to lie on a soft bed in the daytime when everyone was out. I made my way there at a time when I was certain my father would not be home – he was always out in the afternoons. Nevertheless, my hands were trembling when I put the key in the lock, and my heart pounded in my ears as I stepped in.

Only Yaldiyan was at home. I felt a lump form in my throat when I saw that my room was exactly as I had left it – the bed was made and everything was in the same place – as if it had been waiting for my return.

I stood outside that room looking in, quite unable to move. Images of Stefan, life under the bridge, the former judge and the other tramps flitted through my head until I suddenly remembered what I was there for: money. I needed money.

Yaldiyan had money, but I did not dare to ask her for it after all. When she was not looking, I put my hand under her mattress and found what I wanted – her bank passbook. I knew that what I planned to do – steal from my own sister – was wrong, but there was no other way out. I resolved to return the money as soon as I could. Looking in the passbook, I saw that she had 4000 deutschmarks in her account. Reassured, I put the book in my pocket and left.

I went straight to the bank and withdrew 700 deutschmarks, for I was afraid that Yaldiyan would have noticed that her passbook was missing and blocked her account. It felt wonderful to have a thick wad of cash, but the knowledge that it did not belong to me gnawed inside. I knew that this was Yaldiyan's hard-earned money, accumulated from a series of badly paid jobs.

Two days later, Yaldiyan rang me in my flat. She came straight out and asked if I had her passbook. I gulped and lied through my teeth.

'What makes you think I have it? I would never …' I don't know if she believed me, but she did not take any further action, or I would have got into trouble.

A few days later, my conscience propelled me to go back to my father's flat and return the passbook. I had not withdrawn any more money, but I had also not replaced the 700 deutschmarks I had taken, of which I had only a little left. I knew that she would know I had taken it, for no one else had a key to the flat and no one else apart from Tzegehana and I knew where she kept her passbook.

But Yaldiyan never said anything. She did not get in touch with me or confront me, nor did she tell our father about it. To this day, I have never admitted to her that I stole her money. Every time I tried to approach the subject, my courage failed me at the last moment, and I read in her eyes the warning: 'All right, just this once, but never do it again.' And I never did. I hope she forgives me for that one time.

My own life

After I had settled into the new flat, where I was safe and could do as I wished, I was unstoppable. I could finally start living my own life, as I had always dreamed of doing.

I did not succumb to the miasma of hopelessness in that block of flats. The dossers and losers around me spurred me on to do more to help myself because I saw them as evidence of what lethargy would lead to.

My best friend in the young people's home was a girl called Fathma. She and I were the only ones in the home who went to a grammar school. We worked hard and got good grades. I started earning money from part-time jobs at the same time – from paper rounds or at McDonald's to begin with. Then I replied to an ad calling for models, and started getting small modelling contracts from an agency. It was routine work modelling swimming costumes for catalogues and pamphlets, but it paid incredibly well: 1000–1200 deutschmarks per day. Just a few weeks before that, I had not been able to earn so much money in an entire month. I felt very glad to be able to stand on my own two feet.

I was soon able to pay for my living expenses, though I still did not earn enough to pay for the accommodation in the home or for a flat of my own. I was able to pay for cable TV, though, which was a luxury that no one else in the block had. Up to half a dozen people often squeezed into my room to watch a particular programme or film. I found it a little annoying, but I also enjoyed it at the same time: now it was no longer me who had to ask other people for things, but others who came to me.

I did not just squirrel my money away – I sent several African children money regularly and donated some to a charity for the homeless based in a train station which had often helped me when I was on the streets. I also helped my friend the former judge, who was still living under the bridge. Before I started working as a catalogue model, I had worked in a bakery for some time, and had brought him fresh bread rolls which would otherwise have been thrown away every day after the bakery closed.

I lived in the young people's home for two years, in which time I also started on my musical career. Looking back, I often wonder where I got the energy and the time to do everything at the same time: go to school, study, work, help others and make music. I had finally bought myself a keyboard that worked, as well as a CD player and piles of CDs. I listened to all kinds of music and went to lots of gigs and clubs. I had the radio on all the time – when I was studying, when I was doing my homework, and sometimes even when I was sleeping. I mostly watched music programmes on TV, drinking in all the music videos, and soon gained a good idea of how the music industry worked.

Most of the hits were structured around a few chords, a simple rhythm and lyrics that addressed love and loneliness in various different ways, none of them particularly original. After a couple of months of studying the chart hits intensively, I decided that it was surely possible for me to break into the industry.

I sat down at my keyboard and played around with several tunes. I sang in Tigrinya first, then in German, but I liked singing in English most of all. Finally, I decided it was time to take my music out into the world. Through people I had met in clubs, I had got to know some studio musicians, one of whom said he knew someone in a record company. When I asked him, though, it turned out that he only had the man's business card and did not really know him at all. Someone else then said he would be able to sneak us into a semi-professional studio. I took two musicians whom I had only met a couple of days earlier to this studio, and we recorded some songs. We also did one or two live gigs at birthday parties and clubs, but this was not what I really wanted to do. I dreamed of releasing my own CD.

We sent our demo tape to the address on the business card, but it was eventually sent back without even a note. However, about a year later we got financing for a single – only a couple of thousand copies, but at least it was out on the market. It was a total flop and only sold a few hundred copies, probably to friends of the musicians. The rest ended up at flea markets or in the bin. But then a miracle happened – by some roundabout means, the single ended up in South Korea, where it was to become a number one hit two years later.

I was sixteen years old, with no real home of my own, but I had a number one hit single in South Korea. In Germany, musicians were awarded a golden record when their albums had sold a 150,000 copies, but in South Korea only a fraction of the sales were needed to achieve this honour. So when I was awarded one it was no big deal, but it was significant for me, and made me incredibly happy. This was something I would not even have dreamed of not so long ago: I was making music that I liked, getting acclaim for it, was having a lot of fun, and I was making a little money as well. I was flying so high I felt I barely needed to get on a plane to go to Korea to perform at a few gigs and promote my record to the crowds of enthusiastic Korean fans. The start of my musical career was one of the happiest times in my life.

Heart of fire

In the midst of this happiness, I did not forget my friend the former judge, without whose help I would not have made it to where I was. He was the one who had told me I was worth something and would make something of myself when no one else, myself included, had believed it. After I returned from Korea, I went to look for him to tell him about my trip, but when I walked down to the bridge, our old spot was empty. He was not there, and all his things – his mattress, the chairs, blankets and pillows – were gone, too. I walked up and down by the canal looking under the bridges where we had sometimes visited fellow homeless people. But all I found were empty Coke cans and used condoms.

I panicked – had something happened to my friend? I ran back up to the street and looked around. On the other side of the road was a luxury hotel – we had often mocked the finely dressed guests and their ridiculous behaviour, talking about how short the path was between a five-star hotel and sleeping under the bridge. We had got chatting with the hotel doormen, who had sometimes given us a couple of deutschmarks. One of them stood by the revolving doors in his silly uniform now. I ran over to him but, because other hotel employees were nearby, he pretended not to know me and not to know what I was asking about.

'We've driven away all the tramps,' he said shortly. 'The police helped us. They are not allowed to live there any longer because it disturbs our guests.' He had no idea where they had gone.

Aghast, I screamed at him, 'They're not tramps! You don't know anything, you stupid doorman! You're barely educated! You just carry the bags here, and my friend is a judge!' The man did not react, but clicked his fingers a couple of times. Two bellboys hurried over and pulled me away.

I went on with my search, still holding the couple of slices of cake and the bag of fruit I had brought with me. I went on looking for my friend the rest of that day, going to the charity for the homeless based in the train station and asking other homeless people I knew on Mönckebergstrasse if they had seen him. I spoke to every passing tramp, but no one knew what had happened to my friend. When I met up with two friends that evening and told them how upset I was by the whole thing, they were amazed that I still cared about my friends from the streets now that I was successful.

'Senait,' said Mariam. 'You have such good heart – I can't believe it.'

'No,' I said. 'You're wrong. I don't have a good heart.' I was not speaking from false modesty – I really did not feel that I deserved her praise. I thought about how I had crept into my sister's room and stolen those few hundred deutschmarks from her. I remembered how we had fought and how I had pushed her to the floor. I thought of how I had lied to Stefan and how I had shot with a gun during the war. And images of how I had joined my father in winding up the neighbours or how I had disobeyed Uncle Haile to go out in Khartoum flitted through my mind.

'You don't know me,' I said to Mariam. 'My heart is not good, but it burns inside me, and so strongly!' I was not a good person, but a passionate one, full of feelings that sometimes almost consumed me with their intensity. 'Perhaps I have a heart of fire,' I said. From the blank look that my friends exchanged with each other, I knew that my comparison was lost on them. I changed the subject quickly before I revealed too much of myself. We chatted about the latest boy bands, about who was going out with whom, and where we wanted to go clubbing that night.

But my heart of fire had a little goodness in it after all. To this day, I still sponsor a group of African children, some of whom are now teenagers. At Christmas time in Hamburg every year, I used to fill a couple of shopping trolleys with food, fruit and cigarettes and go up and down Mönckebergstrasse distributing presents to the homeless people there. Soon they all knew my name.

'Senait!' they called from a distance when they saw me. I did that because I could never forget how many of them had helped me when I myself had nothing. Secretly, I also hoped to bump into the former judge, but I never met him again.

Once, I asked Mariam, my best friend at the time, if she wanted to come down to Mönckebergstrasse with me to help distribute the Christmas presents. I shared so much with Mariam that I also wanted to share with her these moments of bringing happiness to others. But Mariam did not want to come with me – she used another appointment as an excuse. Later on, I learned from other people that she often complained about my charitable streak, my soft spot for tramps and other aspects of my personality. Our friendship cooled rapidly after that and I soon lost contact with her.

Years later I bumped into Mariam again in a club. She pretended not to recognise me at first, but when I greeted her in a friendly way, she had no escape. She said she felt very guilty about how she had behaved.

'Senait, I spoke badly about you behind your back,' she said.

'I know.' I waved her admission away, for the last thing I wanted was to take revenge. 'I just don't understand the whole thing. I shared my life with you – you were in my flat every day and I was always there for you when you wanted to talk. We were so close – what happened?' I was happy to be able finally to ask the question that had turned over in my mind all these years.

Mariam took a moment to reply. 'I was jealous of you. You had your own flat and everything – it was too much for me. You overcame every difficulty – I just couldn't take it.'

'But we were friends! Why did you never talk to me about it?'

We fell into each other's arms, crying.

That is the way I am: I do not have it in me to hate anyone or think of them badly. I just want to know why people behave the way they do, and I almost always find out why. I don't like pretending that nothing is wrong and just accepting things as they are. I cannot have things eating into me.

That was the first wave of self-awareness I had after I had begun to live an independent life in Hamburg – earning my own money from my own job, living in my own flat, with friends of my own. I did not want to just accept everything as it was – I had done it too often in the past to be able to do it again, and my energy and my time were too precious to me to waste on obstructions. I was like a humming top, spinning away everything negative the people or the environment around me tried to pass on to me. I thought I could go on doing that for ever, but I was very wrong.

Growing up

Strangely, I found everything easier in the first few years after I left home than I did later on. I had embraced a new life filled with an optimism that seems almost foolhardy in retrospect. A lot of things came to me easily: my first flat, jobs, the modelling contract, my first CD, the hit single in Korea and many friendships. That was all much more than a sixteen-year-old could have expected. Perhaps because all this went so smoothly, I underestimated the rocky path that everyone has to negotiate between youth and adulthood.

I wanted to wipe out the shadows of my past, but that proved impossible. I still cannot today, but I no longer want to forget the past. When I was younger, though, I would have done anything to erase those haunting memories, which could leap out at me during the happiest of times. When shopping at the supermarket, I would suddenly have an image of the starving children in the Jebha, or when walking through an underground tunnel to get the U-Bahn, I would suddenly start because I could see myself and my fellow soldiers speeding through the desert at night in a lorry, pursued by enemy soldiers with grenades. In the stairwell of the young people's home I felt as if guns and snipers, or trainers who were trying to hound me to the shooting ground, waited around every corner, so that I was bathed in sweat by the time I got to the door of my little flat.

It was worst at night. I left the TV on when I went to bed – I still do today. I needed the moving images and light to keep the dark memories at bay – I often lay awake for hours, staring at the TV, until falling into an exhausted sleep. It was not just the images from my past, but the people, too, who would not leave me alone. My father tried everything to get me back under his power. He rang me himself or asked friends or my sisters to tell me that he disapproved of my new independence, and was afraid that I would get drawn into drugs, alcohol, prostitution, and so on.

At first, my sisters got in touch with me over and over again, trying to persuade me to go home. It was a paradoxical situation: they were suffering living with my father and would have liked to have escaped him themselves, but they also did not like the fact that I had managed to get away and build my own life. Equally absurd was the fact the our father tried to gain influence over me through my sisters while forbidding them any contact with me. He painted such a bad picture of me that Yaldiyan and Tzegehana began to believe him, and started avoiding me.

Only Uncle Haile gave me any support. After I had run away from home we managed to speak to each other on the phone a couple of times.

'I hear you're living on your own now,' he said.

'Yes,' I admitted. I had not told him that I had run away because I was afraid it would upset him, but since he now knew everything, I decided to speak freely. 'Too much has passed between my father and me.'

Haile merely replied, 'I don't want to interfere. You alone know what you have done and what you want to do. You are grown up now, you are your own woman.'

His wise words brought me to tears. Here, finally, was someone I trusted, who did not blame me for anything, who believed I was capable of living my own life and wished the best for me in my future. It was a life that I fought for with all my might.

Travel

I wanted to see the world, and all on my own, too. I had been forced into travelling so often in the past – herded into a lorry or on to a bus, walking on foot or sitting on a donkey – and been taken to places that I had not wanted to go to: to join the Jebha, to the battlefront, to join my father in Germany. Now I wanted to decide for myself where I was going.

My friends said a girl ought not to travel alone, especially not to exotic countries, but I went anyway. I flew to Barbados, Jamaica, the Dominican Republic, Trinidad, Tanzania, Ethiopia, Eritrea, Turkey and South Korea. The South Korea trip was at the invitation of the record company, but I booked the other trips myself, and went for two or three weeks at a time, carrying nothing but a small rucksack of clothes with me.

Always very busy seeing to the thousand and one last-minute details planning a trip entails, the first day of every holiday was spent catching up on missed sleep, mostly on a beach, for I was never able to sleep on the plane for excitement. In the evening, I looked for a cheap hotel or a holiday flat, and most of the time, I would get an ancient rental car as well. Then I went shopping, cooked myself a big meal and walked through the town, getting to know people.

My friends in Germany could hardly believe what I was doing. 'You're sixteen,' they said (or seventeen, eighteen or nineteen – too young, in any case). 'Girls your age are not supposed to be hanging around on the beach by themselves or going out alone at night. Anyone could attack you, rape you or rob you …' They painted lurid pictures of everything that could go wrong.

But nothing ever did happen to me. I did not dress provocatively or wear any make-up when I was travelling, but instead wore thick dreadlocks tied under a colourful scarf and combat trousers with sturdy Doc Martens. I managed to do everything that everyone said I shouldn't – sleep on the beach, sit by a campfire through the night with total strangers, drink gin or rum and smoke joints, the full works of a Caribbean holiday. I returned home after every trip feeling wonderfully refreshed.

I carried on holidaying alone, unlike my classmates at the grammar school, who went on holiday with their parents to the Baltic Sea or to Majorca, staying in cosy family hotels or in their own summer houses. When I told them about my adventures, they said, 'Are you mad? What would happen if someone tried to kill you?'

'So be it then,' I said. 'I'm not afraid. I want to see the world.'

I can no longer travel so freely today. I have become more cautious. When I was a teenager I could almost have passed for a boy when I tucked my hair under a headscarf. I had a flat chest, and cheeky behaviour to match – there was nothing feminine about me then. I was fearless and confident and full of energy which came from breaking free to live my own life. The feeling that I could conquer the world was better protection than any mace spray could ever have been.

It was not thieves, murderers or rapists that I needed protection from, though, but myself and the storms that raged within me. My newfound independence felt amazing, but it also meant that I had to deal with my problems alone. I am sorry to say that it was alcohol and cannabis that I used to help me cope with these problems. I never tried any hard drugs though they were offered to me many times – I never took coke or heroin, I never even smoked a cigarette. But I drank myself into oblivion, when all my worries and memories melted into a blur. It was often all I could do to stagger into a taxi when I left a bar or a club at night, and sometimes I did not know how I had made it to my own bed. When I woke up the next morning I was filled with shame and self-hatred, but inevitably there were times when I went out and did the same thing all over again that very evening.

Stefan

My problems at that time were not to do with my past or my family, but with my boyfriend, Stefan. He was my first love and I thought he was the man who would determine the course of my life. I am glad that did not turn out to be the case.

Stefan was very spoilt, and often behaved as if everyone around him had to dance to his tune. Despite this, we stayed together for four and a half years – an astounding feat considering all our friends' relationships lasted only a couple of months. Our relationship lasted so long not because it was a good one but because we were co-dependent and because I failed to realise this. He needed me as someone to cling to in his rootless life, someone who was on his side. I needed him because I thought he could offer me a life of excitement, a life worth living.

Stefan took a keen interest in my life. I was glad that he wanted to know about me, but frightened by how he might respond. So, I lied to him about my family, telling him how great my parents were. He soon got suspicious, and kept asking me if he could meet them, but I told him that my father was very busy and my mother had moved back to Africa.

He would have been totally unable to grasp the truth of my family life. He had spent all his life at home with parents who granted his every wish – especially for money – and he had never needed to worry about anything.

I always pretended that I had loads of money and lived it up in the bars and clubs just like Stefan. Money meant nothing to him, for he just had to stretch his hand out to his father for more the next day, but for me, it meant hours of work at McDonald's, at the bakery or, later on, modelling for catalogue shoots. I never told him about any of this, or let him pay for me – I was far too proud. Instead, I gritted my teeth and worked twice as hard.

But my lies, which he saw through one by one, destroyed a great deal in our relationship. I lost his trust, and soon he stopped believing anything I said. He constantly suspected me of being unfaithful to him, though his suspicion was quite absurd, for I felt far too bound to Stefan to think of betraying him. I loved him and I was dependent on him. The intimacy we shared was quite enough for me – in fact, it was much too much for me.

Sleeping with Stefan was like torture for me. I was not in any state to enjoy it. He realised that sex was laden with emotional problems for me, but was not especially sensitive about it. In a bad mood he would call me frigid, or a lesbian. But, if he was feeling affectionate, he tapped my head tenderly and said, more to himself than to me, 'What's going on in that little head of yours?'

I could no more answer that question than he could. I did not want to answer it, for I had not come to the point yet when I could speak freely about my past, let alone about the sexual aspects of it. So I stayed silent whenever we were in bed together. He must have thought I did not care, but I was actually paralysed with pain – physical pain and the pain of knowing its origin.

Poison

Stefan could be extremely charming, but he was also extremely temperamental. Our relationship was a roller-coaster ride, and it was only after a while that I realised why he kept descending into a morass of hatred, aggression and violence.

One day, I found what I took to be a few dirty erasers in his room. I put them in his pencil case, but he kept taking them out and putting them elsewhere. I wondered why he couldn't leave them in the pencil case. Irritated I asked him, 'What do you do with those rubbers?' but he avoided replying.

This went on until once I showed one of them to the cleaning lady who was in Stefan's room. She told Stefan's mother about it, and his mother said to me, 'That's not a rubber, it's hash. They crumble it into tobacco and smoke it in joints.'

I felt incredibly stupid. I had had vague notions that the rubbers were drugs before, but had not wanted to admit the truth to myself. I had hoped that Stefan was clean, but he was everything but that. I started finding bits of burnt foil and bent spoons in his room. Once he told me he was just popping out to the shop in the petrol station, but only returned four days later with incredibly dilated pupils. Then a couple of guys I didn't know started hanging out in his flat listening to pounding techno music all day. Even at that stage, I had already started thinking that this was not the life I wanted and that Stefan was not the man for me.

Things got worse. Once when I was sorting through Stefan's washing before putting it in the washing machine, I found a bag full of white pills. Again, I did not want to see what was before my eyes, and put what I assumed to be 'headache pills' in the medicine cabinet, and when Stefan was looking for the bag in a frenzy a few days later, I told him where I had put it. He grabbed the bag, and, sweating, told me, 'Senait, this is not aspirin. These are the miracle pills that help me keep it all together. It's ecstasy.'

The more I got to know about Stefan's drug habit, the clearer I could see that there was only one direction he could go – downwards. I stayed by his side when he first started taking drugs, and I was still with him when he started losing the plot – until he gave up the fight altogether. He tried to blame me. When he had had too much, he screamed, 'This is all because of you! You're destroying me, you psycho woman, you hysterical bitch …'

After a couple of months, I started believing him. I asked myself what I was doing wrong, how had I brought Stefan to this and how could I help him? But, then, the more I thought about what he said, the less sense his accusations made to me. One day I spoke my mind.

'That's not true, Stefan,' I said. 'I don't take drugs. I don't even smoke. I'm doing well in school. I'm not the one who disappears into the techno clubs for three days at a time. I'm not the one who needs a fix every day just to carry on living. The first time I met you you were prancing around in front of the mirror – there was something wrong even then. You're older than me, too – you were already eighteen when we first knew each other. So you surely must be more grown up than me, more mature. Everyone's got to take responsibility for themselves eventually. You can't just blame it on me. OK, I'm not easy to live with, but you don't seem to be able to live without getting high every day – nothing else matters to you. The only thing I can blame myself for is for still being together with you!'

Though visibly moved by my little speech, it had no lasting effect. Everything carried on exactly as before.

Over time, I got to know more not only about Stefan's life but also about his family's. There could hardly have been a greater contrast between my family and his. My family was barely worthy of the term, but Stefan's family was an intact one – father, mother and son – extremely successful, well-to-do and happy, apart from one failing: none of them had any time for each other. They only addressed problems when they could no longer be ignored – everything else was solved with money. Whatever they didn't have, they bought. From the outside, they seemed to lack nothing, but anything that could not be put on the credit card was swept under the carpet.

Polar opposites

Stefan's parents were very good to me — better than they were to their own son, who they sensed was slipping away from them. They did not want to acknowledge the reason for this — they refused to take his drug habit seriously.

While I was living at the young people's home, I would sometimes go to stay with Stefan's family for a few months at a time, popping back to the home now and then. I did not want to give up my room there because the thought of total dependence on Stefan and his family was anathema to me.

It did not take long for me to be taken fully into the family. His mother introduced me to visitors as her daughter-in-law and his father sang my praises to everyone, telling them how smart, hardworking and beautiful I was. They often invited me to go away with them, always on luxury holidays that I could not have afforded myself. Stefan wanted to hang around in the hotel or the holiday apartment, ideally eating schnitzel and chips, but I had not come to the Caribbean to lie by the pool eating schnitzel and chips. I wanted to see something of the country and its people.

I would have loved to have gone to Africa with Stefan, but he had no desire to go there. 'Urgh, Africa! They eat with their hands there, don't they?' He spoke about the continent I came from as if it was an infectious disease. I could never have introduced him to my family there — he wouldn't have known what to say to them. It would have driven him mad to get up at four in the morning to go fishing with my grandfather or to sit on the floor eating out of a communal bowl with his hands. He thought third world countries were disgusting.

I remember the time when we were walking through Puerto Plata in the Dominican Republic, looking for the market, and a woman gave us some banana fritters to eat. Stefan took a fritter and bit into it, but then went round the corner, spat out his mouthful and threw the rest away. It tasted delicious, but Stefan thought it was full of germs.

Stefan was extremely spoilt. He had 400 deutschmarks pocket

money a week from the age of twelve, and at eighteen he had two cars and a holiday flat by the Baltic Sea to boot. He did not know life any other way, and I could not expect him to take on my version of life. I accepted and understood the way he lived, but I did not like it.

Stefan's father realised how difficult it was for me to earn the money to keep up with Stefan's lifestyle, and now and then he tried to give me money, which I refused. It was important to me to earn my own money, for I would not have been able to look Stefan in the eye and tell him honestly what I thought about everything otherwise. I would not have felt that I was his equal if I had not been able to pay for myself.

Stefan saw no problem in being financed by his parents. Getting a job to earn money for himself never occurred to him, even though his drug habit cost so much. 'Why should I work?' he said. 'I'm going to inherit everything anyway.' He went to his father instead and asked for extra money on top of his allowance. His father handed out a couple of hundred deutschmarks to him the way other fathers give five-mark notes to their kids for an ice-cream.

Stefan was materialistic and possessive, not only about things, but people too. He was used to getting his own way and treating everything and everyone around him as his possessions but he soon realised that he could never lock me in or own me, and that made him angry. He would have liked me to have been dependent on his family – that way he could ensure that I would stay by his side for ever

When my father discovered that I was living with Stefan's family more than I was in the young people's home he was very disapproving. The fact that I was not under his control and that someone else was keeping his daughter hurt his pride, so much so that he rang Stefan's father to offer him money for my board and lodging.

'Don't worry about the money,' Stefan's father said firmly. 'We earn enough. We like having Senait with us. If she wants to go, she can go, but if she would like to stay, she is welcome to stay for as long as she likes.'

My father had to accept this whether he liked it or not. I found the incident deeply embarrassing because I had always lied to Stefan's parents about my family.

Lies

They saw through my lies eventually. Stefan's father said to me one day, 'Senait, we are very fond of you, but please don't lie to us again. We know everything.'

I wanted to sink into the ground. I attempted to explain myself, to describe what it meant to me to live in a perfect family like Stefan's and how it compared to the ruins of my own family, but Stefan's father waved my reply away. 'You don't have to explain anything. It's fine.'

That was the end of the conversation. I will always be grateful to him for his simple acceptance. It was a wonderful feeling no longer to be deceiving him or myself. I had pretended that I had wonderful parents and sisters with whom I had a close and loving relationship. Even though I had never met my mother, I sometimes believed my own lies, which resulted in bouts of depression when the cascade of lies collapsed about me. Friends at school whom I had deceived turned away from me when they saw through my fabrications. 'She's a nutter,' they said. 'She's lying through her teeth. Nothing she says is true.'

Yet I was the one who suffered most from my deception. The only thing which would have hurt me more than lying was telling the truth. What sixteen-year-old would have wanted to admit to her friends that she was being abused – beaten, shouted at and humiliated – by her father every day? Who would not rather have pretended that she had broken her arm in a fall? Which girl would have told her boyfriend that she could not be intimate with him because she had so many wounds – visible and invisible – that made sex intolerable?

When Stefan and I were making out I let him do what he

wanted while I reached for the remote control and flicked through the TV channels. Enraged, Stefan lashed out which pushed me deeper into my cocoon of numbness and silence while he sought oblivion in chemical substances. Eventually we came to terms with the fact that our relationship just wasn't working out – and that I was to lose my first boyfriend to drugs.

Standing on my own feet

The time immediately after Stefan and I split up was a good one. Just before my nineteenth birthday I officially moved out of the young people's home into my own flat. The home was no longer a place of liberation for me but an oppressive environment where most people were much younger and much more messed-up.

I was now responsible for my own life, with no supervision from the social workers or youth office workers at the home. I had found a flat, an apprenticeship and a couple of jobs, for one job was far from sufficient to pay for my living expenses. I had stopped the catalogue modelling because I regarded it increasingly as a form of prostitution. I had also stopped waitressing because I never lasted more than three or four months in a job. I didn't like to be ordered about – I was too proud and impatient and too insistent on doing things my way. I wanted to be my own boss, but I was not there yet.

I spent more and more time working on my demo tapes to develop a musical style of my own and tried working with other musicians, with the aim of getting a recording contract. To make sure I didn't live the life of an impoverished artist, though, I kept a 'safe' career option going at the same time, and started an apprenticeship as a legal clerk. The firm I was working for in Hamburg had just acquired four Arab clients – two from Dubai and two from the Yemen – in divorce cases involving a great deal of money. A twenty-one-year-old woman who had been married to her twenty-nine-year-old husband for a year got a settlement of 4.5 million deutschmarks.

I was impressed that an Arab woman – who normally received

lavish presents from her husband but was otherwise treated like a slave – was rebelling, and getting justice. I threw myself into the job, interpreting from Arabic into German and vice-versa, and really enjoyed the work. I soon started receiving other requests to work as an Arabic–German interpreter or even a Tigrinya–German interpreter. I was able to translate Arabic and Tigrinya – which is spoken in Ethiopia as well as in Eritrea – into German or English almost equally well.

My personal life, however, was not going as well as my professional life. My new boyfriend, Christian, was another spoilt rich kid. He had grown up in boarding school and had very little self-confidence. His father was German and his mother was Iranian – she adored me, and feared nothing more than that her son would get together with a German girl. She called Germans 'potatoheads' and sometimes joked that 'my son will be marrying a potatohead soon. But I don't want a potatohead. I want you!'

Christian's father did not like foreigners, though he had married one himself. Perhaps he just did not like black people. 'Oh God!' he said to Christian in front of me. 'Are you bringing a nigger into the house?'

'What planet are you living on?' I screamed. 'Times have changed and …'

I did not get any further, for he threw me out.

Next came Klaus. He was wonderful, and is one of my best friends to this day.

10

Mother Africa

When I returned to Africa for the first time, as I stepped out of the plane at Asmara, everything I had repressed for so long came flooding back. It was August and the heat was like a wall before me, pressing me back against the cabin door. My throat constricted at the sight of the glaring white light, the blazing blue sky and the crowd of people on the runway. I struggled for air and, as my sisters pressed up against me from behind, I fell down the flight of steps.

As I struggled to get up, Yaldiyan took my arm. 'Senait, I know what it is,' she said. 'You've dreamed about this. You have talked about this in your sleep.'

Yaldiyan told me that I used to sleep talk about how I would grow wings when I arrived in Africa and fly free as a bird. A dozen or so passengers – all black – stood around and listened as Yaldiyan talked. They smiled, laughed and clapped when they heard about my dream. I knew then that I had come home.

I had waited so long for this, scrimping and saving to pay for the journey to find my mother. I knew she now lived in Ethiopia, not Eritrea, but I did not know exactly where or even what her surname was. All I knew was that she was called Adhanet.

My parents had run into each other in Ethiopia a couple of times after my father left for Europe. He had visited Ethiopia but not Eritrea, where he was on the wanted list of deserters since the EPLF had beaten the ELF – of which he was *still* a fanatical supporter. Both my father and my mother – when I eventually met her – told me that they had not spoken when they had bumped into each other. They did not speak about the past, about themselves or about me, their link.

My father had instructed Tzegehana to warn me about my mother. 'Make sure that Senait does not eat anything at her mother's,' he said. 'You have to watch out – she will definitely try to poison Senait.'

I could not understand why my mother would want to do this, yet a little of my father's suspicion seeped into my soul. Perhaps she hated me because I had lived on against her will? With brooding thoughts like this in my head, I flew on to Addis Ababa, the capital of Ethiopia, with Tzegehana, while Yaldiyan remained in Asmara. It took two weeks to find out where my mother lived, and a family friend drove Tzegehana and me to meet her. We were laden with presents: coffee, tea, flour, sugar, oil, fruit and other daily necessities. I stared out of the car window at the rows of low houses, the dusty streets full of people, the beggars, the hordes of ragged women and children, people carrying trussed-up chickens home from the market, the horse carts, the donkeys and the ancient buses belching fumes. It was the first time I had seen all this for years – familiar from my childhood yet also now quite strange and remote.

Meeting

At last we stopped. Had we arrived? Nervous, I got out of the car and stood in the street for a moment, feeling lost, then I pulled myself together and we stepped out of the blazing sunshine, through an open door into a hut. I couldn't see anything at first – like most huts, this one did not have any windows, only a skylight, which was covered with a piece of corrugated iron to keep the heat out. In the confusion, I had forgotten to take off my sunglasses, but gradually my eyes got used to the dim interior and I could make out a few shapes: a wardrobe, a bed, a table, a couple of baskets and boxes. There was a small stove on the floor and a spirit stove for coffee.

A tall, haggard woman sat on a chair in the furthest corner of the hut. Her hair was grey, combed back from her forehead and tightly braided in the customary way, knotted into a large bun. She was wrapped in traditional white robes, and her feet were clad in sandals. She sat motionless, looking at the floor. Only her hands were moving – twisting in her lap. I did not know what to do, so I just remained standing where I was. Her face swam out of the darkness slowly: the high cheekbones, the generous lips. She had strong features – my features. This woman was my mother and she was utterly strange to me.

The family friend stepped forward and said to the woman that her daughter had come. He asked her if she could guess which one was her daughter. My mother pointed at me and said, 'That's my daughter. She looks like her father.'

I felt as if I was leaving the world I knew behind as I walked over to the woman who was my mother and sat down next to her. She stroked my hair gingerly and said, 'You have beautiful hair, Senait.'

I was unable to move or speak at first. It took me a long time to say anything. We finally began to tell each other, haltingly, about our lives. My mother had suffered a great deal during the six years she had spent in prison for attempted infanticide. Later she remarried and had three more children after me: two girls and a boy. A few months after the birth of the third child, her husband had returned from the battlefront, injured and no longer fit for service.

'What am I supposed to do with a cripple?' she asked him. She laid the three-month-old baby on his knee and walked out on them.

I felt stiff and uncomfortable, and incredibly distant from my mother. Sitting there with her felt unreal to me. To think that she had left her injured husband, a small baby and two little children just like that! I wondered if her story of sorrow had any light or goodness in it, and I waited, in vain, for any expression of regret from her. Before me was a poor, despairing woman who did not know what to do with her life. She had as little control over the suffering she had caused as over the suffering she had endured.

I buried my face in my hands and wept uncontrollably. My mother thought I was crying because I was moved by her story, and made jerky movements to comfort me with hands that had never given much comfort. I was not crying for her, though, but for myself – my story, my family and my life. I was crying for the darkness that had been in my life from its very beginning. My mother's story had only let more darkness flood in.

Seeing that I was inconsolable, my mother did what most women in Africa do when they feel helpless. She stood up and started busying herself in the house. She lit a small charcoal fire in the middle of the hut and roasted a few coffee beans which she then pounded with a small iron pestle and mortar. She filled a traditional round earthen coffee pot with water and poured the ground coffee into the pot using a woven fan bent into a V-shape. She put the pot on the fire and fanned it until the viscous liquid bubbled over.

Night fell, and I managed to gain mastery over my feelings again. Watching my mother's practised movements comforted not only me but her too. We resumed talking while we drank the strong, sweet coffee, squatting on the tiny, home-made stools that women traditionally sit on in these huts. I asked her who the father of her other children was and how could I find him so as to track down my sisters and look after them.

'It's not worth it,' she said. 'Don't bother. If you have come to open old wounds, then leave my house.'

The darkness spread over me again. I could feel it seeping into my soul. 'Not worth it?' I asked.

'No,' my mother said shortly, more to herself than to me. 'That man was a good-for-nothing and his children will be exactly the same.'

She was completely wrong, and incredibly pessimistic, in the way that people who are very frustrated and downtrodden can be. But I was unable to reply because I believed her in that moment –

I felt as if I was the product of some evil myself and was convinced that I had come into the world to embody that evil.

I had never felt so despairing about myself before. These two people can't be my parents, I thought to myself, they just can't. Yet there was no doubt: here was my mother Adhanet, and my father was Ghebrehiwet Mehari.

I sat there brooding hopelessly. I couldn't understand how my mother could have so little feeling as to tell me to my face, 'Well, you know, I did not want to live with a cripple, and what was I supposed to do with his children? *His* children ...' She never thought for a moment that it would hurt me to know that because I was just as much her child as my half-brother and sisters were.

I wanted to say to her, 'Now I can see how you could have done it ...' but I stopped myself, thinking, why hurt your mother? She must have felt very intimidated by me: I was educated, attractive, and so much better off than her that I could support her. What else could I do for her?

Sometimes I make the mistake of thinking that other people think the same way that I do — that they, like me, have learned the lessons from their childhood and strive not to be like their parents. It would have been a mistake, too, to have expected my mother to have learned this lesson. Never have I wanted to be less like my parents than when I sat there with my mother, and never have I more wanted to throw off the burden of the past.

Despite all this, I did not hate or despise my mother. I did not feel pity, annoyance or rage. I just felt sad, incredibly sad about everything that had happened, over which I had no control.

We said our farewells after coffee. There was no great ceremony or sign of emotion. My mother seemed to find it perfectly normal for me to drop by from Hamburg to see her in Addis Ababa. She embraced me and asked me to send her money, but did not ask if we would see each other again in the couple of weeks I would be in Africa. She did not want, or did not dare, to ask.

I tottered outside to the car and our family friend drove Tzegehana and me back into the city. It was still early enough for us to go out again, if we desired, but I did not want to see anyone. I went straight to my room and did what I had been longing to do since we had arrived in Africa: I cried and cried and cried until there were no more tears left.

I did go and see my mother once more, but nothing much more happened. She made coffee, we sat in silence for a while, she talked a little, I talked a lot and we exchanged addresses and phone numbers. I don't know what I had been expecting, but I left feeling disappointed.

But something had woken within me. I realised that my roots were in Africa and that I had to come here to learn about myself. I had to talk to the people here, breathe the air of the East African highlands and look at the way the mountains beyond the city rose against the reddening evening sky only to sink into the darkness of a clear starry night. I could find myself here if I reached out with an open heart to the land and its people.

That visit to my mother took place in the summer of 1993. Since then I have been to Eritrea every year, sometimes to Ethiopia as well. I generally go at Christmas time to avoid the incredible heat of the summer. In winter it is like paradise because the temperatures in the highlands never drop below ten degrees celsius at night or rise above thirty degrees in the day, and it is almost always sunny.

I never met my mother again. Apart from the first week of my life, the only other time I spent with her was when I visited her in Addis Ababa on 14 August 1993, stumbling into the darkness of her house to feel her hands, see her face and listen to her bitter story. Exactly one year later, on 14 August 1994, she was sitting on a bus travelling from the mountain village of Adi Keyh in Eritrea to Asmara when the brakes failed and the bus plunged hundreds of metres over the mountainside into a rocky ravine.

It was about seven o'clock in the evening when I visited my mother. She died at almost exactly the same time one year later in that bus. I do not think that this was a coincidence, but fate. I find comfort in thinking that the last year of her life was perhaps her best, not least because of my help. She was free of financial worries and also free of feelings of hatred or revenge, fear of persecution, war and unrest. She would have been able to enjoy her life – inasmuch as the burden of her past would allow her to do so – and I am glad she had that year.

The past

Together with my sisters, I also visited their mother Abrehet, our father's second wife, who lived in Adi Keyh in Eritrea. I will never forget her saying to me, 'Senait, your father has made many mistakes. You are the only thing he has got right, but not through anything he has done.'

Abrehet did not harbour any feelings of hatred or revenge towards my father, only sympathy, not only for her own daughters but for me as well. She told us what our father had done to her and her parents: he had beaten her parents and broken her mother's leg and had kicked her in the belly while she was pregnant with Yaldiyan. We wept to hear all this, and wondered how our father could live with himself. To this day, he has not apologised to any of the people he has caused so much pain and suffering.

My meeting with Uncle Haile in Asmara was more cheerful. It was the first time I had seen him since I had left Khartoum. He lived in Holland now, but was in Eritrea on a visit. Unlike my father, he was able to return to Eritrea whenever he wanted because he was not a political refugee and had also never been in the army. When I told him that his beatings had left a mark on me for life, he only laughed as if to say, 'What do you mean by that?' He did not understand that I had been damaged by his punishments. I see this not so much as his fault as a general problem with the way children are brought up in African culture.

I still thought Uncle Haile was a wonderful person, and loved him more than anyone else – and that was what counted. The beatings and the pain belonged in the past and I understood

My newfound family in Adi Keyh: Abrehet (front, right), mother of Tzegehana and Yaldiyan, her youngest daughter Fiori (front, middle), and two of my father's sisters (standing behind, right). In the middle is a Coptic priest from Adi Keyh.

that he had not beaten us to inflict injury but to show us when he thought we were behaving badly. Uncle Haile was not a disturbed personality like my father – he simply knew no other way of bringing up children.

I have long given up trying to explain to people in Africa that beating is no way to teach children right from wrong. Only when they come to live in Europe do they understand this. I, too, only realised that it was possible to raise children without violence once I was in Germany. There I was free to have my own opinion, and I would not be beaten simply for disagreeing with someone. Recognising that I had rights was incredibly liberating. In Africa beatings and injustice are part of everyday life.

I could not speak of these larger questions to Haile. Africa does not engage in self-reflection or examination of the past. There are no counsellors or therapists to turn to. Violence is not discussed, it is simply accepted. Above all, what matters in Africa is basic survival – where the next meal or drink of water is coming from, trying not to fall ill because a visit to the doctor cannot be paid for. No one has the luxury of examining their feelings. Children do not go to their parents and say, 'Mum, Dad, I have to tell you something', 'I have a boyfriend' or 'I need to go on the Pill.' Strictly speaking, there are no 'mums' or 'dads' in the cosy, intimate way Europeans think of them – the relationships are so different. In Africa, 'mother' and 'father' are better used to describe functions, blood relations or dependencies, but nothing more.

It was these realisations that I brought back with me from my home country, along with the souvenirs of clay coffee pots, woven coasters and small wood carvings. I also took my childhood illness, malaria, which flared up over and over again. I had a couple of jabs every four years to prevent it, but when I missed one dose I fell prey to malaria again a year later. I had just come back to Hamburg from Africa and was staying the night at a friend's. The next day, I woke up feeling like death, with a high temperature.

'Tanja,' I said, 'I'm getting malaria.'

'Yeah, right,' she said, not believing me. She could not imagine someone having a tropical illness in Hamburg.

I started throwing up and was gripped by waves of fever. I felt very weak. All this was familiar to me, it was exactly as it had been in the miserable Jebha barrack where I had experienced my first bout of malaria. I pulled myself together as best I could and begged Tanja to call an ambulance. She finally realised that I was not just suffering a hangover from the bottle of wine we had shared the night before.

When the doctor examined me, he immediately asked me, 'When was the last time you were in the tropics?'

I summoned my last scrap of strength. 'Come on, doctor! I've just come from Africa and I have malaria!' I was right. And I and my African souvenirs had to spend a few days in hospital in a haze.

11

Music

The reoccurence of malaria had reminded me of my physical limitations, which I often put aside in the whirl of my thoughts and plans. These plans centred on the conviction that grew stronger and stronger in me by the day: I wanted a career as a musician. In my experiments on the keyboard, guitar and with singing, I was astounded to discover that I had created songs that I wanted to both sing and hear.

I got together with music producers and looked for musicians I could work with. I listened to mountains of demo tapes, and finally found what I was looking for. I needed musicians who were not wedded to a certain style, but who were as at home playing soul as they were playing pop, rock 'n' roll or funk. It was between these genres that I sought to make my music, along with a good dose of the African rhythms and melodies that I knew from my childhood, as well as the heavy staccato sounds of the Arabic music I had heard in Khartoum. This was a time of experimentation for me – melding melodies from these different influences into a new kind of music that I liked.

Getting to grips with the technology that this required was a constant battle. It was all new to me. Before, I had had to teach myself to read and write music; now I had to learn to write music using a computer program, programme a keyboard and differentiate between different electronic sound effects. I was a total greenhorn, and it soon became clear to me that I would only have a chance of commercial success with my own songs if I became more technically adept.

I did not know if I would make it as a black singer in the German pop market, but I decided to give it a go. I turned up at a casting session at a Hamburg agency two days after the appointed time and started singing without musical accompaniment. I was immediately put into a girl group called Corniche. The group was incredibly poppy and their songs were beguilingly simple, but it was a good start.

I left Corniche when I got sick of all the bitchiness among the members. That was the end of the group, but it was also my springboard to a solo career. After countless sessions in studios, club tours and gigs with semi-professional bands, I signed my first contract as a solo artiste with Polydor in 1999, and was finally able really to let loose musically. I developed what has been named the 'Senait style' – a mixture of rhythm and blues, pop, African beats and German lyrics – and cut a couple of singles. They did not make an impact commercially but got a good critical reception. That was not enough to earn me a living, though, so I also worked on other music projects, including writing some lyrics for the girl group No Angels.

Alongside my work in the German pop world, I made sure that I did not forget my roots. There is a large Eritrean community in Germany, especially in the cities of Frankfurt, Kassel and Hamburg, and I sang at all the Eritrean concerts and festivals that were held regularly. I loved getting up to sing 'our' Eritrean songs, but I also sang some songs of my own.

I met my sisters for the first time in years after performing at an Eritrean youth festival in Kassel. As we stood backstage, it seemed like old times yet different. Only after I had been chattering on about all that I had been up to over the past few years did I realise how much things had changed.

'You travel a lot, don't you?' said Yaldiyan. Her tone was formal and reserved, as if she barely knew me.

I nodded hesitantly.

'Your voice has improved a lot,' she said, distantly.

This would have been a compliment from anyone else, and a point at which to turn the conversation to something else. But, I thought to myself, we are sisters who shared the worst years of our lives – we suffered and overcame hardship together – and here we are making small talk!

I grew impatient, almost aggressive. Adrenalin was still coursing through my body after the concert – the effect of having had the attention of a thousand people focused on me while I had been on the stage.

I almost screamed at Yaldiyan. 'Say something else! Tell me that you've missed me! Anything! I expected more than this!'

She merely repeated, quietly, 'You really have a beautiful voice.'

I started crying.

'Why are you crying?' she asked.

'Why do you think?'

She was silent. She was obviously finding our meeting more and more embarrassing and I could see that she was trying to think of an excuse to leave. I pre-empted her by storming off to the dressing room in tears.

Was it right to have lost contact with my sisters?

The prize

My first breakthrough came at the start of 2003. I was in my late twenties and by now I understood a little more about how the music industry worked. I had written and composed a couple of dozen songs which were stored on my hard disk – they had not been completely arranged yet, but were good enough.

The left-wing newspaper *Berliner Tageszeitung*, popularly known as *taz*, was looking for a candidate to sponsor for selection as the German entry in the Eurovision Song Contest. When they approached my label, Polydor, a boy band was suggested, but this was not what they wanted, so they were told to look on the record company website instead. There they discovered my work and were immediately struck by it. I took my CDs with me when I went to meet the *taz* people and sing for them; and was chosen as their candidate on the spot. I was flattered that they seemed to like everything about me: not just the way I looked, my CV and my background, but also my music, my singing and my charisma.

It was a tough competition, and I came up against people like Elmar Brandt, sponsored by the tabloid *Bild*, who was very popular at the time for his spoofs of Chancellor Schröder. The contest to represent Germany was eventually won by a singer called Lou, sponsored by the well-known pop music impresario Ralph Siegel. The winning song was called 'Let's Get Happy', and it typified the kind of music that Germany generally enters for the Eurovision Song Contest – shallow entertainment that no one can possibly object to. I came fourth with my song 'Heart of Ice' – brooding, cryptic lyrics set to throbbing, melancholic music. It was not a song for the masses, but it did get me recognition and praise all over the country. This was more important to me than winning the contest. As a result, I performed on television and live on stage many times, singing not only 'Heart of Ice' but also many other songs.

Throughout that time I received a lot of media attention, and many journalists solely focused on my previous life as a child soldier and on my experience of being an African woman in Germany, which I did not like. In interviews they asked me if I had ever experienced racist behaviour in Germany, and I constantly said no. I did not like the angle they were taking – and I had never had any racist encounters anyway.

Before the Eurovision selection had taken place, a *taz* editor said to me, 'You shouldn't tell people that you have never experienced racism in Germany.'

'What?' I replied. 'Come on, do you want me to lie? Am I supposed to say that simply because you are a left-wing newspaper?'

The woman was insistent. 'You must have experienced *something* …'

'Never,' I said, holding firm.

What more could I say? What a paradox, I thought, that people are disappointed when I have no racist experiences to recount. They all expected it from me, in line with the stereotypical picture of racism against blacks that is spread by the press.

The question about racism is as predictable as the expectation that I will perform for free at concerts for any humanitarian organisation simply because I am black. I am a professional singer who makes a living from her music, and not even as good a living as other German singers. Why do white singers who are better off than me not sing for third world charities all the time? There are plenty of singers who do not have to struggle to make a living, as I still have to do. Why is it the Africans who have struggled their way out of the misery of their continent who have to pay for the alleviation of that misery? I have, of course, sung for third world charities, and I did so willingly, because I do care about the fate of Africa. But if I had accepted every invitation to sing at fundraising concerts, I would have had to give up on my professional career long ago for lack of time.

The music industry

My whole musical career has been a learning process, and I constantly had to fight to make sure that I got what I wanted. I had to learn to assert my will with my record company so that I did not agree to short-term commercial interests that might have sold a few more CDs but would have harmed me in the long run because no one would have taken me seriously as a musician. That meant that I had to fight against being pigeon-holed by journalists, human rights organisations and other charities as a singer from a third world country who would join them in addressing hunger in Ethiopia and other issues. They did not see that I might want to convey other things through my music.

Other invitations came my way, too. The television presenter Stefan Raab and his team called me to ask if I would like to appear on his show, but I declined. He was pretty annoyed when I instead accepted an invitation to appear on the Harald Schmidt show, which I thought was pretty cool. In considering every opportunity that came my way, I never thought about what other people wanted from me, but what I wanted from them. *Playboy* tried hard to get me to pose nude for them, offering me quite a lot of money, but I said, 'Forget it! I'm not interested!' I could have used the money, but I knew that I would end up losing if I did things which would keep me from holding my head up high later.

People in the music industry call me a difficult person, but I have no problem with that because the people who are called difficult are those who will not obey orders, who say no and who stand up for themselves. The people who work with me are not used to anyone saying no, or not jumping on to the next bandwagon instantly. When music industry supremos see me, a black woman, they pull out the drawers labelled 'Black American music', 'rap' or 'hip-hop'. But these styles of music mean nothing to me, so why should I mould myself to them? Even if I did, nothing good would come out of it because I would not be true to myself. When I say that to people, and explain that I cannot sing hip-hop songs that I have not written, nor do I identify with the music, they call me difficult. I have learned to live with it.

I cannot, and do not want to ignore my past: I am an African woman, and that is very different from being an African American. I'm fascinated by the strong Christian faith of the African Americans and how it provides them with their principles, but I cannot identify with other aspects of their culture at all. Every time I ask a black American if he is African, he completely loses it. Questions like these seem to be a great insult to most Americans because they are extremely racist to the peoples from which they originate. Black Americans are often prejudiced against the continent they come from, or so it seems to me.

I don't feel that the Americans should speak about tradition, history or roots too much. America may be the only world power, but in the cultural stakes, they cannot compare with the peoples they set out to save or whose lives they try to control. I am not anti-America or anti-Americans in general, but I find some of their attitudes, their politics and their exercise of power disturbing.

Despite this, I still sing in English. This has nothing to do with America, but because I enjoy the language. It is a beautiful language and is understood all over the world – it also suits the kind of music I make best. It flows beautifully and is very melodic, and I am lucky to speak it well. Yet I have recently felt a desire to sing more in German because it is a more poetic language, an incredibly multifaceted one. I find that I can convey what I want my audience to hear in my songs very well in German.

12

Today

I decided to move to Berlin in 2002, which was a big step for me. I made the move largely for practical reasons. My record company at the time had just moved there from Hamburg, as had many musicians, managers and other people in the industry with whom I had a lot of dealings. I seemed to be taking the high-speed ICE train to Berlin to see them almost every week.

A friend took me and my stuff – a couple of boxes, a computer and tons of CDs – to the station in his estate car, and I boarded the train for my new life in Berlin, filled with anticipation. After I had settled in, first in Kreuzberg, then in sleepy Schöneberg, and established a routine of going to the post office, to the bank, the supermarket, the greengrocer round the corner, and observed the people in the U-Bahn everyday, I realised that my first impression of Berlin had been wrong. Berlin was not the lively international city that I had thought it to be when I had only visited it to go to the smart offices of recording companies, to parties in trendy bars and to exclusive gigs. It was a dirty, grey provincial town, full of disillusioned and frustrated people living in rented boxes.

I soon began to miss Hamburg, which seemed so bright and buzzy by comparison. People seemed to live their everyday lives there with much more good cheer and openness. It was possible to hang around with laid-back, happy people in Berlin only if you never left the party central areas of Berlin-Mitte and some parts of Charlottenburg, where the 'in' crowd hung out. They never had anything to do with the normal life of the city. But that was not the way I wanted to experience the place.

It was also in Berlin that I experienced racism for the first time, and I then understood why the journalist at the *taz* had been so insistent in questioning me on that point. I had lived for years in Hamburg without a single racist taunt, but all that was to change now. To take an everyday example, I was sitting in a taxi when I asked the taxi driver to raise his window as I was cold. I repeated my request not once but twice, thinking that he was hard of hearing. Then he grunted, 'I take niggers in my taxi, but I don't have to speak to them.' I asked him to stop the car immediately and got out.

Berlin was a rougher place than Hamburg. People seemed to have less respect for each other. I threw a party for my twenty-ninth birthday at the Trompete bar owned by the actor Ben Becker, and worked really hard for a week beforehand to get everything ready. I had booked some musicians to come from Hamburg and spent one day shopping for food and another making African finger food and other party food. I wanted it to be a great evening, and looked forward to seeing people from Hamburg whom I had not seen for months.

The evening started badly when my cigarettes were stolen. I had been speaking to someone, and had left my cigarettes behind me unwatched for a couple of minutes. Later on, my handbag was also stolen. I had had a couple of hundred euros in it to pay the musicians' fee and for their hotel. The bag also contained my mobile phone, my identity card and other personal effects. The thief was brazen enough to ring my cousin Suzy – who was also at the party – from my mobile phone. He had discovered from looking at my identity card that he had stolen the party hostess's handbag. He told Suzy that he would keep my mobile phone and the money, but would leave the SIM card at an Arab takeaway around the corner. He also told Suzy where he would leave the handbag with the rest of my stuff in it. When we went to look for it, the bag had been stolen by someone else. I never got my identity card back.

I was enraged by the incident. Ten days before, I had already had a purse containing a couple of hundred euros stolen in a club. Now I never let my things out of my sight when I go out.

Politics

I have maintained contact with Eritrea through the years. There are only 4.8 million people in Eritrea and probably a few thousand Eritreans in Germany. Most other Eritrean immigrants live in the USA, in Scandinavia or in Australia. They keep relatively strong ties with each other and feel very proud of each other's achievements.

When I last performed at the Eritrean youth festival in Kassel there were representatives of the Eritrean government there, as there always are. This time, however, they came up to greet me, hug me and congratulate me and asked for countless photographs to be taken with me. They wanted to win me over to their side to support Eritrean nationalism and the EPLF, for after years of peace, conflict with Ethiopia had flared up again.

I put a brave face on things, but set the record straight when I went up on stage to perform.

'I'm singing for you,' I said, 'but I can't change who I am. My father is Eritrean but my mother is Ethiopian and I will stand by her. I am singing in your language and I am a part of you.'

There was a tremendous round of applause. Many people in the audience had long had enough of war and of the conflict with Ethiopia, the age-old story of hatred. Even the Eritrean government officials came up and thanked me profusely after the concert.

I only found out the truth behind the official façade when I received an e-mail from a German who took a keen interest in Eritrean affairs. He wrote: 'My wife and I have always admired you. But how could you perform in Kassel in support of the government of Isaias Afwerki? That was betrayal. You yourself were in the ELF, you know how they treated children …'

At first I did not know what the man meant, but when I investigated I found out the devastating truth: to this day, nothing has changed in Eritrea. Children are still being torn from their homes and families and being trained as soldiers. I have seen pictures of Dogali, which lies between Asmara and Massawa: it is a desolate town destroyed by the last war which is now being used by the Eritrean army to train children for the next war against Ethiopia.

The situation in other African countries is much worse, such as in Uganda, where even more, even younger children are being forced to become soldiers. Nowadays there are also smaller and lighter semi-automatic machine guns which children can handle better than the gigantic Kalashnikov I had to carry when I was a child soldier. Arms dealers are conducting a roaring trade with unpredictable dictators all over Africa and with the leaders of countless rebel factions − some of them tiny − which wage senseless wars against each other or against the civilian population, as in Liberia or Sierra Leone. There was a bloodbath like this in Eritrea, too − under the command of the Ethiopian emperor Haile Selassie in the 1960s, soldiers razed many villages in Eritrea, sparing not even the babies, for they wanted to wipe out anyone who could join the rebel armies.

Massacres of this kind no longer take place in Eritrea or Ethiopia, but both countries are still far from democratic even though they call themselves democratic republics. They are both dictatorships − there is no other word for it when a country is ruled by a single party and opposition is not allowed. There are still child soldiers, although they are not as young as they were in my time: the army grabs children of fourteen, fifteen or sixteen off the streets or takes them from their homes to train them as soldiers.

Although the country has not fundamentally changed, the president has. Isaias Afwerki, the current president of Eritrea, was himself a child soldier in the EPLF during the civil war and the war against Ethiopia. His dedication and ability attracted the attention of his commanders in the rebel army and he rose to become its leader, styling himself a 'socialist freedom fighter'. After the victory over the Ethiopians in 1991 and after Eritrea gained independence following a referendum in 1993, Afwerki was celebrated all over the world, and walked through the streets holding children's hands. Today, he is a president like any other – powerful and distant. He travels with his convoy of Mercedes limousines through a country that is largely still suffering from famine, dependent on international aid. He walks around in an army uniform playing politics. Power changes people, and seldom for the better.

Many of my Eritrean friends and relatives in Germany take very little interest in what is going on in Africa today. My cousins Suzy and Ruta, for example, were born in Africa but grew up in Hamburg – they know nothing about Africa and find people from Eritrea an embarrassment. They identify more with American culture and with hip-hop and rap. They always find it funny when I speak in Tigrinya, which they understand from hearing their mother speak it but cannot speak well themselves.

'Senait, you speak Tigrinya like the old people do. You're talking like Grandma. Where did you learn to do that?' They did not mean it as a compliment, but as an insult.

'Well, I made an effort not to forget it and to speak it properly,' I said.

Once, when we were out together, Suzy said to me insistently, 'Please don't speak to me in Tigrinya on the U-Bahn or S-Bahn.' She clearly found it embarrassing.

'What's embarrassing about it?' I asked, and started exclaiming things like 'You coward!' loudly in Tigrinya. My cousins were shocked but no one else in the train had any idea what was going on, so I was able to go on teasing them.

Anger or jealousy

My cousins are a little younger than me, but they seem like children to me. They do not give a thought to where they came from, their past or their family. They do not care that their mother was a child soldier and witnessed murder and killing. Suzy and Ruta came to Germany as babies, so they know nothing of all that.

I swing between feelings of anger and jealousy in the face of their ignorance. I wish that I could live in the carefree way they do, filling my days with buying new clothes, new mobile phones, making friends and catching the latest films at the cinema. Perhaps I exaggerate a little, for of course they are not just occupied with whatever is 'in', but they certainly take great pleasure in throwing themselves into such things.

I often compare the way they pass their days in such a carefree manner with how my mind is involuntarily filled with brooding thoughts and memories because I cannot separate my present from my past. My music is synonymous with Africa and it would not work without my experiences in the Jebha. Those experiences are the source of the fear that repeatedly overwhelms me, and my happiness stems from the love I have in my life despite my past.

I think of my life like the course in accounting skills I had to do as part of my school leaving certificate. The units of the course were not individual, but built upon each other: stock-taking, auditing, ordering. Missing one of these units would have been like leaving a brick missing in a house. Until I left home at fifteen, my life was a catalogue of violence, hatred and neglect, all of which weakened me both physically and spiritually.

It is only today that I can regard what I have lived through as a fight I have won, one which I did not want to talk about until recently – at least not to most people. I have worked my way through a lot of my past, but not through the sexual abuse, which I cannot speak of neutrally or think about objectively to this day. Yet I believe that I would have been able to come to terms with even those moments of my life had I not also had my experience of the war and the ELF to cope with. The combination of all these factors is just too much. I often feel it is harder to come to terms with the past than to have actually lived through it.

I still feel frightened at night and get panicky when I see a gun. I try to rationalise my fears, but the same thing happens again and again. Images from my past appear in my dreams – the swollen corpses next to our camp in Barka come before me – and I need a light on constantly beside my bed.

I leave the television on all the time at home or when I stay in hotels. The voices, movements and colours on the screen make me feel safer and give me the feeling that everything is normal.

I have another, recurring dream: I am as I am today, dressed in western clothing, walking down a street, and a small, ragged girl is walking beside me. That girl is me, and these are the two sides of me that live alongside each other.

When I ran away from home in Hamburg I thought that I would just have to take a deep breath to push everything from my past away, for ever. I had felt invincible, but that was the arrogance of adolescence. I could not shake off my childhood and my youth as easily as an outworn skin. The memories clung to me, sucked me dry and almost destroyed me. I had to learn a great deal of self-awareness and to re-think my past a lot more before I was able to slough it off.

Winners and losers

My mistake had always been to blame myself for everything that went wrong, not others, even my father. I never blamed him for having sent me off to be a child soldier, for example. I did myself harm by thinking of myself as stupid and weak and being unable to accept that I had better qualities.

Yet I was never one of those people who think of themselves as losers in life, and nor am I now. My defiant spirit is what has saved me and helped me to live the life that I do today. When my father told me that I would end up walking the streets of

Hamburg, I was determined to show him otherwise. I swotted like mad in school – twice as hard as before – and got the third-best high school certificate in my form. In the long run, though, I need something more positive to drive me besides defiance – perhaps what I need is maturity.

When thoughts like this go through my head, I think about the people in Eritrea who never go through these agonies of selfhood. I think about people who I admire, performers like Helen Meles, the most famous singer in Eritrea. Her songs are songs of joy, pure and full of conviction – 'We are independent, we are free …' – exactly the opposite of mine. My songs are full of doubt and brooding emotion – 'I don't know what all this is for or where it is going to …' I am the polar opposite of the glowing victor.

Helen sings all the slogans of Eritrean independence which she has internalised and which she has never regarded from a distance. The Eritreans who have fled to Europe or America see the homeland in a different light. Living abroad in homes of our own, where everything is clean, peaceful and well ordered, we begin to wonder at the fact that we had ever fought in wars as child soldiers. Only then do we gain the freedom to think about our lives objectively. In Africa, politics and religion are all tied up with independence for the mother country – that is the only category of freedom they know. The freedom of the individual takes a back seat.

But this freedom that Eritrean emigrants have gained is the very thing that fills us with doubt and fear in comparison to the people who still live in Eritrea. Helen Meles goes up on stage and sings, 'I fight for freedom … yes, we are independent … we are untouchable … we have overcome!' with total conviction, while I sing 'Oh God, my spirit is destroyed …'

I remember smiling ruefully when Lula, an Eritrean friend of mine who had also been a child soldier, told me, 'Senait, I'm proud to have fought in the war.'

Her patriotic feelings had been drummed into her since

My friend Lula when she was an EPLF soldier.

her childhood – by her parents and in school. She spoke with great self-assurance and elaborated on her stories with gusto. Her emotion was genuine, as is that of most of the soldiers in Eritrea. They have been brought up to feel that it is right for them to fight for their country, and all are proud to have done so.

If they were to come to live in Europe their pride would quickly evaporate. No Eritrean abroad is proud to have been a soldier – they realise how terrible it was for them to have been forced to fight so young. There is an asylum in Asmara for people who are tortured with doubts, like I am. They are simply locked up there without any counselling or psychiatric treatment.

If I had grown up in Eritrea and still lived there now, I would doubtlessly think the way Lula does. I know how strong an influence one's surroundings are, especially on someone who has never been able to leave the environment they grew up in.

The same holds true for Germany. What is important to people here is education and belonging to a particular social group or class. Money, careers, power, success and fulfilment are what count here, and fulfilment is primarily attained through gaining material comfort and financial independence.

In Africa, the independence that people strive for is related to the land, and their main concern apart from this is family and childbearing. Everyone in Africa says to me, 'You must have children!' Financial independence is such a distant prospect for them that they do not even think about it. Hardly anyone there strives to succeed in a particular career because there are no careers to be had without emigrating.

I have learned what freedom is in Germany, so I try to fit in with the people and the society here. But the imprint of my past is still with me, and I cannot truly fit in until I have fully come to terms with it. Until then, I will constantly swing between my old and my new selves.

I can choose to repress my past, forget it or come to terms with it. The Eritreans who have stayed in their homeland do not have to make that choice – they do not want to repress the past or forget about it, but are proud of the role the past plays in their lives. They have pride and self-worth, while I torture myself with questions of who or what I really am.

Incredible though it seems, I have learned to love myself in spite of all my difficulties. I like myself, Senait Ghebrehiwet Mehari – yes, no matter who or what she is, I like her. No one knows her as well as I do. It may seem strange to be speaking of myself in the third person, but I do so deliberately. Thinking in the first person means that we follow our thoughts blindly. If we consider ourselves in the third person, we see a great deal more. When I edit my songs or lyrics, I am often struck by what I have written and how exactly it describes an emotion – this recognition comes from being able to step outside myself.

My faith has also helped me. The baptism that my grandparents arranged for me to have in Jerusalem still has meaning for me. I almost never go to church in Germany, I do not even pay the church tax, not because I'm stingy but because it just seems strange to me to have to pay a tax in order to practise a faith and listen to someone tell you how to live your life. From the way I experienced religion as a child, I do not see how being a priest can be seen as equivalent to any other profession, with holiday entitlement, a salary, a bonus and a pension. For me, priesthood is a calling from the heart, a vocation, not a career choice.

In Africa, priests live from the donations of their congregation. Bad priests do not get enough to live on and have to seek out other occupations. I feel that this system is much more honest than the one that operates in Germany. In Africa, people go to church to pray and sing with each other. They go to feel a sense of community with each other, not to subject themselves to an hour-long preaching session, as I have often observed here. It feels more honest to me to pray alone at home than to waste my time going to church services of that sort.

I often pray that I will be able to overcome my past, for I do not want to be a victim of it any longer. I have outgrown the role of victim, and I think I will be able to put it behind me. Illness is the only thing left I still fear. Malaria has not succeeded in getting me down. I have had malaria so often now – even in Germany – that it seems like an old friend. The virus will not die, but nor will it win.

Sometimes I wonder whether everything that has happened in my life was all coincidence. Or was it fate? Destiny? I do not know. One thing I do know is that I do not want pity. I can pity other people but I do not want other people's pity. I would rather have them envy me than pity me. Envy is good because I want to be proud of everything that I do.

I feel that I am gradually entering a new phase in my life. I am not proud of many things that I have done, but I am proud of myself nevertheless. I say that not only because I feel it but because I know I have to think this way in order not to go under. Nobody can get me down now. I have spent six years in therapy, and understand a great deal more about myself as a result. I like this woman called Senait, and I like her not only when she is happy, but also when she cries.

13

Tomorrow

What I want more than anything else in the future is recognition of my achievements – my music, my life and my work. I want to achieve everything that can be achieved in terms of singing and songwriting, and I know that I will succeed. But it will take a little time – I will not achieve what I want until I am at least sixty. I know that sixty is not considered a great age in Europe, but in Africa it is a venerable and wise age at which someone can say, 'Listen, I'm sixty years old – listen to me!'

I know that success – for me, success in my music – is not everything. With success comes money and acceptance, at least from superficial people who are drawn to success, but that does not bring happiness. I want real happiness, not just the appearance of it. I want to have laughter inside, to have children and a family, and to be proud of my life. Sometimes, though, I think that I am expecting too much and ought to have more modest ambitions. So I wish first of all that I will grow old, for otherwise there is not enough time to do everything I intend to do.

I have always dreamed of having children and I know that I will be a great mother. My flatmate Uwe is always apologising for his daughters disturbing me when they come to visit him, but I tell him there is no need. The children – three-year-old twins and an older girl who has just turned twelve – crowd into my room when they come, and have no thought of going out to play or of going home. I love curling up with them on my sofa chatting, reading, playing and watching cartoons together.

I want my children and grandchildren to boast about me one day and ask other children, 'Do you know who my mother/grandmother is and what she has achieved?' And my achievement will be something beautiful and sacred.

I want to die knowing that I have lived a good life. I do not wish harm on anyone, not even my father, even though I may sometimes have sounded like I do. The first thing I want to do when I have earned enough money from my music is to build a house for him in Africa. I have dreamed of doing this with my first million ever since I came to Germany, but now I know that I will need much less than a million to achieve it. My father lives in a small council flat in Kassel at the moment, but I would like to build him a house by the sea in Eritrea in which he can grow old and die in peace.

Like other Africans growing old in Europe, my father wants to return to his homeland. He cannot do so because he has no money and because he has made too many enemies in Eritrea. I am not quite sure how that has come about, and I need to find out a great deal more about his life in order to understand him better. To this day I do not really know my father or what makes him tick. I do not want to judge him solely by his actions – I just want to know the reasons and the thinking behind them.

I would like to know where my path in life will take me. It is a path that has veered close to death several times and I have been saved so many times that I think it is more than coincidence. I feel a power keeping me on this earth, a strength that protects me, leads me and keeps me from death.

One-third of the Jebha soldiers are estimated to have survived – mostly the older and more experienced soldiers who could run faster, shoot more accurately and survive long marches. The child soldiers were much more vulnerable in every battle. It seems a miracle that both my sisters and I survived that living hell.

I have always refused to kill, and I have been extraordinarily lucky in not having been made to, because God has been on my side. Realising that, I feel that my fate is entirely bearable. I don't want to change anything about my past, and I know that everyone can take responsibility for his or her own life.

I do not fear death because I have my faith. I believe in the afterlife, wherever that might be, but I do not want to die yet. I want to live first, enjoy my life to the full, make myself and other people happy with my music.

14

Epilogue

The publication of *Heart of Fire* turned my life upside down. Requests for interviews on radio and TV flooded in and I was asked to appear on many TV talk-shows. Such interest in the book was immensely appreciated.

At the end of 2005, I decided to take a break from the hefty publicity schedule and to return to Africa to revisit the places of my childhood. I particularly wanted to visit my family in the highlands of Eritrea, and also to meet a man called Luul in Addis Ababa, Ethiopia, who had written claiming to be my only living brother. Khartoum, capital of Sudan, which had provided refuge through my teens was also on the itinerary.

In all, this trip was an adventure – but not always an easy one. Amazingly, Luul turned out to be my brother; we share a physical resemblance and a similar outlook on life. His life has been strewn with tragedy, but he is able to see the good in his experiences. On the trip, I also discovered many other members of my family as well as Luul.

The visit to Khartoum, however, was much more difficult. Sudan has embraced a far stricter form of Islam than had been the norm when I lived there, but I was lucky enough to be able to revisit the scenes of my childhood and meet some former colleagues of Uncle Haile.

Just as I was due to return to Asmara, I learned that Eritrea was on the verge of a new war with Ethiopia, this time over a tiny stretch of a half-deserted mountain ridge. The roads to the town of Adi Keyh, which lay on route, were blocked and the situation in Asmara was volatile. Soldiers were patrolling the streets of the capital, looking for under-aged recruits. This news was both shocking and saddening, I decided to abort the rest of my travels and return to Germany.

Back in Berlin, though, I felt at home in a different way. While my heart was at home in Africa, my head was at home in Berlin. Work on a new CD started almost immediately and I continued to speak at public events on behalf of UNICEF and other aid organisations. The book tours also started again. By this time *Heart of Fire* had been translated into English, Italian, French, Dutch, Swedish, Hungarian, Polish and Slovenian. But mostly my time was spent at home writing *Wüstenlied (Desert Song)*, an account of this latest trip to Africa which was published in Germany in May 2006.

The publication of this new memoir attracted an enthusiastic response from the public, but also an increasingly critical one. Some members of the Eritrean community living in Germany claimed that I had lied about my childhood: they said that the army camps I described had actually been schools, and there had been no famine or drought in Eritrea, nor were children used as soldiers. But, thankfully, other Eritreans came to my defence. The controversy resulted in members of the audience at readings nearly coming to blows with each other. It was terrible. How can people claim to be against violence, yet use force themselves to defend their arguments?

The announcement that *Heart of Fire* was to be made into an international film inflamed the Eritrean diaspora. Some turned to the German press to publicise their claims of falsehood in my story; accusations were repeated in a TV magazine, but proof of their claims could not be provided, meanwhile the aid organisations that I am involved with – UNICEF, the German 'White Ribbon' campaign, and the 'Red Hand Day' organisation – swiftly backed me and proved my detractors wrong: child soldiers had indeed been used in the war between Eritrea and Ethiopia, and hundreds of thousands of people had died of hunger in the regions described in *Heart of Fire*.

The film of *Heart of Fire* is currently being shot in Kenya and we hope it will be screened in spring 2008. It has since come to light that the Eritrean government – who would not permit *Heart of Fire* to be filmed in Eritrea – had put pressure on the Eritrean community in Kenya not to participate in the film. This attitude saddens me. It displays a paranoia that must result from decades of doggedly fighting for independence even after their allies had fallen away. Where I am concerned this paranoia is completely unfounded. I have repeated made it clear that I do not oppose the current regime in Eritrea, nor am I working to political ends. My mission has always been, and still is, to draw attention to and thereby alleviate the suffering of children and young people who are forced to become soldiers in armed conflicts, now and in the future, regardless of whether these take place in Eritrea or in other parts of the world.

At times my private life is overwhelmed by my public one but I am pleased to report that last year I moved in with Boris and our son Zeon was born in April. The controversy over *Heart of Fire* coincided with my pregnancy so I am looking forward to more peaceful times in motherhood, though no less interesting ones.

Senait Mehari
May 2007

Acknowledgements

I would like to thank Lukas Lessing, who has helped me write my story down after a series of long and intense conversations. He has journeyed into my past with me, and accompanied me to the scenes of my childhood.

I would also like to thank my literary agent Liane Kolf as well as my agent Jobst-Henning Neermann and his wife Katja for their support.

To Uwe Lehnfeld and Norma Aronez and their three darling children, I would like to say thank you for being family to me. It is wonderful to have you in my life.

Thank you also to my publishers Droemer Verlag and everyone working there.

Senait Ghebrehiwet Mehari

July 2004

Child Soldiers

Child soldiers are a phenomenon of recent history – children would have stood no chance against adult soldiers in the times when battles were waged with swords or bows and arrows, nor even when wars were fought with old-fashioned guns with a sharp recoil. It was only with the invention of the American M-16 machine gun and the Russian AK-47 – better known as the Kalashnikov – that an untrained, malnourished girl could be sent into battle.

Wars nowadays often take place in poor, underdeveloped countries and child soldiers help to save on resources, for they eat less than adult soldiers and demand no pay, apart from a few inexpensive drugs to keep them going. Children learn quickly and there is no shortage of them – in Africa and south-east Asia, every second person is under eighteen years of age – as high birthrates replace the dead quickly. Slaves may have had trading value for their masters in days of old, but child soldiers today are dispensable wares.

The numbers

At the moment, about 22 million children and young people in Africa, Latin America, Asia and eastern Europe are trying to escape being drawn into war, into killing or being killed. According to research by the United Nations, more than 300,000 children and young people under eighteen are fighting in official armies, in militias or local warlords' armies. In Europe, thousands of young people under eighteen have fought in civil wars, such as in Kosovo. In Africa, there are around 120,000 child soldiers, mostly in Rwanda, Angola, Congo, Sierra Leone, Ethiopia and Eritrea. Children as young as five are put to work as delivery boys and girls or as spies. Between 1986 and 1997, 2 million children died in battles, and 6 million were injured, some crippled for life.

Girl soldiers

It is only in war that there is equality of the sexes in Africa. Girls and women fight alongside boys and men with equal rights. This is enshrined in the law of Eritrea. Military service is compulsory for both sexes and 35 per cent of the soldiers are women, welcome replacements for the armies decimated by war and hunger. There has never been any official acknowledgement of the fact that there are child soldiers – the authorities attribute any instances to errors made as a result of missing birth certificates.

Eritrea: a war-torn land

In 2900 BC, the Horn of Africa was called 'the land of the gods'. Gold, incense, ebony, ivory and slaves were traded there. The land that is Eritrea today belonged to the mighty kingdom of Aksum, of which modern-day Eritreans are still proud. This pride is undented despite the thirty-year war for independence against Ethiopia (1961–91) and a bloody border conflict, again with Ethiopia, over a stretch of desert land (1998–2000).

The thirty-year war for independence was the longest war in Africa in the twentieth century, and cost 65,000 lives out of a population of 3.7 million, 1.9 million of whom were under eighteen. In contrast, the fierce border conflict claimed 100,000 lives in barely three years, and reached new heights of violence against children. Generals on both sides sent thousands of child soldiers into battle in waves to break through against regular troops. Over a million civilians – almost a third of the population – were displaced as they fled the war.

Eritrea wrested its independence from Ethiopia in 1991 even though the Ethiopian army was larger and had much better weaponry, and was supported by the Americans and the Russians. The victory was all the more astonishing considering that the different factions of Eritrean freedom fighters were fighting each other at the same time. One of the factions was the Eritrean Liberation Front (ELF), an Islamic-oriented group that was founded in Cairo in 1960. It was also known as the 'Jebha', which is Arabic for 'battlefront'. This was the army that Senait fought with. In the 1980s, the ELF lost the battle to the Eritrean People's Liberation Front (EPLF), a socialist revolutionary party also known as the 'Shabhia', which is Arabic for 'the people'. The EPLF forms the basis of the government in Eritrea today, headed by President Isaias Afwerki.

Eritrea is officially a democratic republic, but it is a single-party state without free elections. The press is dictated to by the government and there is insufficient separation of powers in the state for it to be seen as a democracy from a western perspective.

Eritrea today

Even though the war has ended, the economic situation in Eritrea is still very weak. Many refugees are only now returning to the their home regions, many of which are landmined. Humanitarian organisations estimate that about 60 per cent of the population requires food aid to survive. The situation is made worse by the drought that has lasted for several years, which has destroyed harvests for the most part. Tribal customs and adherence to traditions make for a rich cultural heritage, but also hold the country back. Ninety-five per cent of women in Eritrea still undergo circumcision today, mostly clitoridectomy, in which the clitoris is removed. Some women are subjected to infibulation, in which the clitoris and the labia minora are removed and the labia majora sewn together. This is the most appalling form of genital disfigurement known.